The New Taste of
CHOCOLATE
Revised

The New Taste of
CHOCOLATE
Revised

A Cultural and Natural History
of Cacao with Recipes

MARICEL E. PRESILLA

TEN SPEED PRESS
Berkeley

Library of Congress Cataloging-in-Publication Data
Presilla, Maricel E.
  The new taste of chocolate : a cultural & natural history of
cacao with recipes / Maricel E. Presilla ; photography by
Penny De Los Santos.—Rev.
    p. cm.
  Includes bibliographical references and index.
  1. Cookery (Chocolate) 2. Chocolate. I. Title.
  TX767.C5P74 2009
  641.6'374—dc22
                                        2009026130

ISBN 978-1-58008-950-0
Printed in China
Cover and book design by Toni Tajima
Food styling by John Carafoli pages 142, 144, 147, 151, 158, 163,
    164, 167, 172, 175, 177, 186, 188, 193, 200, 202, 205, 206,
    209, 211, 216, 218, 220, 224
Food styling by Wesley Martin pages 134, 136, 152, 169, 179, 190
Props by Maricel Presilla
Additional recipe testing by Sarah Wallace and Jim Koper

10 9 8 7 6 5 4 3 2 1

First Revised Edition

The following material is reprinted with permission:
Pages v (portrait), 1 (background), and 4 (right) by Ismael
    Espinosa Ferrer. Author's collection.
Page v (backdrop): Courtesy of Biblioteca Real Jardín Botánico,
    Madrid, CSIC.
Pages vi, vii: Maya vase shown in the title page with woman
    pouring chocolate from one vessel to the other in the Maya
    underworld. Princeton Vase (Late Classic Maya, c. AD 750).
    Rollout photograph K511 @ Justin Kerr.
Pages viii, ix, 11 (top), and 12: Rollout photograph K4464 @
    Justin Kerr.

Page 4 (left): Courtesy of The New York Public Library.
Page 6: Courtesy of The North Carolina Museum of Art,
    Raleigh, North Carolina.
Page 11: Photo by Cameron McNeil.
Page 13: Rollout photograph K6418 @ Justin Kerr.
Page 14: Rollout photograph K1599 @ Justin Kerr.
Page 15: Photo by Reynold C. Kerr. Courtesy of the Proyecto
    Arqueológico para la Planificación de la Antigua Copan
    (Colgate University) and the Instituto Hondureño de
    Antropología e Historia.
Page 16: From the *Codex Mendoza*, MS. Arch. Selden. A.I., folio
    47r. Courtesy of the Bodleian Library, Oxford.
Page 18: From the *Códice de Yanhuitlán*. Courtesy of the Instituto
    Nacional de Antropología e Historia, Mexico.
Page 21: From the *Códice Tudela*. Courtesy of the Museo de
    América, Madrid.
Page 24: Penn Museum watercolor by M. Louise Baker, 1926,
    object 165062, image no. NA 11701. Courtesy of the Univer-
    sity of Pennsylvania Museum of Archaeology & Anthropol-
    ogy, Philadelphia.
Page 25: Courtesy of Giraudon, Paris.
Page 26 (left): Courtesy of the López Memorial Museum Collec-
    tion, Manila.
Page 30: Courtesy of Fondo Cultural Cafetero, Colombia.
Page 32: Courtesy of CEGA, Caracas, Venezuela.
Page 33: Courtesy of The New York Public Library.
Page 38: Photo by Kike Arnal.
Page 42: Courtesy of Chocovic S.A., Spain.
Page 43: Quote reprinted with permission from Alfred A. Knopf,
    Inc., New York.
Page 44: Map by Susan Ziegler.
Page 47: Photo courtesy of The New York Public Library.
Page 49: Photo courtesy of Frances Bekele, Cacao Research Unit
    (CRU), Trinidad.
Page 58: Photo by Alejandro Presilla.
Page 70: Courtesy of Gladys Ramos Carranza.
Page 71: Photo by Kike Arnal.
Page 82: Courtesy of Steven Wallace.
Page 86 (top): Photo by Kike Arnal.
Page 88: Photo courtesy of Silvio Crespo.
Page 89: Map by Susan Ziegler.
Page 102: Document courtesy of Silvino Reyes and Ana Karina
    Flores Luxat.
Page 109: Photo by Kike Arnal.
Page 119 (backdrop): Courtesy of Galerie Rauhut, Munich.
Page 123: Courtesy of The New York Public Library.
Page 131: Photo by Stefan Hollberg.
Page 148: Photo by Cameron McNeil. Courtesy of the Insti-
    tuta Hondureño de Antropología e Historia and the Early
    Copan Acropolis Program of the University of Pennsylvania
    Museum.
Page 181: Photo courtesy of Gonzalo Galavís.
Page 185: Photos by José Buil Belenguer. Courtesy of the Archivo
    General del Estado de Veracruz. Collección Juan Manuel Buil
    Güemes.
Page 187: Popul Vuh. Rollout photograph K5615 @ Justin Kerr.
Page 189: Courtesy of the Museo Nacional del Prado, Spain.
Page 191: From the *Códice Azoyú*, folio 21. Courtesy of the Insti-
    tuto Nacional de Antropología e Historia, Mexico.

To the memory of my grandmother,
Pascuala Ferrer Matos, who was born with cacao,
and for my family, the Ferrer clan of the Yauco River
and Baracoa, who still live with cacao.

With gratitude to my aunt, Ana Luisa Espinosa Ferrer,
and my father, Ismael Espinosa Ferrer,
for remembering it all so well.

Contents

Acknowledgments

In 1999, I went back to Cuba to revisit my first memories of cacao. I found my paternal family, the large Ferrer clan, still clinging to their cacao and coffee farms in Cañas on the Jauco River, the same remote place where my Spanish great-grandfather and his Cuban wife settled after their wedding in 1889 and where he was buried next to cacao trees. My heartfelt gratitude to Manolo, Mireya, Manolito, Eve, Nelson, Jaime, Blas, Faustino, and Evelio Ferrer, and the ones who are no more, for the gift of cacao.

Special thanks to my friends and associates Silvino Reyes and his wife, Ana Karina Flores Luxat, the owners of Hacienda La Concepción, for drawing me into cacao farming and the cacao bean trade. I would also like to thank the workers of La Concepción, Wilfred Merle, Beatriz Escobar, Juan Sardi, and the cacao workers of APROCAO for letting me experience cacao farming from the inside. My thanks to Francisco "Pancho" Bolívar, a member of Chuao's cooperative, and the children of Chuao for their assistance.

I owe a great debt of gratitude to renowned scientists, the late Humberto Reyes and his wife, Lilian Capriles de Reyes, for teaching me about the intricacies of cacao agriculture. I am very grateful to Gladys Ramos Carranza, the former head agronomist of the Campo Experimental San Juan de Lagunillas, for introducing me to Guasare cacao. I am indebted to Nancy Arroyo for her support during my work at the Estación Experimental Chama in the flatlands of Lake Maracaibo. My thanks to Kai Rosenberg in Choroní. In Bali, I enjoyed the warm hospitality of cacao bean trader Chris Hayashi and the members of the Tabana cacao cooperative, Koperasi Cacao Tunjung Sari. Cacao farmer Gusti Ayu Nyoman Saneh and her son I Gusti Made Budiatmika opened their house to me with characteristic Balinese charm. My thanks to Anne Schmidt of the Fairchild Tropical Botanic Garden in Miami for useful leads in Bali and for organizing the Fairchild Chocolate Festival every year, where horticulturists Nori Ledesma and Richard Campbell are doing a fantastic job promoting cacao.

In Trinidad, cacao grower Philippe Agostini allowed me to roam over San Juan Estate with overseer Pooran Ramdoolar, who guided me through the maze of the Cheesman Field. My gratitude goes to Dr. David Butler, the former head of the Cocoa Research Unit in Trinidad, for allowing me to watch the work of cacao scientists at close range. With Dr. Thayil Sreenivasan, an expert on cacao pathology, I took a look at cacao's many scourges. Dr. Darin Sukha guided me through the International Cocoa Genebank while morphology expert Frances Bekele was my cacao muse; not only did she help me identify the pods I collected in Trinidad, but she answered every query with patience and enthusiasm. My thanks to CIRAD researchers Olivier Sounigo, a molecular biologist, and plant pathologist Jean-Marc Thévenin.

At Miami's ARS station, geneticists Dr. Raymond Schnell and Stephen Brown and molecular biologist Dr. David Kuhn gave me insight on the center's main cacao programs. My thanks to Mike Winterstein, an agricultural science research technician at ARS, for taking the time to help me explore the center. My gratitude to geneticist Dr. Juan Carlos Motamayor of Mars, Inc. for his friendship and for answering my many questions on his groundbreaking research on cacao genetics and classification. I am also indebted to Harold Schmitz of Mars, Inc. for invaluable information on issues of chocolate and health and for keeping me abreast of the latest scientific research. Warm thanks also to Judy Whitacre, research scientist Eric Whitacre, as well as Rodney Snyder and Doug Valkenburg, all of Mars, Inc.

For rekindling my passion for the ancient Maya, I am primarily indebted to archaeologist Michael Coe and archaeobotanist Cameron McNeil, who could not have been more generous with information and resources. Jeffrey Hurst, a biochemist at Hershey's, Inc., cheerfully shared technical information about his work. My thanks to ethnobotanist Nat Bletter for his insight on cacao in Bali. My appreciation to researcher Elin C. Danien and conservator Lynn Grant of the University of Pennsylvania Museum of Archaeology and Anthropology, for bringing to light the luminous art of Chamá. I also owe thanks to archaeologist Robert J. Sharer for sharing photos of objects excavated at Copan.

My deep gratitude to Jorge Redmond, president of Chocolates El Rey, for giving me the opportunity to assist in the birth of a world-class Latin American chocolate. César Guevara, was a most valuable font of information on cacao agriculture in Venezuela. Rand Turner was generous in providing products for recipe tasting. Thanks to Roger Thürkauf, formerly of Suchard and Maestrani, for important lessons in chocolate manufacturing. My gratitude to my cousin Jorge Ferrer, the chemical engineer of the chocolate factory of Baracoa, for introducing me to another side of the Cuban cacao industry.

Silvio Crespo, former technical director of Wilbur Chocolates, gave me a glimpse of the inner workings of the North American chocolate industry of old. With Robert

Steinberg and John Scharffenberger I had the fortune of witnessing the birth pangs of an exciting new North American chocolate. Many thanks to Terri Richardson and his assistant Peter Dea for going out of their way to help me in this project. Thalia Hohenthal of Guittard Chocolates taught me a memorable lesson on the science of cacao butter. My gratitude to Gary Guittard, president of Guittard Chocolates, for his ongoing support. Marc Cluizel has been a supporter of Venezuelan cacao and a friend to farmers. Special thanks to cacao broker Roland Sánchez and to Pierrick Chuard of Plantation Chocolates who shared information on the Ecuadorian cacao industry. The work of progressive cacao growers Nazario Ryzek (Los Ancones) and Joseph Locandro (Finca Elvesia) in the Dominican Republic have given me great hope in the future of Dominican cacao. Thanks to those who provided products and information: Marc Cluizel of Cluizel chocolates; Art Pollard of Amano, Alan McClure of Patric Chocolate; Shawn Askinosie of Askinosie; Gary Guittard of Guittard Chocolate, Carolina Gavet and Pierre Coater of Valrhona; Mario Snellenberg of Chocovic S.A.; Jean-Jacques Berjot of Barry-Callebaut; Bernard Duclos of República del Cacao; François Pralus of Pralus; and Mark Scisenti of Kakawa Chocolate House.

Many thanks to Susana Trilling for her kind assistance; chefs Marc Bauer and Vicky Wells, my pastry teachers at FCI, for all things chocolate; Mirza Salazar and Paloma Ramos, my assistants, for their devotion; and Raquel Torres for inviting me to apprentice at her restaurant in Xalapa, where drinking hot chocolate was a ritual. In 1992, I had the fortune of meeting food historian Sophie D. Coe at an Oldways conference in Spain; her spirit lives on in her indispensable book *The True History of Chocolate*, which was completed by her husband, anthropologist Michael D. Coe. Harold McGee taught me more about the science of cacao fermentation than any textbook. My sincere appreciation to chocolate artist Elaine González, who took me under her wing. My profound gratitude to my friend and fellow food historian Anne Mendelson for her invaluable work on my manuscript. Anne read my work with a sharp eye, correcting my mistakes and offering learned advice. Special thanks to the dynamic Ten Speed Press team. First, my heartfelt gratitude to my first editor Lorena Jones, who edited with sensitivity and intelligence. Thanks to her unwavering support *The New Taste of Chocolate* is a beautiful book that makes me happy. My deep gratitude to current publisher Aaron Wehner for enthusiastically encouraging this new edition. Melissa Moore, my new editor for this project, was a dream to work with; the steady, intelligent hand that I needed to keep me focused. My thanks to publicist-turned-managing-editor Lisa Regul for helping promote this book. I was lucky to work with talented art director Toni Tajima, who translated my vision into thoughtful and elegant designs for both editions. I am also indebted to creative director Nancy Austin for giving me the freedom to do justice to the beauty of cacao.

In Venezuela, I teamed up with photographer Roberto Mata, whose field photography make this book truly special. Grateful acknowledgment to Venezuelan photographers Kike Arnal and Gonzalo Galavís for their important contributions. I am thankful to Ten Speed for enriching this new edition with the food photography of Penny De Los Santos. Her vivid photos and the thoughtful styling of veteran food stylist John Carafoli capture the spirit of my cooking and my organic vision of chocolate and cacao. My gratitude to my father, Ismael Espinosa, for his line drawings, and to Justin and Deborah Kerr for providing the rollout photography of Maya vases. Thanks also to Susan Ziegler for her hand-painted maps. Many thanks are due to the people and institutions who have granted reprint permissions and supplied visual materials, specially Rose Mary and Rainer Rauhut, and Joseph González and Ralph E. Magnus.

Special thanks to all the enlightened chefs and chocolate experts who have contributed their recipes and insights to this book. Clay Gordon, Mark Christian, and Curtis Vreeland kept me abreast of many new developments. My thanks to Alexandra Leas and the members of the Manhattan Chocolate Society for allowing me to participate in their Porcelana chocolate tasting. My gratitude to my friend and business partner at Zafra, Clara Chaumont, for holding the fort while I was working on this book. Many thanks to Maria Guarnaschelli for her cheerful, steadfast support. I owe much to my friends Marc Aronson and Marina Budhos, who have shared the joy of chocolate at my table and to Nelly and Saul Galavís for being the most generous hosts I could ever hope to find in Barquisimeto. I owe an enormous debt of gratitude to food journalist Miro Popiç and his wife, Yolanda, and their children, Maikel and Veronika, for becoming my family in Caracas and for letting me turn their house into a cacao warehouse and busy center of operations. This is a better book because of Miro.

Finally, my eternal gratitude to my husband, Alejandro Presilla, who has encouraged me to take a plane at a moment's notice to do my work right. Alex has helped me photograph and pick cacao pods in many steamy plantations, lending his considerable technical skills—and equipment—every time I needed to set up a makeshift photo studio in the clearing of a forest, a hotel room, or our dining room. This book also belongs to him.

GROWING UP WITH CACAO

For many people, tasting just a small piece of chocolate can trigger a flood of memories, whether it's of their first Hershey's bar or that special cake baked for a birthday or a graduation. It's not quite like that for me. I am fortunate to be a Latin American with long memories drawn from something closer to chocolate's origin. I first got to know it as a fruit.

A STRANGE AND WONDERFUL FRUIT

When my father told me about big, strange-looking fruits that sprouted right out of the tree bark and were filled with the beans that are the source of all chocolate, I formed a mental picture of thick-skinned papayas full of fragrant Hershey's chocolate kisses. Then one day he brought home about a dozen cacao pods from his mother's family farm at the eastern end of Cuba, about eighty miles from our home in Santiago.

They were large oval fruits of many shapes and hues: some rounded and smooth, others longer with bumpy skins and long-ridged grooves, colored in splendid shades of orange, russet, yellow, and green. I was entranced until my father cut open the first pod. Instead of chocolate-colored beans to eat like candy, I found a strange

In the upper Jauco River region of eastern Cuba, cacao farmers carry cacao pods, fruits, and coffee beans in *catauros*—sturdy baskets made with *yaguas*, the hard sheathing bracts of royal palm leaves. My cousin Carlos Espinosa takes a newly made *catauro* to our family's hilly cacao grove.

1

mass of lumpy, tan-colored seeds enclosed in a sticky, glistening ivory pulp that did not even smell like chocolate.

My father scooped out the inside of the pod and gave me some of the pulp to suck on. It had a refreshing sweet-tart flavor and a wonderful aromatic quality that today reminds me of lychees. If you ever taste fresh cacao fruit, you will understand what attracted people to it long before the discovery of chocolate.

I would have eaten the lot happily, but my father, who is an artist, had other plans. He had brought them back to paint. For days I had to endure the sight of those luscious pods arranged in a basket until they shriveled up. I still remember how much I longed to eat that cacao and to go to the place it came from.

Several years later I visited the farm, high in the forested mountains of the upper Jauco River, not far from the southeastern tip of the island. My great-grandparents, Desideria Matos and Francisco Ferrer, who originally came from Alicante, Spain,

settled in this isolated and godforsaken area at the end of the nineteenth century. As the Cubans put it, they quickly became *aplatanados*—that is, they went native like plantain trees. In their new home at Cañas, they began a typical anything-and-everything, mixed-growth farm, living off the land by growing and processing the things they needed, right down to their own home-roasted coffee beans and home-crushed sugarcane juice, which they used for sweetening when they couldn't get commercial sugar. Cacao was sold for cash.

The cacao farm was small and lush, with the deceptively chaotic look characteristic of the tropics, where many kinds of plants are crammed together in a planned give-and-take. My father's elderly uncles and their children tended the cacao growth and harvested the fruit with sharp blades fixed on long poles. The pods were collected in a rustic rectangular basket called a *catauro,* made from the woody fruit sheath of the royal palm. The men cut open the pods with machetes, removed the mass of beans embedded in the white pulp, and squeezed out as much pulp as they could by hand. Then the beans were spread out on a cedar tray fitted with wheels to dry in the sun. At night, or when it rained, the tray was wheeled into a thatched shed. After a few days, the pale tan beans changed to a reddish brown and were ready to be bagged for sale.

TAKING CHOCOLATE INTO THEIR OWN HANDS

Meanwhile, at the ranch house, another batch of beans was being transformed into chocolate. The aunts and cousins roasted the cacao outdoors—like coffee beans—over a wood fire in a large blackened kettle. Then, they ground the roasted beans into a sticky, fragrant paste in a hand-cranked corn grinder and mixed it with sugar and flour. They rolled the paste between their palms to make balls the size of duck eggs. These were set out to dry. When needed, they grated chocolate off the hard

surface, dissolved the gratings in water or milk, and heated it to make a thick hot drink.

How powerful and knowledgeable these women seemed to me, taking chocolate into their own hands! Later I would always remember that I belonged to those who live with cacao and know it personally, as a tree, a fruit, an ordinary household preparation.

Today thousands of such people still live in the cacao-growing regions of Latin America, where the plant originated and chocolate reached its early heights of development. For them, this is a fruit as rooted in the land as potatoes. They are not mystified or intimidated by even the finest commercial chocolates. They, too, have taken a batch of beans and made chocolate.

The chocolate that so fascinated me was meant to be consumed as a drink—the way the Maya and Aztec ruling classes and their subjects knew cacao, the way it is mainly used throughout Latin America today. Wherever cacao grows in the New World, someone is harvesting the beans on a small farm or buying them by the kilo at a market to make the same kind of cacao balls for drinking chocolate that my peasant family made at Cañas.

That early memory links me with Latin American chocolate at its plainest and most democratic, economically extended with thickeners. Yet the Ferrer clan's rough-and-ready drink also lingers

LEFT: Cacao balls (center), made with Criollo cacao and flavored with aromatic spices, for sale at Mérida's central market in the Venezuelan Andes.
RIGHT: Street signs in Papantla, a vanilla-producing town in northeastern Veracruz State, Mexico, announce the arrival of freshly harvested cacao beans from Tabasco and Chiapas and homemade chocolate.

---

in my memory when I taste the sophisticated hot chocolate of small artisanal producers in other Latin American regions, from Oaxaca in Mexico to the Paria Peninsula in Venezuela. The complexly layered interaction of fine, skillfully treated cacao with half a dozen Old and New World spices transports me to Spanish colonial drawing rooms with elegantly gowned ladies sitting on low, cushioned stools to sip frothy, spiced hot chocolate from hand-painted gourds or thin porcelain cups.

BRIDGING THE INFORMATION GAP: Getting to Know Chocolate from Bean to Bar

In 1994, when I was asked to be a marketing consultant for Chocolates El Rey, a respected Venezuelan producer, I began to taste, travel, read, correspond, and experiment with an eagerness

Drying Cocoa.

LEFT: Traditional drying sheds on the island of Trinidad.
RIGHT: Luis Ferrer, my father's uncle, built this cacao drying
house atop a steep hill overlooking the Jauco River. This drying system—with minor structural variations—is found all
over the Caribbean, from Martinique to Trinidad. The beans
are spread on a wooden platform that can be wheeled under
an A-frame shed at night or during rain.

far beyond what was required of me. Once again
I found myself drawn to aspects of the subject
that didn't seem to be a part of the general European and American chocolate experience. I saw
that even at high levels of connoisseurship, there
was an information gap—a lack of communica-
tion between those who consume and cook with
chocolate and those who produce it.

Probably the watershed events in my realization were the Venezuelan tours on which I led
groups of American and European chefs and
journalists through some of the finest cacao plantations in the world. As they walked through the
farms, I saw their vision of chocolate expanding
to take in the living tree and everything that goes
into its nurture.

The true appreciation of chocolate quality
begins with a link between the different spheres of
effort. To know chocolate, you must know that the

candy in the box or the chef's creation on the plate
begins with the bean, with the complex genetic
profile of different cacao strains. Think how
impossible it would be to make fine coffee with
the coarse, acrid beans of *Coffea robusta*. You must
know also that the flavor of the finished product
further depends on people carrying out careful,
rigorous harvesting and fermentation practices.

Today, most informed cooks and diners appreciate the many intertwined factors that add up to
quality in products like tea, coffee, cheese, and
wine. Somehow chocolate was slow to receive the
same scrutiny. My Venezuelan trips showed me
that chocolate lovers were eager to bridge the gap
when offered the opportunity. I detected something cooking, a quiet revolution in the perception and enjoyment of chocolate. I started to see a
deeper understanding of cacao's essential nature
among a new breed of chocolate manufacturers in
developed nations, spearheaded by new outreach
efforts on the part of enlightened growers, manufacturers, and researchers in some cacao-producing countries.

Now, perhaps, you will understand the original
mission of this book: to encourage as many chocolate lovers as possible to marvel at the pre-Columbian beginning and Spanish colonial flowering of
chocolate. I wanted them to understand the many

factors—genetic, chemical, environmental—that determine the quality of chocolate at all stages, from the fertilized flower to the foil-wrapped bar. I wanted to take them inside the thinking of the scientists who identify and develop important cacao strains. And I wanted them to see the human face of cacao farming. The life of a plantation worker in the Third World should mean as much to the chocolate lover as that of the chef who transforms a bar of chocolate into a work of art.

It has been wonderful for me to see how these issues have gradually become a part of people's awareness in talking about chocolate. I like to think that my book had something to do with it. I can't count the number of times that chocolate makers, chefs, and food lovers have told me how much they appreciated my book and how it changed their perception of this wonderful food.

But cacao and chocolate history have moved fast in the last eight years. Today anyone trying to sketch an overall picture must reckon not only with breathtaking new developments in fields from archaeology to modern cacao genetics, but with a swift tide of geopolitical changes that are redrawing the world map of chocolate. The chocolate industry also has changed, both to satisfy the new expectations of savvier consumers and to adjust to new realities in the world cacao supply.

It is for these reasons that in a surprisingly short time, I knew that I would have to revisit the book. I began to glimpse both a richer past and a brighter future for chocolate than I could have imagined even as recently as eight years ago—together with agricultural challenges that have the potential to destroy or transform the industry.

More than two hundred years ago, Carolus Linnaeus, the great Swedish founder of modern botany, bestowed on the cacao tree the scientific name *Theobroma cacao,* or "food-of-the-gods cacao." Truly, for many people, chocolate is as close to celestial as any food can be. But I hope that through this book you will find an equal fascination in the story of its roots in the earth, and learn to see it as a food of the people.

Workers take baskets of freshly harvested cacao beans to be weighed at the farmhouse of Hacienda la Concepción in Barlovento, Venezuela.

A NATURAL AND CULTURAL HISTORY OF CHOCOLATE

A Venezuelan plantation worker once said to me, "Where there is cacao, there is life," referring to both his own livelihood and to the nurturing relationship between cacao and the land. No tree has more to teach us than cacao, when we take the trouble to see it in its own environmental and biological context.

In nearly every part of the world where cacao trees are raised today, they are surrounded by other useful plants that shade them at different points in their life cycle. The true cacao—*Theobroma cacao,* Linnaeus's "food of the gods—is perfectly adapted to the demands of the humid New World tropics, which lie roughly within the latitudes of 20 degrees north and 20 degrees south of the equator. At least twenty remarkably similar wild Latin American cousins in the *Theobroma* genus live in the shadowed forest understories today. One of them, *T. bicolor,* or *pataxte,* is a food crop in Mexico and Central America. Another has enough culinary merit to have become an important domesticated crop of its own: *T. grandiflora,* the prized *cupuaçu* fruit of the Brazilian Amazon. These plants share the habit

OPPOSITE: *A Man Scraping Chocolate,* circa 1680–1780. This seventeenth-century Spanish painting shows a man grinding cacao nibs on a three-legged, slightly concave stone *metate,* which is heated from below to facilitate the grinding process. Chocolate pieces are set to dry on a sheet of paper.
RIGHT: *T. grandiflora (cupuaçu)*

7

Theobroma speciosum. This cacao relative bears stunning clusters of dark red flowers.

of putting forth flowers from cushionlike patches on the trunk (a condition called "cauliflory") and displaying all stages of flower and fruit growth year-round.

The origin of cacao is a subject mired in controversy, but most modern scientists argue that cacao first grew in South America. Recent DNA analysis pinpoints two areas that gave rise to different genotypes, or genetic makeups. One was the Amazon River basin, with Peru as the center of greatest biodiversity. The other lies in modern Venezuela, south of the udder-shaped Lake Maracaibo and in the foothills of the Venezuelan and Colombian Andes.

In the beginning, the different members of the cacao complex found their local niches—and incidentally, spread different parts of an original genetic dowry according to nature's own choreography. Then an unknown chain of events transformed sturdy wild plants occupying well-based environmental nooks into a particularly valuable crop transplanted into precarious new circumstances.

CACAO ENTERS THE KITCHEN

Historians have not established when, how, or why cacao began to be carried north. But its real culinary history begins far from its place of origin, in the tropical lowlands of the region now known as Mesoamerica. The variety of cacao native to northwestern South America seems to have been established here by the second millennium BC.

Mesoamerica is the area between central Mexico and western Honduras, including all of Guatemala, Belize, and El Salvador. It was here that unknown discoverers first took the uses of cacao to new stages. Like other peoples, they must have begun by using cacao as a fruit, for the sake of the sweet white pulp. Even today, cacao furnishes Latin American cooks with both fresh and fermented drinks. But a more complex history unfolded when someone looked past the gooey white interior of the multicolored cacao fruits to the almond-sized seeds enclosed in each pod.

Some historians speak of this development as a miraculous leap, pointing to the fact that a cacao seed (officially "bean") in its natural form is an unpromising and usually bitter object. But it's not that simple. The culinary investigation of the beans seems logical and inevitable, given the systematic way in which the pre-Columbian peoples of Mesoamerica approached most of their standard foods. What they did with the astringent but oil-rich beans was spread them out to dry in the sun, roast them on clay *comales* (griddles), and then grind them on stone slabs—everyday techniques used with such common foods as chiles, pumpkin seeds, and corn. The miraculous part is not that they tried the same procedures on cacao beans, but that these procedures chemically transformed it into something almost unrecognizable—chocolate. The sweet pulp either softened and melted by itself or was rinsed away with the fibrous material ("placenta") holding it together. The interior of the beans fermented to some degree in the sun; other compounds were formed during roasting. Grinding the roasted seeds released their oils along with other volatile substances produced in the earlier treatments, creating an irresistibly fragrant paste that could be shaped into little cakes or balls and dried for future use.

This is not a dim historical footnote en route to real chocolate, meaning modern chocolate industrially processed for candies and cakes. The first Mesoamerican discoverers of chocolate achieved the great feat of domesticating the plant and growing it in an ecologically sound way. They arrived at a sophisticated knowledge of chocolate's culinary possibilities, combining it with a wide array of other ingredients—vanilla, herbs, flower petals, chiles, maguey sap, honey, mamey sapote pits, and achiote—to create flavors and effects that make our uses for chocolate pale in comparison. This traditional concept of chocolate has never wholly died out in Mexico and other parts of Latin America. Mixtures like this still exist. They were, and are, used in a variety of hot and cold chocolate beverages, though "beverages" is really a misnomer. The cuisine of Mexico and neighboring regions has always been rich in drinkable foods that fit no European category. Chocolate became prominent in two branches of the family: flavorful gruels and porridges (from quite thin to nearly solid) based on ground corn, and highly prized creations with frothed toppings, like the Veracruzan *popo* or the Oaxacan *tejate*.

Before the Spanish arrived, frothed drinks were often used as sacred offerings (a use that persisted into modern times in scattered spots). Even today they retain some ceremonial aura. In Oaxaca the froth on the top of chocolate drinks represents a gift of personal vigor or essential force from the one presenting to the one receiving the drink. The idea of a chocolate-enriched corn gruel also survives today in the universally popular Mexican *champurrado* and its many Latin American cousins, like the *chorote* of Tabasco and the Ecuadorian *chocolate con máchica*, chocolate thickened with toasted barley flour.

BORN IN THE NEW WORLD

Since the first edition of this book, many avenues of investigation, from linguistic discoveries to genetic and biochemical analysis, have dramatically converged to alter our entire understanding of early cacao.

What people began the Mesoamerican chocolate story, and when? Educated guesses used to point to the mysterious Olmecs, who lived along the southernmost part of the Gulf coast of Mexico (today's southern Veracruz and Tabasco) between 1200 BC and 300 BC, and who spoke a language related to the modern Mije-Soquean family of languages. They are clearly the ancestral people of Mesoamerica, creators of cities and monumental sculpture that bespeak high civilization. Their complex political system, based on the sacred power of kings, is thought to have laid the foundation for Maya civilization. A term that archaeologists have deciphered in Classic Maya glyphs as *kakaw*, which we now know has its origins in the Mije-Soquean language family, gave rise to the Spanish word *cacao*.

Much excitement greeted the discovery in 1987 that two pre-Classic Maya pottery vessels unearthed three years earlier at Rio Azul in the Petén region of Guatemala and dating from AD 500, contained chemical traces of cacao. The analysis was performed by W. Jeffrey Hurst of the Hershey's Company research labs. This was the first of many contributions that Hurst was to make to the field of cacao archaeology using high-performance liquid chromatography and other methods to identify the chemical composition of archaeological food residues. Since cacao is the only Mesoamerican plant containing theobromine and caffeine, these are the chemicals that Hurst used as markers to detect the presence of cacao. But the importance of the Río Azul finding went much further. In fact, it would be the Rosetta stone for scholars trying to crack the whole code of Maya writing, which until then had barely yielded to intensive efforts. On a vessel that had tested positive for theobromine, a gorgeous stirrup-handled pot with a lock-top lid, David Stuart successfully decoded two appearances of the fish-shaped glyph signifying *kakaw* (see page 11). (Michael D. Coe had isolated and examined this glyph earlier on sequences running around the rims of elegant vessels, which he had dubbed the Primary Standard Sequence, see page 12.) It was a pioneering triumph for the young discipline of Maya epigraphy, or the study of inscriptions.

This was just the beginning of many discoveries that have kept extending both the timeline and the geographic scope of early chocolate history. Later findings at Colha, Belize, where archaeologist Terry G. Powis found spouted pots containing cacao residue in Maya tombs, pushed back the date of the earliest cacao use an entire millennium, to 500 BC.

Since then, at the northern Honduran site of Puerto Escondido in the Lower Ulúa River Valley, anthropologist John S. Henderson and his team found shards with cacao residues—identified by the presence of theobromine and caffeine—dating to 1400 to 1100 BC. For the researchers, the narrow neck of the Puerto Escondido vessels suggests that they contained not chocolate but a fermented drink made from cacao fruit pulp. Today's Latin America has a wealth of similar mildly alcoholic fermented drinks made from corn, fruit, and even tubers like yuca, known collectively known as *chicha* (there's a roster of other local names).

There was more to come. As Michael Coe relates (in the newest edition of *The True History of Chocolate*, an invaluable work first written with his late wife, Sophie D. Coe), even more startlingly ancient remains of cacao have now been traced to what he calls "the first pottery-using culture of Mesoamerica," in a Pacific coastal region that interestingly enough would eventually be the great cacao-producing area of Soconusco in today's Chiapas State in Mexico (see map on page 16). The work in progress that he mentions there has since yielded more conclusive results. A 2007 paper by Terry Powis and seven other scholars, including Coe, establishes that residues of a cacao beverage dating to 1900 to 1500 BC were found on a pottery shard at the site of Paso de la Amada, a village once occupied by the early fishing and farming Mokaya people.

Almost simultaneously with the Paso de la Amada discovery, Powis and his colleagues also identified cacao in a bowl from the Olmec site of El Manatí, on the Gulf Coast of Mexico, tentatively dated at 1650 to 1500 BC. Though obviously much remains to be discovered, at the very least we now know that the use of cacao was well established in two separate areas of Mesoamerica before Maya civilization appeared. It is also clear that people were harvesting and using cacao at locations where it grew abundantly—places that remained commercially important sources of cacao throughout the colonial period and even up to today.

There has been a still more recent discovery in the United States that may revolutionize the study of ancient trade routes, and that shows how far-reaching the influence of Mesoamerica must have been. In 2009, University of New Mexico anthropologist Patricia Crown called on Jeffrey Hurst's expertise to test a collection of tall cylindral clay jars covered with abstract designs found at the Pueblo Bonito site in Chaco Canyon, New Mexico, home to the ancestors of today's Pueblo Indians. Three shards tested positive for theobromine and caffeine. Thanks to these findings, we now know that cacao traveled to today's New Mexico between AD 1100 and 1125. How did it get there? Michael Coe believes that the Chaco Canyon dwellers must have received it from the Mexican highlands, perhaps through trade with the Toltecs in the same way that they got live macaws and their feathers in exchange for turquoise. The Toltecs, in turn, must have obtained it from cacao-growing regions on the Pacific Coast or the Gulf Coast, or Maya territories farther south.

THE MAYA: Guardians of *Kakaw*

Maya glyph for cacao.

It was the Maya who brought chocolate making to a high art. Building on the foundation left behind by other cultures of Mesoamerica, they expanded on it and developed a body of skills and knowledge that they would transmit to other peoples, including the Aztecs. The Maya, who became ascendant throughout southern Mexico after the waning of Olmec power, left an indelible mark on an area encompassing the Yucatán peninsula (their heartland) and neighboring southern Mexican regions, as well as today's Belize, Guatemala, Honduras, and central El Salvador. During a golden age lasting from about AD 250 to 900, they built great city-states supported by advanced developments in agriculture and canal building. Their monumental sculpture and architecture are still awe inspiring, and their complex hieroglyphic writing system recorded extraordinary Maya achievements in mathematics and astronomy.

It also recorded the importance of cacao in Maya society. When scholars began deciphering the mysteries of Maya writing, one of the first signs they were able to understand was the one for cacao (see left). The symbol for cacao first iden-

JAGUAR CACAO: *PATAXTE*

Cacao actually has a botanical cousin that used to be nearly as important in Mesoamerica as today's main player. It is *Theobroma bicolor* (known as *pataxte* in southern Mexico and *balamte* among the Maya), a species of the same genus as cacao that has been cultivated as long as *T. cacao* and that also produces seeds capable of being processed into chocolate. The Maya seem to have used both. Biochemist Jeffrey Hurst recently analyzed *pataxte* seeds bought at a Central American marketplace and found that they contained more theobromine than caffeine. This could be an important clue when looking for residues of *pataxte* and cacao in ancient Mesoamerican vessels. In ancient Maya culture, these two *Theobroma* species seem to have been almost complementary twins, like yin and yang in Chinese cosmology. The ancient Maya called *pataxte* the jaguar tree. Even today, *pataxte* has masculine associations, perhaps because its reticulated surface is like that of a scrotum. Cacao seems to be the feminine side of the pairing because the pod resembles a woman's breast.

tified on the Río Azul jar appears on hundreds of pottery remains. The Primary Standard Sequence (see below) running around the rim of vessels used by nobles regularly include formulaic statements of their contents, in which cacao and/or its *pataxte* cousin is a frequent "ingredient."

Tree-Fresh Cacao

From both glyphs and actual pictured scenes on Maya pots we have been able to learn that chocolate made using particular recipes was drunk by kings and nobles. There is also evidence that it was used by people of all classes, particularly during rites of passage, but only the upper ranks had drinking vessels made of anything as resistant to decay as fired ceramics. The upper ranks also used more perishable painted vessels, the gourds of the calabash tree (*Crescentia cujete*); of these, only the paint now survives. Such paint residues have been found in the western Honduras site of Copan, together with small, delicately decorated ceramic vessels modeled after gourds. It is not surprising that we know more about chocolate in luxurious than in humble surroundings. But my guess is that for everyday purposes people drank chocolate from gourds.

Dozens of Classic Maya pots and jars, included along with other furnishings in burial chambers, depict chocolate as a crucial, central element of opulent feasts. These beautifully painted, thin-walled vessels testify to the importance of the occasion and the prestige of chocolate. It is probable that these were not anyone's commonplace chocolate vessels, but rare, expensive articles reserved for special feasts and meant to figure in an elaborate system of reciprocal party giving and gift giving. (Bishop Diego de Landa, writing of the early post-Conquest Yucatán in 1566, specifically mentions cacao as among the requirements of a noble feast, and states that hosts were obliged to present the guests with such gifts as cups or vases, "as fine as the host can afford.")

We also know something about the range of cacao uses among the Maya. We know they consumed the pulp itself and juice made from the cacao fruit pulp, which continued to be drunk as it had been by the earlier peoples who left remains at Paso de la Amada and Puerto Escondido, in both fresh and fermented forms.

The inscriptions deciphered from Classic period drinking vessels and funerary offerings point to the existence of a well-established cacao-chocolate terminology. In addition to "tree-fresh cacao" and "green cacao" (probably meaning the mucilaginous pulp and juices made from the sweet pulp, respectively), there was "bitter cacao," "honeyed cacao," and most importantly "foamy cacao." Foamy toppings eventually came to be one of the glories of chocolate drinking among the Maya.

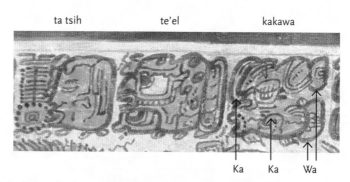

The Maya glyphs for tree-fresh cacao come from the Primary Standard Sequence (see top band on pages viii and ix) of the celebrated seventh-century Buenavista vase, from Buenavista del Cayo in Belize.

ABOVE: The image above is from a polychrome Maya vase showing a Maya lord seated on a low platform with a frothy achiote-colored cacao drink and a pot of tamales below.
RIGHT: Achiote pods from the Jauco River in Cuba.

Again and again the vase paintings depict scenes of chocolate drinking among the governing elites. In one particularly stunning example from Guatemala (pictured above), a royal figure is seated on a low platform next to a cylindrical pot of some cacao beverage crowned with the frothed topping that marked the most prestigious versions of chocolate. The slightly reddish color of the topping shows that the cacao had been ground with achiote paste, one of the classic elements in Maya chocolate.

Achiote, which is often called annatto by European writers, was the pre-eminent food dye of pre-Hispanic Mesoamerica. The small hairy pods of this tropical bush enclose tiny seeds surrounded by a waxy substance that imparts a strong reddish-orange hue to foods.

Modern Central American cooks make achiote paste by boiling the seeds or soaking them in water to free their waxy coloring substance, which precipitates into a pasty sediment.

We know that chocolate colored with achiote had the symbolic meaning of a sacrificial victim's blood, the sacred fluid that was the fuel of the Maya ritual universe.

On another vessel, we see two nobles bearing bouquets of blossoms that archaeologists have conjecturally identified as the fragrant and sweet-spiced "ear flower," *Cymbopetalum penduliflorum*, a highly valued addition to the best Maya (and later Aztec) chocolate. (The name clearly derives from the fleshy contours of this fragrant flower of the *Annonaceae* family.) The chocolate pictured in such images usually contained an array of other ingredients, ranging from vanilla, Yucatecan all-spice, maguey sap, and the honey of the native Mesoamerican stingless bees to dried chiles (probably small and very hot, like the *Capsicum annuums ululte* and cobanero chiles still used in the Guatemalan highlands).

By a corner of the seated dignitary's platform stands a bowl that scholars identify as containing the corn gruel now called atole, still a classic fixture of Mexican cuisine. There are many versions of atole, some made with fresh corn and many more made by cooking ground, nixtamalized (lime-treated) corn in water until enough starch

A Maya vase showing nobles bringing a tribute of flowers (possibly ear flowers to season cacao) for a Maya ruler. Passion River Region, Guatemala, c. 683.

dissolves to partly thicken the liquid. Spices and seasoning are sometimes used in today's atoles, but early Maya versions are thought to have been still more imaginatively flavored. To students of pre-Hispanic food history, the relationship between corn and chocolate is a provocative issue. One is the basic, necessary staff of everyday life, the other the food most synonymous with luxury and status. But they both bore mythical associations with cosmic life cycles, and it is clear that the two were indeed combined in Maya cuisine. In today's Yucatán and the other Maya lands, we find thick atoles flavored with chocolate like the *tanchucuá* (*tanch'ukwa* in Maya), which is perfumed with fragrant allspice and served with tamales on the Days of the Dead (see recipe on page 196).

Another tantalizing detail in this same picture is the dish before the platform, containing tamales topped with what certainly looks like a rich red-brown sauce that could possibly contain cacao. Researchers have long wondered whether or not chocolate was used as an ingredient of cooking sauces in the Maya period. It seems like a logi-

cal inference given the wealth of epigraphic references to cacao on Maya vases, but until recently conclusive evidence has been lacking.

Now, however, the archaeobotanist Cameron McNeil, in studying the early Classic vessels excavated by archaeologist Robert J. Sharer at the Maya site of Copan in western Honduras, has found that two vessels that contained (respectively) fish bones and turkey bones also had traces of cacao. The analysis, carried out by Jeffrey Hurst, McNeil's collaborator in this project, provides certain evidence that cacao was being used in cooking sauces for protein-based dishes as early as AD 450. At the same time, McNeil and Hurst discovered traces of cacao in a vessel designed for tamales. More recently, in the spring of 2009, Hurst found traces of capsaicin, the chemical marker of hot peppers, in the vessels containing cacao and turkey bones. So sauces with some form of ground cacao and chiles may be far older than anyone has suspected.

I am certain that they were nothing like the Mexican sauces that people think of today in connection with chocolate and chiles, such as the seventeenth-century *mole poblano*, with its baroque melding of pre-Hispanic flavors and a whole panoply of Old World spices. Rather, they were likely similar to still-surviving examples, such as the simple but delicious preparation of cacao nibs and tiny hot chiles that today's Kekchi Maya at Alta Verapaz in Guatemala use to season foods like *chompipe* (turkey). Pre-Hispanic cacao-and-chile-based sauces may have been slightly more elaborate, but I doubt that they contained anything more exotic than perhaps allspice, achiote for coloring, ground pumpkin seeds or corn masa (nixtamalized corn dough) for body, and perhaps tomatillos for acidity, thinned with water or cooking broth. (See page 217 for my attempt to re-create a Maya-style "proto-mole.")

The Copan excavations have marked a shift in methodology that may help researchers see the role of cacao in broader contexts. At one time nearly everyone assumed that the presence or absence of cacao residues could be inferred by the shape of a vessel. If it didn't look like a tall drinking vessel, it wasn't worth examining for evidence of cacao. Now, however, the Copan team is sending vessels of all shapes and forms (even platters) for chemical analysis. This enlarged focus means that researchers are thinking of other culinary roles for cacao.

Archaeobotanist Cameron McNeil scrapes the interior of a Maya pot, excavated by archaeologist Allan Maca at Copan, for food residues. The scrapings will be sent to Jeffrey Hurst's laboratory for analysis. Research of this kind has yielded much knowledge of Maya food, especially chocolate.

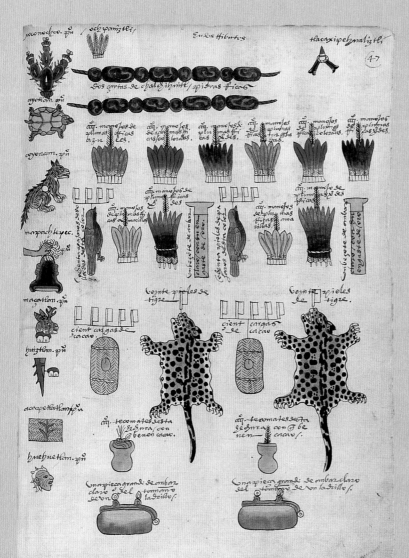

This folio from the sixteenth-century *Códice Mendoza* records the tributes paid to the Aztec rulers twice a year by the subject cacao-growing region of Xoconochco (Soconusco). Besides jaguar skins, cotinga feathers, and the prized green stone chalchihuitl, Xoconochco provided Tenochtitlan with 200 loads of freshly harvested cacao and 800 gourds from which to drink chocolate. According to the sixteenth-century Spanish chronicler Fray Toribio de Benavente (Motolinía), a load of cacao was equivalent to 24,000 beans.

Descripcion del Destricto del Audiencia de Guatimala by Antonio de Herrera, 1601/1622. The "Audiencia" (a Spanish colonial political division immediately below the viceroyalty) of Guatimala encompassed Guatemala, Honduras, Nicaragua, and Costa Rica. The map shows the important cacao-producing areas of Tabasco, Chiapas, and Soconusco.

THE ROMANS OF MESOAMERICA: The Aztecs

Many people today connect chocolate with the Aztecs. But they could not have discovered it on their own: the cacao tree would not grow anywhere near their strongholds in the high central valleys of Mexico. Cacao cannot tolerate conditions like those of the great Aztec capital Tenochtitlan (on the site of today's Mexico City) on relatively exposed terrain without the dense forest shade that the tree requires. Nor can it withstand the winter chill that invades these altitudes.

Nonetheless, the Aztecs knew and prized cacao early on. When they conquered large parts of Mexico starting in the late-fourteenth century, they eagerly adopted and extended the uses of cacao they found in cacao-growing regions to the south. Cacao itself was a spur to conquest, as had been the case with Soconusco (*Xoconochco* in Nahuatl) in today's Chiapas State. At any rate, when the Spaniards began poking around the Mexican Caribbean and Gulf coasts just before 1520, cacao was one of the most extraordinarily valuable items traded on the mainland. The large and powerful class of Aztec merchants engaged in long-distance trade bartered for cacao, as well as cotton, feathers, and the precious red dye called cochineal, on journeys to Tehuantepec and other southern provinces. To satisfy appetites in Tenochtitlan, porters (*tamemes*) routinely carried cacao hundreds of miles without benefit of either wheeled carts or beasts of burden, simply fastening cords (*mecapales*) over their foreheads to support their packs.

The post-Conquest chronicler Diego Durán, author of *Historia de las Indias de Nueva España* (History of the Indies of New Spain), describes how the cacao trade became mired in hostilities when the southerners decided that the goods the Aztecs brought for exchange (for example, cakes of dried edible algae and larval fish from the lake on which the capital was built) were "of little value" compared to such royal treasures as cacao. Attacking the offending mechants and trying to stir up resistance to these bad bargains, they instead found that they had called down the wrath of Tenochtitlan, which subdued them by armed force and thenceforth secured a steady supply of cacao as tribute.

In the post-Conquest illustrated manuscript called the *Códice Mendoza* (opposite), there are records of cacao tributes being sent in baskets, jars, or bales to the capital from five southern provinces. The cacao beans of Soconusco were particularly valued, and the *Códice Mendoza* records an annual tribute of some two hundred loads of 24,000 beans each.

By then cacao beans had taken on the status of legal money, a role that the Aztecs had picked up from the Maya. Bishop Landa's sixteenth-century account shows that the Spanish conquerors had already found the Maya of the Yucatan conducting transactions with both "cacao beans and stone counters." Apparently the equation of cacao with money was widespread in Central America. Columbus's one and only encounter with cacao illustrates the relationship between cacao and currency. In 1502, on his fourth New World voyage, Columbus, who was accompanied by his teenaged son Ferdinand, intercepted a party of Indians in a massive canoe off the coast of today's Honduras. Ferdinand wrote of the surprising fuss the people made over some nuts that they carried with them, immediately stooping to rescue any that dropped "as if an eye had fallen from their heads." Since neither group spoke the other's language, the reason would remain a mystery until Cortés's army marched into Mexico seventeen years later.

Just as the Dutch and English invaders of North America found that the Indian wampum (shell-beads) was more useful currency for fur-trading purposes than their own money, the Spanish found themselves supervising "cacao currency" for a long time. As late as 1750, the Spanish viceroy, the Count of Revilladiego, enacted regulations for Mexico City *pulperías* (general stores) requiring them to accept both small coins and cacao beans as change.

AS GOOD AS GOLD

> The cacao dealer customarily has a large quantity of it and has plantations of cacao, and brings it out to sell. The good dealer in this commodity, the beans that he sells are all fat, solid, and select. And he sells each thing separately, in one place the ones that are fat and solid, and in one place the ones that are small and hollow, or broken, and in one place their broken-up pieces. And each kind by itself: Those from Tochtepec, those from Anáhuac, those from Guatemala, those from Guatulco [Huatulco], those from Xoloteco, whether they are whitish, or ashy, or red.
>
> —Bernardino de Sahagún (1499–1590),
> Historia general de las cosas de Nueva España

Nearly all that we know about cacao and chocolate among the pre-Hispanic Aztecs comes from accounts written down after the Conquest—a sharp contrast to the Maya, who left a wealth of visual evidence long predating the arrival of Europeans, but received fewer and briefer Spanish-language descriptions (Bishop Landa's *Relación de las cosas de Yucatán*, "Narrative of Yucatecan Affairs," is one of our few sources). Some of the earliest written information about the Aztecs occurs in first-hand reports by the invaders, especially Cortés himself and one of the officers who accompanied him in 1519, Bernal Díaz del Castillo.

These two observers paid great attention to anything smacking of wealth. Struck by the use of cacao beans as specific units of money (commodities ranging from turkeys to sex had their known price in cacao) and by the notable social prestige attached to chocolate as a drink, they were predisposed to be interested. They observed the Emperor Moctezuma II drinking frothed chocolate with a degree of ceremony clearly marking it as an exalted food.

We do not know how clear the first invading Spaniards' grasp of Aztec society was, but there is no doubt that when their hosts presented them with cacao and invited them to partake of prepared chocolate, the gesture was meant as a great honor. They saw that cacao ranked with gold and gems in records of solemn offerings to the dead, and they gathered that its use was restricted to certain prestigious classes. Among the honors accorded to warriors who returned victorious from battle was being allowed (like members of the nobility)

The *Códice Yanhuitlán* (1532–1556) documents the consolidation of Spanish political and economic power in Santo Domingo Yanhuitlán and other Mixtec towns in Oaxaca, Mexico. Yanhuitlán was an important central point in the cacao trade between the cold highlands of Mexico and the warm cacao-producing region of Soconusco during the early colonial period. Here we see the Dominican friar Domingo de Santa María, known for his evangelical work among the Mixtecs and his knowledge of agriculture.

to enter the imperial palace, wear sandals and cotton garments, and consume cacao. The army drank it even on the march. Durán describes the provisioning of Aztec soldiers sent to subdue the cacao-growing southern provinces, and mentions that they were given rations of ground cacao, both loose and shaped into small balls—presumably easier to carry and prepare than whole beans requiring processing.

Bernardino de Sahagún: Unparalleled Chronicler

The first wave of Spanish missionaries brought one of history's most remarkable observers of Aztec civilization: the Franciscan friar Bernardino de Sahagún, who dedicated most of his life to compiling a monumental account of the Aztecs in their own language and translating it into Spanish as *Historia general de las cosas de Nueva España* (General History of the Affairs of New Spain), believed to have been completed in 1569. It remained unpublished at his death in 1590, and did not come to public knowledge for another two and a half centuries. Had Sahagún not gone to many elderly survivors of the Conquest and asked them to tell him their memories of the old ways in their own words, we would not possess a fraction of the knowledge that we have. For the last twenty years, I have been consulting the original Spanish text every time I have a question about food in Aztec civilization and always find a wealth of detail that not only answers my questions but leads me in new directions.

The *Historia general* preserves something close to firsthand accounts of life in the heyday of the Aztec court at Tenochtitlan, recording customs that survived into the earliest years of Spanish rule. Cacao's importance can be glimpsed when Sahagún explains that it was proverbially called "heart and blood"—a treasured substance specifically meant to be drunk by lords and distinguished persons "because it was worth much and there

was very little of it. If one of the common people drank it, if they drank it without sanction, it would cost their life. For this reason it was called *yollotli eztli*: the price of blood and of heart."

The *Historia general* presents cacao as an unmistakably elite food in a royal city that, like imperial Rome, depended on a crucial network of roads for bringing objects of trade or tribute to the great hub of empire. (Elsewhere, Durán's *Historia de las Indias* tells us that the rulers maintained storehouses filled with cacao along with other precious possessions like jewels or feathers—gifts or tribute from neighboring and subject provinces. These hoards were for the emperor's personal use, but were drawn on for other purposes, such as ceremonial gift giving at feasts. The imperial storehouses supplied cacao allotments to members of the warrior class, who also could purchase it in the public market and could expect to receive gifts of cacao and the all-important corn when they passed through any town on campaigns.)

The *Historia general* devotes much space to the selling and buying of cacao. Merchants who specialized in this product were known as *cacahuateros;* they seem to have been wholesale dealers. At the great and impressively organized market of Tenochtitlan, retail sellers offered both cacao beans in many grades and particular seasonings that Sahagún tells us were prized as additions to chocolate: *tlilxochitl* (vanilla), *ueinacaztli* (ear flower), and *mecaxochitl* (the elongated flower stalk of *Piper auritum,* or hoja santa).

Sahagún also describes women selling ready-made cacao drinks at the market, giving many basic details of skilled chocolate making that would be the foundation of artisanal techniques up to this day:

> "She who sells premade cacao for drinking first grinds it in this fashion: At the first [grinding] she breaks or crushes the beans; at the second they are slightly more ground; at the third and last they are very well ground, being mixed with boiled and rinsed corn kernels; and

being thus ground and mixed, they add water [to the mixture] in any sort of vessel [vaso]. If they add a little [water,] they have beautiful cacao; if they add a lot, it will not produce a froth. To make it well the following should be done and observed: It is well to know that [the cacao] is strained; after straining it is lifted up high so that it will pour in a good stream, and this is what raises the froth, and it is put aside. And sometimes it gets too thick and is mixed with water after being ground; and whoever makes it well makes and sells the cacao well made and beautiful, such as only the lords drink: smooth, frothy, vermilion, red, and pure, without much corn masa [I conjecture that pure and "without much masa" are synonymous]; sometimes they add many aromatic spices and even bees' honey and some pink-tinted liquid; and cacao that is no good has a lot of masa and a lot of water, and so it doesn't make a froth, only a bubbly scum."

Chocolate fit for lords, from this passage, apparently was chocolate judiciously mixed, but it also leaves much unsaid. The beans would first have been ground on a *metate* (grinding stone), shelled, then put through a three-stage crushing with increasing pressure to break them into coarse nibs, then smaller bits, and finally something fine enough to form a paste. The kernels of "boiled and rinsed" corn probably refer to the nixtamalized (lime-treated) corn used for most cooking purposes. The amount of water and corn added to the mixture was obviously a crucial determinant of excellence, as measured by the amount and quality of the froth on top. The raising of a froth—the feature most visible to chocolate connoisseurs—required repeated pourings from one container lifted above shoulder height into another on the ground, as depicted first on a Maya vase (see background illustration, page vi) and most famously in a sixteenth-century post-Conquest Aztec codex (see opposite). But the effort would go for naught if the mixture had been cheapened by too much corn (today we'd have to say cornstarch or other thickener) or thinned with too much water. Adding just the right amount of corn was the hallmark of a skilled artisan who could make "pure" (that is, unadulterated) chocolate fit for lords, but also of an honest market-seller who gave you value for your money.

Sahagún also describes family ritual offerings at the home *oratorio* (shrine), where containers of different foods were solemnly placed. Among them were diminutive gourds of a size to accommodate tiny amounts of chocolate—and here for the first time the friar-anthropologist varies his usual

THE THREE CUPS

"*Las Tres Tazas*," excerpted from a nineteenth-century newspaper article by Colombian writer José María Vergara y Vergara (1831–72), vividly depicts the painstaking preparation of hot chocolate in the highlands of colonial Colombia.

The cacao came from Cúcuta [the Colombian Andes], and to grind it they had observed every rule of the art, so carelessly forgotten by today's cooks. They had added aromatic cinnamon to the cacao mass and had moistened it with wine. Immediately thereafter, each bar had been wrapped in paper, to be left to rest for eight years in a cedar chest. Nor, to make the hot chocolate, had they forgotten the instructions of the wise. The water had boiled once, when they first added the chocolate bar, and then this mixture was boiled twice, allowing the chocolate bar to dissolve gently. . . . Prepared in this fashion, the chocolate exhaled such perfume. Such perfume! The flavor of that chocolate was just like its aroma.

Greek muse, you of ingenious fictions, please tell me: How the devil could the perfume of that colonial chocolate reach the noses of my compatriots today!

OPPOSITE: *Códice Tudela*, sixteenth century. A Mexican woman prepares a chocolate drink with a frothy head by pouring the liquid back and forth between two vessels.

term "cacao" to write *cacaoatl,* or "cacao water," his closest approach to the later word "chocolate." (The first published use of "chocolate" in the modern spelling occurs in the Jesuit Joseph de Acosta's *Historia natural y moral de las Indias,* "Natural and Moral History of the Indies," in 1590, ten years after the slightly more Aztec-sounding *chocollatl* surfaces in the Spanish physician Francisco Hernández's *Historia natural de la Nueva España,* "Natural History of New Spain," published in 1615.)

Chocolate also was served in elaborate fashion at banquets called "foot-washings," given by the powerful class of merchants to celebrate the completion of trading journeys. The host, having notified the company associates and senior partners of his safe return, invited them to a ceremonial dinner involving particular dishes and marked by offerings to the god of fire and the patron god of merchants. He took special pains over the "excellent cacao" served in gourds at the close of the meal, with the two gods each also receiving a gourdful as an offering, before distributing reeds filled with tobacco for smoking. And this was followed, as in Maya banquets, by gift giving, especially cacao-related items like serving bowls, cacao beans, flavorings, and tortoiseshell *paletas* (sticks) to stir the cacao drinks.

The most lavish of all the merchants' banquets were those involving the sacrifice of slaves and the eating of their flesh. For these, still more astonishing amounts of equipment and food had to be provided before the invitations went out. The host had to secure a supply of everything from corn and chiles to turkeys and dogs. The cacao-making supply included twenty *cargas* (24,000-bean lots) of beans and from 2,000 to 4,000 flat sticks or rods for stirring the drink.

Sahagún pays very close attention to the gourds used to drink chocolate, explaining that some were decorated with "diverse paintings," and were accompanied by tortoiseshell spoons or sticks called *aquauitl* for stirring the cacao. Other gourds were painted black and sat on stands made of jaguar or deer pelt. He also describes gourds pierced with holes to strain the cacao and larger ones in which the cacao "was lifted on high [for pouring]."

THE SPANISH:
Colonial Transformations

The Spanish arrived in the New World at the zenith of Mesoamerican chocolate culture. They were presented with a spectacle summing up the full panoply of pre-Hispanic chocolate achievements over a span of close to 2,500 years, until the sixteenth century. It's important to understand that the Spanish deeply entered into the spirit of what they found. Through them, the major aspects of chocolate use for drinking in ancient Mesoamerica were preserved and disseminated throughout many of the Latin American colonies and as far away as Spain itself and even its distant Asian colony, the Philippines.

What always impresses me most in the early accounts is the pre-Columbian peoples' awareness of cacao and its qualities. Let's go back for a moment to the first true cacao, the one that originally grew in South America, along with many wild descendants of the first cacao ancestor or ancestors. In reality, true cacao trees (*Theobroma cacao*) were never uniform copies of a standard model. There must have been many built-in variations in each of the principal genotypes. But the one we are concerned with in its adoptive Mexican home—the strain that might have originated around the northern Andean foothills and in the flatlands below Lake Maracaibo, or perhaps (as some scientists will still argue) arose independently in Mesoamerica—had certain strongly expressed qualities that help determine the character of any chocolate made from it.

The cacao that grew in Mexico is distinguished by large, plump beans. When cut open, the raw beans reveal very pale, pure white to light pink cotyledons (seed leaves). The taste is somewhat bitter

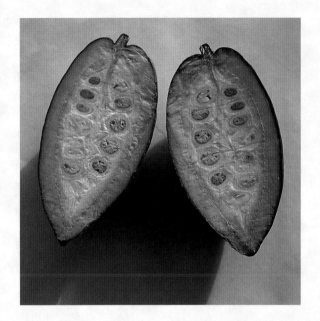

From svelte cacao trees with their outlandish fruits to a box of seductive bonbons, there is an improbable distance that does not look any shorter when the fruit is cut open. The first impression is of slimy lumps embedded in a nameless whitish substance that recalls squashed insect larvae or other unpleasant sights. The whiteness is disconcerting because when we think of chocolate, dark brown is the key color we recall.

FAR LEFT: This transverse section of an unripe Porcelana pod from western Venezuela shows the characteristic pure white and light pink cotyledons of a true Criollo pod with red skin.

but not unpleasantly astringent. When the beans are fermented and roasted, faintly nutty or delicately herbal overtones in the raw cacao deepen into a more pronounced accent of nuts, and other flavor notes from fruity or flowery to spicy can be detected.

Wherever this first strain of cacao was domesticated in Mesoamerica, it took on a slightly different local character, or *goût de terroir*. Sahagún's account makes it clear that shoppers in the Aztec marketplace were knowledgeable—and choosy—about the beans shipped north to them from cacao-growing territory. They paid for quality and were always on the lookout for adulteration. The best dealers arranged their stores of cacao by place of origin, as we might distinguish between Blue Point and Cotuit oysters.

When the Spanish colonists began their own chocolate experiments within about a generation after Cortés, they continued to observe the crucial distinctions they had learned from the Aztecs and to judge chocolate on the basis of nuances in the different original cacaos from which it was made. Later they would attach names like *cacao dulce* (sweet cacao) or *cacao blanco* (white cacao) to the whole complex of superior cacaos that they had found being grown in Mesoamerica and later in Venezuela. But the name that would endure was Criollo, or "born in the New World."

Surely there were better and worse grades of cacao in pre-Hispanic Mexico. But without exception, all belonged to the Criollo strain—which has tragically disappeared from the Mexican cacao supply in modern times. Today cacao experts conduct search missions to odd corners of Chiapas and Tabasco or other southern parts, desperately trying to follow up rumors of a farm that preserves just a few trees of Criollo, or something with light-colored beans that might be Criollo.

Like other Spaniards, Cortés was quick to see that in Aztec society cacao was a road to riches. Even before the murder of Moctezuma, he was thinking of how to cash in on the bounty of New World flora and fauna, including cacao. In 1519, he wrote to his royal master, the emperor Charles V, to report that he had requested and been given a grant of land for a Pacific Coast plantation, on which Moctezuma had already been diligent enough to plant two

A Maya vase from Chamá, a cacao growing region in Alta Verapaz in the Guatemalan highlands, showing a chieftain being carried in a hammock. Rollout watercolor of the Ratinlixul vase from Guatemala by Mary Louise Baker. c. 1926.

thousand cacao trees. Cortés was careful to spell out the implications of this statement for Charles, who probably had never heard of the plant: "Cacao is a fruit like the almond, which they grind and hold to be of such value that they use it as money throughout the land and with it buy all they need in the markets and other places." The rest of the farm was to be a combination of the local staples (corn and beans), Mexican ducks, and livestock (chickens, dairy animals) probably brought from the Spanish colony of Cuba. (In other words, this "gift" of Moctezuma was meant to secure the Spaniards a self-sustaining base of operations, with the additional advantage of one highly lucrative cash crop.) Cortés's Spanish companions estimated the value of the whole at 20,000 gold pesos.

THE DRINK OF ARISTOCRATS:
Old World Transformations

Did Cortés know that Moctezuma's drink would soon be as sought after in Europe as the East Indian spices Columbus had expected to discover? It was not long in making its way to Spain. Michael Coe believes that the first chance for the Spanish court to sample chocolate as drunk by the New World natives came with a delegation of Kekchi Maya Indians who arrived in 1544 bearing the sort of rich gifts they might have given to their own overlords. The main chieftain (*cacique*), Don Juan Aj Pop'o Batz, came carried in a sort of hammock by two porters to present the gifts to the future Philip II, including 2,000 quetzal feathers, painted gourds, and containers of beaten chocolate. (We can see a similar scene of a chieftain carried in a hammock accompanied by a colorful entourage on the Ratinlixul polychrome Maya vase dating from the eighth century from the site of Chamá in Alta Verapaz, see above). Chocolate and cacao soon became economic pillars of Spanish enterprise. And by degrees, people in Spain adopted the habit of drinking chocolate.

Within fifty or sixty years, the custom had spread to France, Italy, England, and most parts of Europe. Meanwhile, the taste for drinking chocolate had already taken hold in the Spanish colonial cities of Mexico like San Cristóbal de las Casas in Chiapas—where women were known to drink gourdfuls during mass. In colonial Caracas, chocolate drinking was all the rage, and the wives

of the cacao barons drank it at the lavish midafternoon soirees called *agasajos,* as was the fashion in Spain.

This Hispanicized chocolate was inspired by what Cortés had found the Aztecs drinking, and it emphasized the idea of a complex, heavily spiced mixture. The Spaniards even embraced some of the porridge dishes the Indians had created, such as chocolate thickened with *pinole,* a blend of ground, toasted corn and spices such as vanilla and achiote (annatto). They turned one former option into a requirement: adding a sweetener. It was the Spanish who first married chocolate and sugar, which they and the other European colonial powers were busy planting with African slave labor throughout the Caribbean. Pre-Hispanic Mexico had no sugar; cooks used honey or the sap from the heart of the maguey plant when they wanted to sweeten chocolate. Starting around the late-seventeenth century, another development may have occurred simulta-

Detail from *The Cup of Chocolate* by Jean-Baptiste Charpentier le Vieux (1728–1806). A French aristocrat drinks chocolate from a delicate porcelain cup.

neously in Europe and colonial Mexico: the use of chocolate as a spice or flavoring in savory dishes, like Sicilian caponata, Catalan *estofats* (braised dishes), and several of the hybridized Spanish-Indian moles of Mexico. But the lion's share of attention to chocolate during the seventeenth and eighteenth centuries went to its incarnations as a beverage.

One thing that didn't change—at first, anyhow—was the association of drinking chocolate with high social standing. Chocolate arrived in Europe with the aura of an exotic luxury for the cognoscenti. Both the making and the drinking involved special pains and paraphernalia. First someone had to roast the beans, carefully judging

ABOVE: The *metate* became as much at home in Spain, France (where it was called "the Spanish stone"), and the Philippines as in Mexico. A Chinese servant in Manila grinds Criollo beans on a Mexican *metate*.

RIGHT: Mole is a thick, baroque sauce that is made with dozens of ingredients, including chocolate. These are the ingredients for a traditional mole from Xalapa, Veracruz. All are processed in sequence, each at its own time.

the degree of doneness so that the beans developed full flavor without scorching.

The shelled beans were crushed and placed on a stone slab modeled on the Mexican *metate*. The slab was set over a brazier to warm the beans enough to bring out the essential oils as, by degrees, they were ground to a grainy paste with other ingredients. (Before the age of mechanization, *metates* had an amazing intercontinental and multiethnic career wherever chocolate went.)

The mixture might feature several spices (often cinnamon and anise, with or without nutmeg and some form of chile or other pepper), essences (rose water or orange-blossom water), ground nuts (typically almonds, hazelnuts, pine nuts, and/or pistachios), such New World ingredients as achiote and vanilla, Old World rarities (ambergris, musk), and, of course, sugar, which was still a food for the rich. Any dry ingredients

not ground with the chocolate had to be pounded to a powder and sifted.

The rich cacao oils would tend to form a layer on the top when the mixture was combined with hot water or (a European innovation) milk. The new breed of chocolate aficionados generally skimmed off some of the fat, and partly offset the effect of the rest by beating up a froth on the drink. Bypassing the many foaming agents that were, and still are, made from native Mexican plants, they frothed the chocolate by the technique (also Mexican) of repeatedly pouring it back and forth between two vessels, or whipping it with a clever device called a chocolate mill (*molinillo*) in which wooden rings rattled briskly around a stick twirled

Molinillos.

HUMORING CHOCOLATE DRINKERS

Every new food arriving in Spain from the Americas had some medical tests to pass. For the arbiters who wrote about food and health, it was vital to know how novelties like tomatoes, chiles, vanilla, squashes, and potatoes affected the "humors" of the body, a concept taken from ancient Greek and Roman medicine.

The still-prevailing theory of humors held that bodily and mental health depended on a proper balance among four bodily humors derived from the "elements"—earth, air, fire, and water—and expressing the respective principles of cold, warm, dry, and moist belonging to those elements. The bodily fluids—blood, black bile, yellow bile, and phlegm—each associated with a different organ, embodied four different combinations of physical principles: warm and moist, cold and dry, warm and dry, and cold and moist. Any one person had a "temperament" created by interactions among these forces. Any one food was made up of the warm-cold-moist-dry principles, which occurred in different degrees; some foods might have mixtures of contrary qualities. The art of medicine was to achieve an ideal balance of humors in the patient, for instance, correcting the excessively "warm" and "dry" tendency of "bilious" people through judicious doses of "cold" and "moist" foods like lettuce or cucumbers.

Chocolate was difficult to classify, since it didn't seem to resemble other drinks. The expert who tackled the problem in greatest detail was Dr. Juan de Cárdenas, who traveled in Mexico in the late sixteenth century and wrote the treatise *Problemas y secretos maravillosos de las Indias* (Enigmas and Wondrous Secrets of the Indies), published in Mexico City in 1591. Cárdenas describes cacao as mingling contradictory qualities in complex fashion. He considered raw cacao damaging, but the difficulty vanished when it was toasted and mixed with the ingredients favored by the native people.

He thought that plain cacao contained both "cold and dry," "warm and moist," and unusually "warm and dry" properties. A dangerously earthy (cold and dry) basic substance in cacao solids was responsible for many ill effects, from "anxieties and melancholy fits" to dropsy (edema). This stuff coexisted with the airy (warm and dry) nature of the fat that rose to the top of chocolate and the fiery nature of some bitter principle that provoked headaches and strange sensations. But the terrible effects of cacao were miraculously tamed by toasting the beans and adding certain ingredients. Cárdenas singles out and describes in loving detail the local flavorings "ear flower," *mecaxochitl* (the long, thin flower spike of the hoja santa plant, *Piper auritum*), and vanilla. In his opinion, both these and the commonly used achiote had just the right therapeutic balance to tame the "malice" of cacao. The particular benefit of most spices was supposed to be that they were "warm" and "dry," but Cárdenas thought the New World seasonings had these attributes in a milder, less extreme degree than East Indies spices like cinnamon. In other words, chocolate as made by the natives with local spices and atole (which also had a tempering effect) converted all the harmful effects of raw cacao into dietary virtues. The only part that he disapproved of was the much-loved froth, as being nothing but air that will fill the stomach with wind. Otherwise Cárdenas considered the drink healthful.

In a way Cárdenas was rationalizing his own enjoyment and acceptance of the way chocolate was made in the Americas and putting it in the scientific context of the times. And we find that the techiques and practices that he considered wise and healthy have been used from his day to the present in Latin America and Spain. In Mexico, overroasting cacao beans is still a popular technique to counter the underlying bitterness. The long reign of chocolate with aromatic spice mixtures was another example. Long after medical opinion had stopped recommending spices as a "warm and dry" counteractive to the properties of cacao, people went on instinctively using them—roasted to temper their heat. Instead of honey, which was deemed too "hot" in combination with spices, the more neutral sugar became the favorite sweetener. The custom of adding atole, or some other grain-based thickener like *pinole* or barley flour, also persists today.

between the palms. At first, Spaniards drank chocolate in *xícaras* (gourds), often lavishly decorated, or clay *tecomates* (cups modeled on gourds). Soon exquisite porcelain cups resembling the gourds were being manufactured for the serving of chocolate, and a special pot had been devised with a built-in mill.

The Spanish quickly took over the role filled by pre-Hispanic lords and administrators who had supervised the Mesoamerican cacao trade. Within a decade or two they were conducting a thriving business in cacao from every growing region, especially cacao-rich Guatemala. Partly adopting a custom they had observed among the Maya and Aztecs, Spanish estate administrators began collecting tribute in the form of items such as cacao from towns and estates. A complex bureaucracy grew up involving the people of local villages, a native *alcalde* (town magistrate) who collected tribute from them, and the *encomenderos* (crown-appointed administrators who held grants for the labor of a certain number of Indians).

During this turbulent epoch, the colony of New Spain underwent a transition from a barter-based to a money economy that placed high emphasis on cash crops, especially cacao and the precious dye-stuff called cochineal. One result was that the indigenous peoples—those not wiped out in the waves of disease that rapidly struck the New World—began to adopt some of the conquerors' attitudes toward profit as well as purchasable luxuries. The changes are often mirrored in the records of local *cabildos* (town councils), which despite the Spanish name were solidly rooted in the native communities and illustrate collisions between the older and newer value systems. In *Mesoamerican Voices,* a wonderful anthology of native-language records from the colonial era, I found a striking example in which the members of a *cabildo* in Tlaxcala, east of Mexico City, complain about commoners swaggering about with the air of patricians. Such people expect to buy food with the profits of cochineal instead of planting

corn, beans, and the old crops in the spirit of the old subsistence economy. Worse yet, they squander the money on luxuries like the best chocolate ("very thick and full of cacao") and contemptuously reject what doesn't meet their standard.

Cacao fortunes were made in sixteenth-century Mexico, Guatemala, Honduras, Nicaragua, and El Salvador. Soconusco and other growing centers began shipping cacao to distant parts, including other colonial capitals, such as the splendid city of Lima.

But just as a taste for chocolate spread to every rank of colonial society, smallpox and other epidemics swept over Central America's lands of cacao. Abandoned cacao orchards became a common sight; production fell disastrously behind the demand of the burgeoning market for fine chocolate in Mexico City and elsewhere in the New World. But Mesoamerica's bad luck meant cacao opportunities elsewhere.

THE NEW CACAO COLONIES

It was during the decline of Mesoamerican cacao farming that entrepreneurs' thoughts turned to South America. The first place to figure importantly was Venezuela, where cacao was native and where the Spanish chronicler López de Velazco had observed it growing during expeditions between 1571 and 1574. The moment was perfect to fill the gap. The cacao was also perfect, since it was of the fine Criollo strain that Cortés had found in Mexico. Probably cacao was being planted on a commercial scale by the turn of the seventeenth century. In any case, 1607 is the date of the first recorded shipment of a load from La Guaira (the port of Caracas) to Cartagena de Indias in Colombia, the major Caribbean port city from which the fleet of Spanish galleons sailed to Veracruz in New Spain (today's Mexico) or directly to Spain.

Venezuela soon began a golden age as an exporter of cacao as fine as any from Soconusco or any other Mexican growing center. Throughout

Europe, the names Maracaibo and Caracas were synonymous with first-class Criollo cacao. By the eighteenth century chocolate drinking was a passion for Venezuelans from top to bottom of society. Whereas the Maya and Aztecs had drunk it with ceremony, usually at the end of meals, people in Venezuela guzzled it like coffee fiends. José Rafael Lovera's history *El cacao en Venezuela* (Cacao in Venezuela) cites three general types mentioned in a 1736 report on consumption and export statistics. According to this document, people drank chocolate at all hours of the day, in gourds much larger than ordinary drinking glasses. Chocolate bordered on a drug habit, and slaves and laborers were said to complain of headaches if they couldn't get their "fix."

The report mentions three general types or styles, each corresponding to different social levels. The most prevalent was *cerrero* ("rough and ready," but also meaning "bitter"), essentially nothing but cacao dissolved in water without sweeteners or flavorings, and it was drunk as freely as water among the country people of the interior. Later the term would be also applied to coffee.

The next type, *chorote,* seems to have a more complicated history. Some historians have used a passage in an early post-Conquest account, Fray Pedro Simón's *Noticias historiales de las conquistas de tierra firme en las Indias Occidentales,* 1627 (Historical Accounts of the Conquests of Tierra Firme in the West Indies), to argue that *chorote* harks back to a pre-Hispanic Venezuelan use of cacao among the Cuica people, involving ritual offerings of the "butter" skimmed from the boiled drink. In any case, by the eighteenth century *chorote* was chiefly drunk in the cities and was made by boiling ground cacao in a pot and letting it cool until the top layer of cacao butter could be removed and set aside for other purposes. There remained a thick layer of cacao solids at the bottom of the pot under a clear liquid that was poured off, leaving the defatted solids to be shaped into little balls that would later be dissolved in water along

with muscovado sugar, or what Venezuelans call *papelón,* to be served to guests. *Chorote* was said to have served as the lunch and dinner of Venezuelan slaves and laborers. (Interestingly, the word *chorote* is used for a cold drink of toasted ground cacao and boiled corn, sometimes with sugar, in Tabasco, Mexico, and just for plain chocolate in the cacao-growing region of Baracoa in northeastern Cuba.)

"Chocolate," the most elaborate of the three, was the kind of fragrant mixture beloved throughout the Spanish colonies. In Caracas, it was prepared with premade hand-shaped balls of ground chocolate that also contained some form of sweetener (sugar or honey), some amount of toasted corn for thickening the drink and helping to raise a froth, and various seasonings. Cinnamon was the usual spice, together with ginger and allspice; vanilla and ground almonds were less frequent additions. Though commercial pressed chocolate tablets superseded the handmade balls, the latter survive in parts of Venezuela today, often in elaborately and vividly spiced versions (see recipe, page 181).

Foreign observers reported that spiced chocolate was the first thing taken by the upper class at the morning and noon meals. There was also a custom of consuming something salty together with the chocolate. Lovera quotes a late-nineteenth-century German traveler who describes with distaste how peasants in the Venezuelan Andes would take chocolate at three o'clock in the afternoon together with a fresh cheese called *queso de mano.* I have seen the same thing myself, also at the traditional three o'clock *merienda,* in Bucaramanga in the Colombian Andes, but with saltier cheeses like Edam and Gouda, which are dunked in the hot chocolate (see recipe, page 221) and left to soften until they can be scooped out with a spoon. Along the Colombian coast, chocolate is traditionally accompanied by cheese arepas or the queso blanco (fresh cheese) used in arepas (see recipe, page 219).

Colombia ("New Granada," at the time of the viceroyalty) became a repository of very old colonial chocolate customs. In the capital, Bogotá, the custom of serving afternoon chocolate was and is universal. Poor people turned it into a simple meal with bread; the more affluent served it in fine china, accompanied with elegant little pastries as well as cheese. Over time, however, the pre-Hispanic thickening of corn was replaced by wheat flour.

The great sixteenth-century fortified Caribbean port city of Cartagena had easy access to the best cacao from all parts of the colonies, as well as some local Colombian cacao from the Magdalena. It also had more cosmopolitan—perhaps Mexican—chocolate traditions. (Bogotá probably relied more on what was grown in Andean plantations in Cúcuta.) Teresita Román de Zurek's wonderful

Afternoon Chocolate in Colombia, watercolor, by Joseph Brown (1802–74). The cult of hot chocolate flourished during the colonial period in the cool highlands of Colombia, and in cities such as Bogotá. Brown's vignette of the traditional afternoon repast shows an Indian woman serving hot chocolate to a European visitor.

cookbook *Cartagena de Indias en la Olla* provides some charming insights into colonial history. For instance, she cites eighteenth-century travelers who relate that chocolate was known there only as cacao. Even black slaves drank it daily after breakfast, buying it from street vendors who sold gourds of a common version heavily thickened with corn, premade and requiring only heating. She also cites the Swedish sea voyager Gosselman writing a century later that it was the custom to have chocolate on rising at six o'clock; a few hours later people ate a substantial breakfast including chocolate and cheese, followed by cold water. (The custom of drinking cold water after chocolate seems to have been almost a norm; Gosselman says that some "creole" families took chocolate "five or six times a day, always with great amounts of ice water.") Chocolate and cheese were also a usual part of dessert, being served along with sweets made from honey or the local brown sugar (*panela*), again with a chaser of cold water. And in a latter-day echo of Aztec fashion, the meal ended with the smoking of cigars.

Chocolate also had a long colonial tradition in Peru, where the port of Callao near Lima received cargoes from the older colonial port cities (though cacao from the Cajamarca region close to the Peruvian Amazon was also sold along with cacao imported from Bolivia). Rosario Olivas Weston, a Peruvian culinary historian, cites a petition sent to the city council by the Lima chocolate-makers' guild in 1787 that provides many insights into the state of affairs. Among other things, the guild proposed an ordinance to fix prices for cacao according to quality and place of origin. They ran a gamut from two reales (a coin of small value) for cacao beans from Guayaquil in Ecuador to two pesos (or sixteen reales) for beans from Soconusco. Between these extremes we find ready-made chocolate from Guayaquil at three reales, and a range of beans at different prices: four reales (Jaen de Bracamoros o Montaña in Peru), eight reales (Panama), twelve reales (either Martinique or Caracas), and fourteen reales (Magdalena in Colombia). The range of prices shows that the Lima chocolate makers were as familiar with the qualities of lesser and finer beans as their Mexican predecessors. We can also see that by this date cacao was commercially grown in Peru; there were fertile river valleys on the eastern side of the Andes supplying cacao to cities like Lima and Cuzco. On the scale of quality this local cacao seems to have been considered lowest common denominator, as shown by the price. But it gave all kinds of people a chance to develop a taste for chocolate, ordinary or elegant.

The Lima chocolate-makers' guild, however, wanted to put restrictions on chocolate—not only restrictions meant to bar competition by unlicensed, untaxed sellers and to subject the rest to official supervision from guild masters, but others that prohibited anything beyond a narrow range of proper, refined ingredients. Among the banned ingredients were vanilla, "Oaxaca powder" (*pinole*), ground ambergris, "Chiapas pepper" (allspice), sesame, popped amaranth, ground corn, and "Quijos cinnamon" (a cinnamon substitute from Quijos Province in Peru). Another similar petition from 1785 asked that the composition of chocolate be limited to cacao, white sugar, and (real) cinnamon—ensuring a refined product easy for the guild masters to supervise and legislate. A 1785 document specifically excludes not only such dubious substances as "sheep's liver," but also corn, the popular unrefined sugar called *chancaca*, and "other spices." It is an early example of the approaching trend toward views of pure chocolate that would later prevail in much of the Americas and Europe. Spices and aromatic flavorings fell out of favor with mainstream chocolate makers—although there were two survivals. Latin Americans (at least some) retained a taste for chocolate flavored with Old World cinnamon, and the New World vanilla became a standard ingredient in European-style chocolate.

By the reign of Charles III (1759–88), cacao and chocolate shipments were regularly reaching the royal court from the cacao-producing colonies. María del Carmen Simón Palmer, author of *La cocina de palacio, 1561–1931* (Palace Cuisine), explains that cacao shipments were important enough to be sent directly to the royal keeper of the jewels (*guardajoya*), instead of being handled like other foods. One recorded shipment in 1759 contained "50 turrones of Soconusco cacao, 4 crates of chocolate in cakes, 2 crates of pinol powder, and 12,000 vanilla beans." Among the royal gifts of food that Charles sent to Italian relatives, as well as the pope, were chocolate, vanilla, and cinnamon.

Colonial Peru, like Venezuela and Colombia, had been a place of nearly nonstop chocolate drinking since at least the seventeenth century. The Peru-born laywer Antonio de León Pinelo, who worked for the Royal Council of the Indies, discussed New World chocolate at length in his widely distributed book, *Question moral si el chocolate quebranta el ayuno eclesiastico* (Moral Question, Whether Chocolate Breaks the Religious Fast), published in 1633. He indicates that "In Lima, it is drunk in mornings and sometimes evenings, always hot, because it is seldom used cold (though that is increasing). At this court there is no proper order, because some people drink it at all hours from morning to evening as often as possible, and what stops them from having more is the expense, not lack of a yen."

Even in the first years of independence (beginning in 1824), chocolate continued to be indispensable. Rosario Olivas Weston, author of the history *La cocina cotidiana y festiva de los limeños en el siglo XIX* (The Daily and Festive Cooking of the People of Lima in the Nineteenth Centruy), quotes the nineteenth-century traveler Johann Jakob von Tschudi as saying that at Sunday *almuerzo* (brunch) black servants would even froth each guest's chocolate in the cup, sometimes so dexterously that the froth almost completely filled the cup, leaving only a couple of spoonfuls of liquid. The usual accompaniments were toasted

SERVING CHOCOLATE

Regardless of local preferences in the ingredients that went into chocolate, some things remained nearly unchanging among Ibero-American chocolate drinkers. The actual preparation was amazingly similar from place to place. Everyone dissolved drinking chocolate in water (later, cow's milk, almond milk, or—in the Philippines—coconut milk) in a tall narrow earthenware pot, similar to pre-Hispanic chocolate pots. In affluent households copper eventually replaced clay as the material of choice, and a straight horizontal handle was added. The shape of the pot was perfectly suited to frothing the chocolate with a handmill, or *molinillo* (see page 26).

As time went on, it became customary to transfer the chocolate to a more elegant porcelain or silver pot for table service. The new pots kept the same shape— but with an innovation, a hole in the lid to accommodate the handle of the *molinillo*. Chocolate pots enjoyed a long reign among Ibero-American chocolate drinkers. They remained popular into the nineteenth century, until chocolate was eclipsed by coffee even in the greatest Latin American strongholds of chocolate.

Nineteenth-century *coco chocolatero* from Venezuela.

As in the rest of colonial Latin America, the vessel preferred by the Venezuelan upper classes for drinking hot chocolate was a hollowed-out coconut, polished and decorated with sgraffito designs and carved motifs. These are the descendants of the Aztec painted gourds that Sahagún described. (Cold chocolate was served in a shallow two-handled silver cup called a *tachuela* or *tembladera*.)

A fine survey of the subject, Carlos F. Duarte's *El arte de tomar el chocolate* (The Art of Drinking Chocolate), has wonderful illustrations of coconut vessels for chocolate. Probably the idea of using coconuts as vessels had come from Mexico and spread everywhere in the New World tropics that coconut palms grew. The most elegant had silver rims and handles, and usually rested on delicate silver bases. Like their classic Maya antecedents, they often bore the name of the owner. The nineteenth-century Venezuelan example pictured here, courtesy of the historian José Rafael Lovera, and now at his cooking school CEGA, in Caracas, bears a silver tag with the name Heraclia Trejo de Fernández, 1878.

When chocolate drinking was first introduced in polite Spanish and colonial society, the wobbliness of gourds (*xícaras*), coconuts, and ceramic vessels (*tecomates*) modeled on their shapes presented a certain danger to the well dressed. The story goes that after witnessing a lady's dress ruined by a spill, Peru's viceroy, the Marquis of Mancera, invented a clever serving piece that would eventually be called *mancerina* in his honor. It was a small plate with a ring-shaped support surrounding a hole in the middle; the outer part of the plate formed a saucer for holding party fare like small pastries, and the chocolate vessel fitted into the ring.

Everywhere in Latin America we find evidence of how deeply people valued artifacts connected with chocolate, from a poor Guatemalan woman's grinding stone to valuable silver or porcelain pots and cups. We know of their importance because they are among the articles most frequently mentioned in wills. The Guatemalan woman asked that her *metate* be used to pay for two masses for her soul. Rich people made careful inventories of chocolate paraphernalia to be bequeathed to family or friends. Duarte's book includes examples of wills mentioning such articles as silver-studded coconuts, silver *mancerinas*, silver *tembladeras, and* copper chocolate pots. Before the coming of coffee, Latin America was indeed a world ruled by chocolate.

bread and cheese (queso fresco or a buttery kind). In the evenings, visitors were welcomed with lavish spreads called *agasajos* (receptions) featuring chocolate with biscuits, accompanied by a plethora of ices, cold fruit drinks, and pastries.

These descriptions point to a pan-Latin or—more accurately—an Ibero-American chocolate culture with shared tastes and customs built on earlier Mesoamerican foundations. When the use of chocolate flowered in Spain in the seventeenth century, giving rise to a constellation of social rituals and usages, it was inevitable that people would start exchanging experiences across boundaries and oceans. Spaniards returning from New Spain brought with them favorite recipes or preferences, which would undergo transformations on Spanish soil. But that was just the beginning. The dawning Spanish chocolate culture went back overseas with Spanish soldiers, sailors, government bureaucrats or overseers, and members of holy orders—who did not necessarily stay put in one colony but often were transferred from, say, Mexico City to Lima or Caracas. In other words, chocolate customs and ideas flowed freely from city to city in both Latin America and Spain.

THE GENETIC PLOT THICKENS

The pleasures of the chocolate pot ultimately arose from African slave labor. The need for slaves came out of a New World labor crunch that developed after millions of Indians died—apparently of diseases brought by the conquerors—just as Old World demand for the new taste sensation of hot chocolate began to expand beyond everyone's wildest dreams.

This new imported labor supply enabled cacao production to barely hang on in Mexico during the late seventeenth and eighteenth centuries. At the same time, production expanded in South America and Caribbean centers like the French colony Martinique. But after a time, discerning judges began to find that some of the cacao com-

West African workers sun-dry Forastero cacao beans on raised, movable wooden trays.

ing from the South American plantations was surprisingly inferior. This is where the genetic plot thickens. It is difficult to document exactly what happened at just what date, but the end result is clear: At some point in the eighteenth century (possibly earlier), a new source of genes was introduced into the world's commercial cacao stocks. The consequence was a widespread and lasting change in the quality of chocolate, and the repercussions are still being felt today.

To understand what happened, we must return to the several genotypes of true cacao that originated in South America. The most recent research indicates an extremely complex picture. Scientists have recently been able to classify cacao into ten genetic groups or clusters (see page 54). But this is a very new development. People who work with cacao and chocolate still use the unscientific names inherited from an earlier stage of understanding. They talk about domesticated cacao being classified into two major branches, with a third that is a hybrid of the two. The first is Criollo, the northern South American strain that came to Mesoamerica and was introduced to the Spanish. (There is a potentially confusing coincidence here, since in parts of South America like Bolivia and Peru, the word "Criollo" applies to local native strains of cacao in contrast to those brought in from elsewhere.) The second major branch of cacao is Forastero, a general term for cacaos from several parts of South America, including the Lower Amazon, the Guiana region, the Upper Amazon, and the coastal area of Ecuador, home of the prized Nacional. A third type, Trinitarios, are hybrids believed to have been created when Lower Amazon Amelonados were crossed with Criollos in Trinidad.

In historical sources the use of these terms is far from consistent, but even today they are standard for most writers. The newest research shows that though the term Criollo still makes sense, Forastero covers a number of genetic groups with complete imprecision. Actually, the old *"Forastero"* is now known to be nine genetic clusters as dif-

ferent from one another as they are from Criollo. It is like lumping Albanians and Finns together as "Europeans"—useful in some circumstances, hopelessly inadequate for more detailed understanding. In light of the newest research, I have debated whether to adopt the new classification in this book and have decided that for purposes of general discussion it is still helpful to keep the old umbrella terms. However, where it is vital to draw clearer distinctions, I will use the new system.

The need to distinguish between types of cacao arose only as the business expanded. For several generations after the Spanish and Portuguese conquests, Amazonian cacaos remained unknown to the chocolate trade. But their day was coming. By the mid-seventeenth century, both of these Iberian powers had discovered luxuriant stands of something they recognized as cacao growing wild or semiwild on the South American mainland, especially in coastal Ecuador and along the course of the Amazon and its tributaries. Here the native people knew it as a fruit; most probably it had never made the great leap to chocolate.

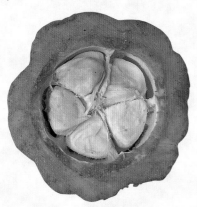

BELOW: A transverse section of an Upper Amazon cacao shows the thickness of the husk (cortex, or pericarp) and the spatial configuration of the beans within the pod, with five rows of flat beans attached to a central placenta.

LEFT: At least 10 percent of the cells making up the tissue of the seed's two cotyledons contain anthocyanins (among other polyphenols). These chemicals give non-Criollo cotyledons a deep purple color. The cotyledons of the majority of non-Criollo cacaos feature varying shades of purple, with a few exceptions: the white-cotyledon Brazilian *catongo* (*Theobroma leiocarpa*), which is a mutant form that contains no anthocyanins, some Amazonian cacaos, and a few hybrids.

OPPOSITE: A smooth-skinned Forastero Calabacillo pod.

Anyone acquainted with Criollo cacao would have found the other cacao strains strangely foreign, which is actually the meaning of the word *forastero*. The fruits of a Lower Amazon cacao known as Amelonado (which is now the name of one of the nine genetic clusters formerly gouped under Forastero) seem to have been the first "foreign" strain to have been introduced in the lands of the "classic" Criollo. They were thick-skinned and exhibited a variety of pod types. Some were smooth and rounded, others warty. The beans within the pods had a flattened rather than plump shape, and the interior of the beans, the cotyledons, were a medium or deep purple instead of white or rosy white. The differences in taste were just as obvious. The raw beans had a harsher bitterness than the familiar Criollo type. When fermented (a process that took longer) and roasted, they retained an acrid, sour quality and a different aroma. The chocolate made from them was strong-flavored but flat, with nothing of the mellowness and complexity of chocolate made from Criollo beans. Yet Amelonado cacao had some overwhelming advantages. The trees reliably produced many pods with a large bean count and appeared very hardy, which was becoming much more important to growers.

BLAST! TRINITARIOS ARE BORN

The introduction of new genetic material primarily from the Lower Amazon into colonial plantations was linked to the problems growers were beginning to encounter with their treasured Criollo cacao. During the chocolate boom, the Spanish had found it impossible to revive Mexican production to pre-plague levels. Indeed, Mexico became a net importer of Venezuelan cacao as early as the seventeenth century, and Spaniards put their eggs in other baskets. Early on, the Spanish took Central American cacao—probably from Nicaragua—to the valleys of Venezuela's central coast and to the Hispanic Caribbean islands. Criollo types probably

passed from Venezuela to the neighboring island of Trinidad (a subject mired in controversy) at an uncertain time.

All seemed well at first. The Venezuelan producers made fortunes in the lucrative cacao trade, now supplying Mexico as well as Europe. But by about 1725 they found themselves facing disaster. A series of epidemics swept over the cacao groves; probably the first recorded one was a mysterious event that wiped out the plantations of neighboring Trinidad in 1727. An English account calls it a "blast," which at that time commonly meant "blight." The Valencian Jesuit Joseph Gumilla, an eyewitness of the catastrophe, saw the barely formed cacao pods falling when they were only the size of an almond and announced that it was a divine judgment on people who didn't pay their tithes to the church. After a few years, the grow-

Two Trinitario pods.

ers tried to reestablish their plantations with stock brought from the Orinoco basin in eastern Venezuela. Mainland trees rapidly crossed with the remains of the old Criollo growth on Trinidad. Growers found themselves with a hybrid cacao—hardier than Criollo and better tasting than the newly introduced cacao—which they named Trinitario, after the island. Recent DNA research shows that the parents were Criollos and Amelonados.

A page from *El Orinoco Ilustrado* by Joseph Gumilla, 1741. Nothing escaped the keen intellect of the Valencian Jesuit Joseph Gumilla, the great historian of the Orinoco River. He recorded the life of Indian communities, flora (including cacao) and fauna, and even the trials and tribulations of the farmers of neighboring Trinidad. Here, he notes that only the cacao trees of N. Rabelo, a pious farmer from the Canary Islands, were spared from the "blast"—a sure sign "that God had rewarded his punctuality" in paying the tithe to the church.

16 EL ORINOCO ILUSTRADO,
(como lo confieſſan aquellos Isleños) que eſte fuè caſtigo de Dios, por la culpable omiſſion en pagar los Diezmos. Y à la verdad, en eſte caſo atò ſu Mageſtad las manos à la critica; porque como dixe, quitò el *Cacao* à todos, menos à N. *Rabelo*, oriundo de Tenerife, una de las Islas Canarias, que era el unico, que pagaba, y proſigue pagando, con toda puntualidad, ſu Diezmo, no ſolo de los arboles, que por aquel tiempo tenia fructiferos, ſino de los que ha ido añadiendo, y vàn fructificando: ſi ſe quiere replicar, que la hacienda de *Rabelo* tal vez eſtà fundada en mejor migajòn de tierra, y en ſitio mas abrigado; reſponden los miſmos vecinos de la Isla, *que no*: y que Dios ha premiado à eſte ſu puntualidad; y que todavia reprehende con eſte exemplar, ſu mal conſiderada omiſsion.

Aunque no nos haviamos apartado mucho de ella, bolvamos à mirar, con mayor cuidado, la miſma Isla: toda ella combida, y provoca à ſu cultivo, con la abundancia de otros frutos. (yà que por ahora eſtà privada del mas principal) Ella tiene ſuficiente gentio para defenderſe de los enemigos, como ſe ha viſto ſiempre, que ha ſido acometida; porque ella miſma es ſu mayor defenſa, con la continuada eſpeſura de boſques impenetrables: la practica ha ſido retirar ſus haberes, mugeres, y chuſma: ponerſe en emboſcadas, y dexar entrar al enemigo por los dos unicos caminos
nos

(marginal notes:) Examinaſe mas la materia.

Otras excelencias de eſta Isla.

Ella miſma, por ſu naturaleza, es ſu defenſa.

A PROMISCUOUS LOT

The genetic relationships of modern cacaos are tangled. We can surmise that the original Criollos and the new stock introduced in Latin American plantations underwent not one but hundreds or thousands of crossings and backcrossings since growers stumbled on what they called Forasteros. Several races may have previously hybridized here and there in the wild to form different subvariants.

It is not clear that Trinitario itself ever was just one single strain resulting from one encounter of two original parents. The name now applies to many different cacao clones—that is, groups of plant specimens propagated by grafting slips onto pieces of rootstock in order to preserve the genetic identity of a single parent. But it is certainly clear that a plethora of offspring came into being in many cacao-growing regions as soon as people started planting the different cacaos together, and that only DNA analysis can unscramble the resulting mixes of genes. The other fact beyond dispute is that the more new genes got into the world cacao supply, the less accustomed consumers became to the taste of chocolate made with pure Criollo cacao.

From the eighteenth century on, the share of the so-called Forastero cacao grew by leaps and bounds. Today it accounts for more than 90 percent of the cacao used by the world's chocolate manufacturers.

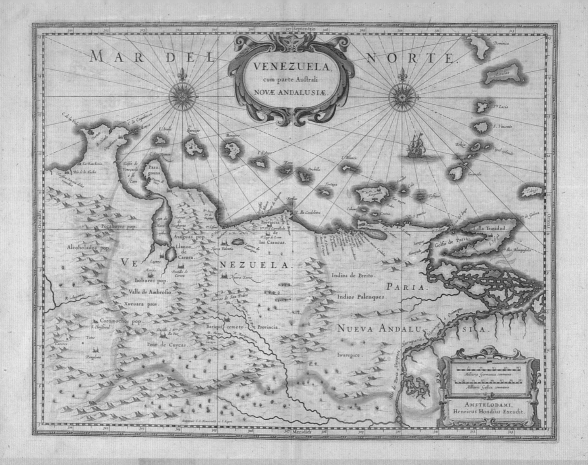

FROM VENEZUELA TO TRINIDAD

Many theories have been made about the nature of the original Trinitario population of the island. We surmise that the cacao brought to Trinidad years after the blast must have been the Lower Amazon Amelonado, or—if spontaneous crossing between the two genotypes had already been going on—they must have had a lot of Lower Amazon genes in their makeup. E. E. Cheesman, a botanist working at Trinidad's Imperial College of Tropical Agriculture who wrote a seminal work on cacao in 1944, speculates that the Trinidadian planters found stock new to them in the area around Ciudad Bolívar on the lower course of the Orinoco. The late Venezuelan scientist Humberto Reyes suggested that hybridization might have occurred first in the Orinoco delta. The cacaos of this area, Reyes added, exhibit the wide range of morphological variations (see page 62) found today in Trinitarios, including white or pale violet cotyledons. He inferred that Criollo could have been easily carried from the foothills of the Andes through the river network that led to the Orinoco and then to the delta area, because in the eighteenth century, trade and most contacts between Trinidad and Venezuela took place through the Orinoco River.

ABOVE: *Venezuela cum parte Australi Novae Andalusiae* by Henricus Hondius, 1642. This dramatic Venezuela map extends from Rio de la Hacha to Trinidad and the mouth of the Orinoco and includes the Lesser Antilles up to Dominica.
RIGHT: The Orinoco River.

FROM NUANCED LUXURY
TO DAILY SNACK

European and colonial Latin American connoisseurs knew a lot about the origin of their chocolate. They did not generally use the names Criollo
or Forastero, but they identified most cacao by the
name of the area in which it was grown. Soconusco and Caracas (*Caraque* to the French, *Carack*
to the English) beans were considered the crème
de la crème. The Soconusco came from an area of
Chiapas that used to send cacao tribute to Aztec
emperors; the Caracas came from the Venezuelan
regions that sent cacao to the port of La Guaira,
near the city of Caracas. Equally valued was Maracaibo cacao, brought from the foothills of the
Venezuelan Andes and the southern environs
of Lake Maracaibo and shipped from Maracaibo
port. Cacao dealers and chocolate makers might
even have vied for beans from a single prestigious
plantation, such as the fabled Venezuelan estate of
Chuao. These highly valued cacaos were among
the purest Criollos surviving after Forasteros and
Trinitarios invaded the world market, and they

A copper etching by Benard of an artisanal chocolate shop in
France, from the *Encyclopédie*, 1715. The workers in this small
shop are shown carrying out the same basic operations performed by the women in pre-Columbian and colonial times.
The dried beans are (1) roasted, (2) winnowed, or shelled,
(3) ground with a mortar and pestle, and (4) ground again
with flavoring ingredients into a very fine paste on a heated
metate-like grinding stone.

commanded high prices. The quality of the beans
could be tasted in the finished chocolate—until a
new technological age dawned.

For many years cacao beans were roasted and
ground into a thick, grainy paste (cacao mass or
liquor), by methods differing very little from the
pre-Columbian *metate* grinding, except that during the eighteenth century small factories succeeded in carrying out the work on a somewhat
larger scale. Then, in 1828, Conrad Van Houten of
the Netherlands developed a way of mechanically
extracting most of the fat from the cacao liquor,
resulting in "cacao butter," which could be used for
anything from soap to suppositories, and the partly
defatted "cocoa," a compacted mass of solids that

could be sold as it was ("rock cocoa") or ground to a powder. This cocoa furnished a quick drink far easier to make than the traditional hot chocolate. In addition, the cacao liquor and cacao butter could be recombined by confectioners in any proportion to make something even more lucrative: eating chocolate.

In Europe, cocoa technology began the transformation of chocolate from an exquisitely nuanced luxury to an inexpensive daily snack. The voluptuous and costly spices of the old-style hot chocolate were abandoned in the industrial product. Cocoa mixed with sugar soon became a drink of the masses. It contained no extraneous flavors, yet paradoxically the basic chocolate flavor mattered less. What the cocoa drinker was tasting was not the essential, whole cacao itself, but an industrially broken-down and reconstituted part of it. Often the original cacao was further dena-

tured by Van Houten's other contribution, an alkali treatment that made the cocoa mix more smoothly while darkening the color and offsetting the natural acidity of poorly fermented or poor-quality beans.

The next step forward was a smoother chocolate. The product made by the early European commercial chocolatiers had a distinct graininess, which was not a fault but an intrinsic quality of the food itself. This was eliminated by a process introduced in 1879 by the Swiss Rodolphe Lindt. He added another stage to the process of grinding the roasted cacao with sugar. The Lindt innovation, known as "conching," was to agitate the ground mass—either unmodified, or more often, adjusted with additional cacao butter—in a sloshing-and-kneading apparatus called a "conche," which was inspired by the Mesoamerican *metate*. The mass was processed for hours on end (usually more

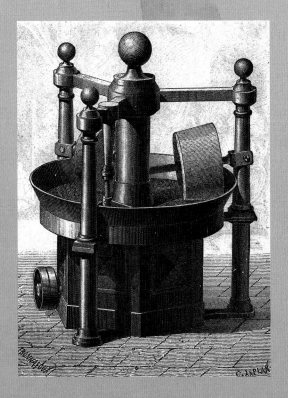

THE MÉLANGEUR

The mélangeur (shown here in a wood engraving by Spamer, from *Orbis Pictus*, 1874) is one of the most versatile and long-lasting inventions of the industrial revolution of chocolate manufacturing. in the nineteenth century. In Cocoa: All about It, Richard Cadbury, under the pseudonym "Historicus," described it:

The pure Cocoa is, in the first place, incorporated with white sugar in what is called a "Melangeur." This mixing machine consists of a round granite revolving slab, forming a pan, the sides being of steel. Into this receptacle the Cocoa and sugar are poured, and two sets of heavy, stationary, granite rollers bruise the thick mass, which is reduced to the consistency of dough. A double knife, the action of which is similar to that of a screw propeller, continually revolves just above the rotary stone slab, and distributes the Chocolate as it passes.

—Richard Cadbury, 1896

Reméleuse, Moulage, Claquette, 1870. This French print shows chocolate-making machines for mixing, molding, as well as vibrating molds to get rid of air bubbles.

than twenty-four, sometimes more than seventy-two). This partly rounded off the edges of the sugar crystals. When made into candy, the resulting mixture had a silky way of melting that soon came to be considered the norm for all chocolate; the frequently used name "fondant" chocolate refers to this melting property.

Conched chocolate proved to be easier to use in baking. It had its oddities and tricks, which can still puzzle uninitiated cooks, but when handled correctly, it amalgamates smoothly and completely with cake batters, cookie and pastry dough, and custard mixtures. Plain ground chocolate was not sufficiently emulsified to do this. If you look at old cookbooks, you will notice that they contain very few recipes for chocolate in any but beverage form until about 1890 to 1900.

With these advances, chocolate could now be manufactured very cheaply on a huge industrial scale. It could be eaten—drinking chocolate had nearly disappeared except in the form of cocoa—by a cross-section of society from beggars to duchesses. Everyone became familiar with the faces of smiling children on the labels of favorite brands—Fry's or Cadbury's in England, Menier or Poulain

in France, Lindt or Suchard in Switzerland, and later, Hershey's in North America.

ANONYMOUS CHOCOLATE

From the early industrial history of chocolate into the twentieth century, fine manufacturers used high-quality beans to produce their best chocolate blends. But the desire to create a uniform product that would carry their company's imprint, and the urge to keep their formulas secret, contributed to the divorce of chocolate from its place of origin. Even excellent chocolate had become faceless and anonymous, for the great majority of consumers had no way of seeing and judging the cacao from which it was made. Only a scattering of small factories in Europe and Latin America kept alive the old customary ways of making chocolate.

As the price of chocolate went down, so did the quality of the cacao supply. The more careless manufacturers were happy to buy mixed batches of beans with scant regard to their quality. Over-roasting and some conching often helped to reduce or mask the acidity and bitterness of cheap, unfermented Forastero beans and create a more

XOCOLAT FAMILIAR

A yellowing notebook dating from 1888 found at the old offices of Xocolat Arumi (today the Barcelona company Chocovic) contains recipes written in an elegant nineteenth-century hand, giving precise measurements for chocolate blends prepared specially for several local families. This was the so-called *xocolat familiar* (family-style chocolate). Some not only list flavorings—such as "Chinese" cinnamon (possibly cassia cinnamon) or pine nuts, a Catalan favorite—but also identify the type of cacao or blend of cacaos used in the recipe: Caracas or Guayaquil, or a mixture of the two. In these personalized recipes, we find the familiar hierarchy of quality and price.

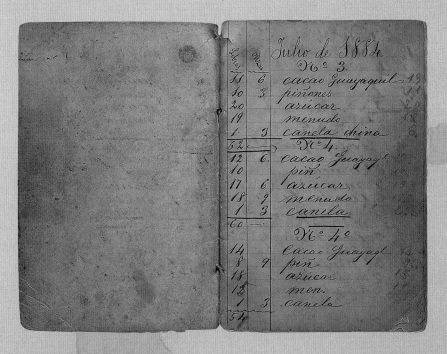

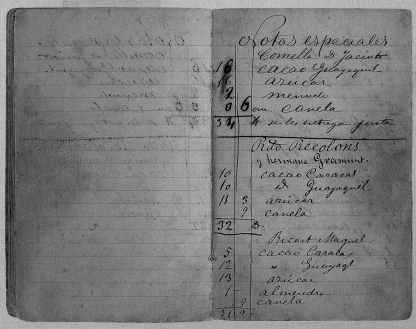

neutral-tasting end product that would reward a purchaser with exactly the same flavor and texture year in, year out. The practice of adding dried milk to the chocolate mass to make milk chocolate (a process introduced by the Swiss manufacturer Daniel Peter in 1879, the same year as Lindt's conching breakthrough) put another layer of distance between the consumer and the direct flavor of good and bad cacao.

CACAO ON THE MOVE

A new life had begun with the coming of cacao; what had happened earlier did not matter. Sugar mills and distilleries, plantations of sugar and coffee, old tales and legends, had disappeared forever. Now the groves of cacao were developing, and so were new stories of how men fought for possession of the land. The blind folk singers were carrying to the remotest country fairs the names and deeds of the men of cacao.

—JORGE AMADO, *Gabriela, Clove and Cinnamon*

Follow the equator, and you'll find cacao. Because of its particular climatic requirements, cacao was fated to become a Third World crop. Starting at the end of the seventeenth century, the Spanish carried it eastward to the Philippines, Java and other islands of present-day Indonesia, and the Malay Peninsula. The Portuguese made cacao-planting forays in some of the same areas. But their big contribution came in the nineteenth century when they conclusively established a Lower Amazon cacao from Bahia (Brazil) in West Africa, where the French also took up cacao cultivation. For a time, all the colonial powers (including the English, the Dutch, and even the Germans) sought to get a finger in the chocolate sauce.

All this activity had tremendous consequences. Once the European colonists in the New World became aware of the South American cacaos that would later be called "aliens," or *forasteros,* it was only a matter of time before entrepreneurs would begin exploiting the enormous wild cacao reserves of the Amazon River basin and the northern Ecuadorian coast. By the end of the eighteenth century, the "new" cacao was on the move within the New World, and soon it would be on its way to Africa.

In the colonial and early modern era, the upper part of the Amazon River system had not been fully explored. The first wild cacaos discovered by settlers were the kind that grew along the Lower Amazon. It was this prolific, hardy tree, called Amelonado on account of its melon-shaped pods, that would facilitate an explosive nineteenth- and twentieth-century increase in the world supply of cacao.

The growth of the cacao industry brought thousands of Africans from Angola, the Congo area, Dahomey, and Calabar to Venezuela between the seventeenth and nineteenth centuries. Today their descendants tend the cacao farms and plantations of Barlovento and the coastal valleys of the state of Aragua.

1. Mexico, 2. Guatemala, 3. Honduras, 4. El Salvador, 5. Nicaragua, 6. Costa Rica, 7. Panama, 8. Colombia, 9. Ecuador, 10. Peru, 11. Bolivia, 12. Cuba, 13. Dominican Republic, 14. St. Lucia, 15. Grenada, 16. Trinidad, 17. Venezuela, 18. State of Pará (Brazil), 19. State of Bahia (Brazil), 20. Ivory Coast, 21. Ghana, 22. Togo, 23. Nigeria, 24. Cameroon, 25. Fernando Pó (Bioko), São Tomé, and Principe, 26. Madagascar, 27. India, 28. Sri Lanka, 29. Java, 30. Malaysia, 31. Philippine Islands, 32. Sulawesi, 33. Papua New Guinea, 34. Solomon Islands, 35. Fiji, 36. Hawaii, 37. Samoa Islands, 38. Bali, 39. Vietnam. The red areas show cacao-producing regions.

Cacao did not stand still under the control of Spain and its rivals while chocolate was winning new converts. After establishing cacao plantations in the Caribbean, Spain tried to expand to other sites, hoping to corner the European market. But their ambitions were soon thwarted. Cacao trees require conditions like those found in their first American homes and failed to produce even as far north of the equator as the Tropic of Cancer or as far south as Capricorn.

West to East, East to West

The promise that speculators saw in cacao would cause many thousands of Africans to be transplanted westward to Venezuela, Ecuador, Brazil, and the Caribbean islands and East Indians to islands like Trinidad. It would draw smaller numbers of Europeans in the same direction to seek their fortunes as landowners, farm supervisors, or merchants. French planters coming from Haiti settled in Cuba and Trinidad after the Haitian revolution at the end of the eighteenth century. They were followed in the nineteenth century by Corsicans who also settled in the Paria Peninsula in Venezuela. Vast plantations tended by slaves (or after emancipation, day laborers or tenant farmers) were scattered over millions of acres of tropical forest.

The cacao boom also sent cacao traveling the other way across the Atlantic, and millions of trees were planted in the regions that are modern-day Nigeria, Ghana, Cameroon, and the Ivory Coast, eventually making Africa the largest world supplier of cacao. It also poised the economic survival of large regions or whole countries on a steadily narrowing genetic base.

For some reason, Brazil initially lagged behind the Spanish colonies in promoting cacao culture, to which it gave an official blessing only in 1679. But in 1746 the French settler Luiz Frederico Warneau transplanted some cacao seedlings—though only as ornamentals—from Pará to a plantation on the River Pardo, not far south of Ilhéus on the east coast of today's state of Bahia. It proved to be a fruitful environment for growing cacao. At that time Bahia was sugar country, one of the major destinations of the slave ships. But the new European chocolate technology, starting with Van Houten's cocoa process in 1828, signaled golden opportunities for expansion in Bahia. A ragtag wave of workers poured in from all over Brazil. Soon Amelonado cacao (locally called *Brazil comum*) replaced sugar as the region's leading source of wealth. By 1906,

Brazil—mostly meaning Bahia—was the world's greatest cacao producer.

At the same time, Amelonado-type cacao was being planted in most of the Caribbean sugar dominions. In the late-nineteenth century, it began its rise to the great cash crop of West Africa.

Aside from the special case of Venezuela, there are a few areas of the cacao-growing world where Amelonado did not come to dominate the industry. The trees that the Spanish first brought to the Philippines were Criollos, and as cacao spread westward to Indonesia and Malaysia, Criollo was the

In the nineteenth century, Corsicans settled in Trinidad and the nearby Paria Peninsula in Venezuela. They became landowners and farm supervisors like Arsenio Borthomierth, the second-generation Corsican who managed La Concepción farm in Barlovento, Venezuela, who holds a Criollo pod.

Bahia from *A New Map of South America, Showing Its General Divisions, Chief Cities & Towns, Rivers, Mountains, & Dedicated to His Highness William Duke of Gloucester* by Wells, Oxford, 1700. From the late-nineteenth century until recent outbreaks of witches' broom disease, the Brazilian state of Bahia was the largest cacao-growing region in Latin America.

foundation of the first plantations (though profit-minded growers later brought in Trinitarios and various hybrids, followed in the second half of the twentieth century by Amelonados). A major factor in keeping Criollo afloat in this part of the world after it had been overshadowed elsewhere was the growth of the milk chocolate industry. Trinitario cacao brought to the island of Java from Venezuela was bred with the island's Criollo cacao and evolved into a strain famous for the attractive light color of the beans even after roasting, a marked cosmetic advantage in the finished product.

The other anomaly in the story of the global takeover of Lower Amazon Amelonado is Ecuador. Geneticists conjecture that it was home to some singular cacao strains long before the Spanish colonial period. One of these was a cacao traditionally called "Nacional" and long thought to be some unusual Forastero variant. (In the new classification system, Nacional is recognized as a specific genetic cluster in its own right.)

At around the turn of the nineteenth century, Ecuador charged in to flood the market with a lesser-quality cacao. To dealers, it was known as "Guayaquil cacao," after the port from which it was shipped, but its popular nickname was "poor people's cacao." But other genetic material was already in Ecuador—a Criollo or a hybrid from Trinidad generically called "Criollo from Venezuela," that had crossed with Ecuador's native Nacional cacao. These hybrids produced a better cacao, which was sold under the umbrella name of "Esmeralda," after the humid northern province where it was grown. Another region of Ecuador on the upper Guayas River became known for another of the plant's still unplumbed genetic mysteries: Arriba, a unique type of Nacional cacao. It combines a good basic flavor with a distinctive flowery bouquet that people in the chocolate business can recognize immediately.

Descendants of the first Trinitarios and a wide array of other hybrids continued to be fitfully explored wherever growers wanted to upgrade the flavor of their cacao. Yet the overall Criollo element on the world's cacao plantations has been shrinking from disease and neglect for close to two hundred years. With a few exceptions, Criollo cacao all but disappeared from its old Mexican and Central American strongholds, replaced by plantings of Amelonado that the growers considered hardier. Some Mexican plantations in Chiapas State have a few Criollo trees. In the area of Chinandega in Nicaragua, there are still pockets of a fine Criollo strain formerly called "royal cacao" or *cacao real*. This cacao is known for its large warty,

East Indian workers in Trinidad get ready for the cacao harvest. The men hold long poles fitted with sharp blades for picking cacao.

red pods with curved pointy tips, which are probably identical to the remaining Criollos growing in the central coastal valleys of Venezuela. In 1995, a team of scientists from the Smithsonian and Trinidad's Cocoa Research Unit discovered scattered Criollo trees growing wild in the mountains of Belize, probably relics of Mayan times. Previous expeditions had also found isolated wild Criollo trees in Mayan "sacred groves" in the Yucatán and in the Lacandon forest in eastern Chiapas. But only in Venezuela did a large spectrum of Criollo cacao and hybrids with high-Criollo germplasm manage to survive. This is why Venezuelan cacao never lost its special reputation among dealers and chocolatiers who knew quality.

Disease: The Achilles Heel

Unfortunately for everyone from cacao dealers to peasants in the new cacao-growing regions, the supposedly hardy trees of the Lower Amazon proved to be vulnerable to disease. Wherever large plantings were made, sooner or later a pest or disease would appear that would wipe out a crop within days or cripple a whole plantation within a year or two. Some scourges would make their way from one established growing region to neighboring ones. Others occurred in new regions where cacao turned out to present a virgin target to some local virus, fungus, or insect.

Names like "witches' broom," "capsid," "swollen shoot," "black pod rot," "frosty pod," and "cocoa wilt" came to strike terror into entire communities or nations. The vagaries of weather—capable of creating disaster in their own right—could also create new opportunities for disease or threaten the lives of the all-important shade trees. A seemingly innocent plant like the Amazonian *cupuaçu* or the African kola tree might turn out to be a host for one of cacao's many emerging enemies. Considering what a harsh mistress cacao could be, it is not surprising that eventually the great estates of the colonial period began to be broken up. In most of the world's cacao regions only small farmers remained to tend the chancy crop on tiny plots of ground with little between them and ruin.

Around the turn of the twentieth century, cacao-growing nations and major chocolate companies began to apply scientific methods to the problems of cacao, and the study of varieties evolved into a precise search for the most highly productive, disease-resistant cacaos. The early-twentieth century saw the founding of research centers and experimental stations, of which the Imperial College of Tropical Agriculture (today a part of the University of the West Indies) on Trinidad soon became the greatest. It was at this point that some of the formerly overlooked Upper Amazon cacao strains entered the commercial picture.

By now, the technique of cloning the best stock was being practiced on some advanced plantations on a large scale. In the late 1930s, geneticist F. J. Pound of the Imperial College of Tropical Agriculture on Trinidad began a series of cacao-collecting expeditions—later continued by others—among the wild stands of cacao trees along the western Amazon and its tributaries coming down from the Andes in Peru and Ecuador. Their hope was to infuse new blood, or at any rate new genes, into the vulnerable cacao supply. Over a period of decades, scientists from the Imperial College of Tropical Agriculture planted seedlings from chosen specimens on several farms, among them Marper Farm, which today stands as a relic of Trinidad's pioneering effort against cacao diseases. The likeliest candidates were cloned and crossed with one another as well as with select Trinitario cultivars (selected from the best original Trinitario population of the island). The most

---

The first record of cultivated cacao in Indonesia dates from 1778. Presumably Criollo cacao had arrived in Java from the Philippines at an earlier date. However, the genotype that produces the coveted bean known to the trade as Java A or fine ("*edel*") cacao is technically a Trinitario—the progeny of Java's native Criollo population and a single Venezuelan Trinitario tree brought to the island in 1888 and planted in Djati Roenggo estate.

Moniliophthora perniciosa, the pathogen responsible for the dreaded witches' broom disease, has a complex life cycle. When the fungus first infects a cacao tree, it lives between the cells of the plant and causes abnormal growth of the infected area. In most cases, the tree will put forth a flush of seemingly healthy new leaves. But when the fungus invades the cells of the plant and kills them, it enters a saprophytic phase during which it receives nourishment from the plant's dead tissue. After six to seven weeks, the flush of leaves shrivels and dies out, resembling a broom.

LEFT: Plant pathologist Jean-Marc Thévenin examines a dried-out witches' broom sample at the pathology laboratory of the Cocoa Research Unit.

RIGHT: Members of the 1952–53 Anglo-Colombian cacao collection expedition to the Colombian Amazon.

successful resulting trees were cloned for commercial distribution. The criteria of success were simple: high yields and immunity to disease and pests.

The field of cacao research blossomed. In cacao-growing nations around the world, government- or industry-sponsored research facilities began studying the potential of the Trinidadian clones and Trinidad Select Hybrids (TSH) and advising farmers on their use. One of the most dramatic results was a second movement of cacao germplasm around the globe. This time the germplasm came from Upper Amazon strains and the so-called Ecuadorian Refractarios, chosen for their apparent immunity to disease, and was circulated with greater efficiency and knowledge. The overall share of Criollo in the world supply dwindled even further. Yet the long-term consequences of this "new" germplasm were no miracle. For many decades the last thing the researchers (and most growers) thought of was what kind of chocolate the new cacao cultivars would make—some of the disease-resistant plants produce acidic and bitter-tasting chocolate. Moreover, the very efficiency of modern breeding and cloning programs turned out to be a mixed blessing. It rapidly caused the genetic basis of commercial cacao, already narrowed through long reliance on Amelonado types, to shrink more. After a few generations, farms planted with many clones of a few alleged wonder stocks proved more susceptible than anyone had guessed to new troubles and diseases—and some of the old ones as well.

The last decades have been catastrophic ones in some of the world's most fruitful regions. The Bahian plantations are close to ruin, devastated by witches' broom. Ecuador's cacao industry has been collapsing throughout the twentieth century. Its prized Arriba, already in serious trouble, received what may have been the coup de grâce from the 1982 to 1983 and the 1997 to 1998 climatic disruptions of El Niño. (Already in 1937, F. J. Pound had reported that this valued strain showed little real resistance to witches' broom disease.)

Cacao

THE PROMISE OF CACAO

Given the dire circumstances of cacao today, it may seem perverse of me to describe this as a time of immense hope and promise, but in many ways it is. Several factors are contributing to the writing of an epochal chapter in the history of chocolate.

The first is DNA analysis and genome mapping. Today scientists stand on the threshold of a revolutionary breakthrough in the knowledge of cacao. (A team of researchers at the USDA Subtropical Horticultural Research Station in Miami has begun sequencing the complete cacao genome; see page 53). For the first time, we have the realistic prospect of being able to identify the genes responsible for precise traits in cacao (and the chocolate made from it), and also to trace just where and how different strains split off from some ancestral *Theobroma* and from one another. We are in a position to study the makeup of cacao's wild *Theobroma* cousins and perhaps adapt some of their survival strategies to combat the cultivated plant's natural enemies.

Allied with this effort are pioneering studies of tropical ecosystems and the environmental adaptability of cacao. We are starting to learn more about the interrelationships among organisms (for example, the best insect pollinators for low-yielding strains). On experimental and some commercial farms, growers have found that cacao can be raised successfully on open ground with little shade as long as it is well irrigated—a discovery that might open up new cultivation areas, but has triggered misgivings among environmentalists about effects on existing ecosystems. The consensus seems to be that traditional shaded environments are less invasive.

OPPOSITE: *Metamorphosis Insectorum Surinamensium* by Maria Sibylla Merian, 1705. This copper engraving shows cacao pods from Dutch Guyana.

Deforestation in areas where cacao originated threatens to destroy the genetic diversity of this marvelous plant. It is encouraging to see that concern over the genetic erosion of cacao has led to its designation as a priority crop for conservation. At the heart of the effort to conserve cacao's biodiversity is the creation of germplasm banks—safe havens for wild varieties of cacao that are now threatened.

The very term "germplasm bank" conjures up a world of test tubes. But a cacao germplasm bank is really halfway between a large plantation and a botanical garden. There scientists and agronomists keep thousands of cacao trees (domesticated and wild) from all over the world, for conservation, research, and use in plant-breeding programs. Most cacao-producing countries have their own limited germplasm banks, but only the International Cocoa Genebank of Trinidad (ICG, T) and the Centro Agronómico Tropical de Investigaciones y Enseñanza (CATIE) in Turrialba, Costa Rica, have been designated as universal collection depositories. Of the two, Trinidad has the largest number of accessions (close to three thousand).

There are other signs that we are about to enter a new era for cacao. Major research institutes are now beginning to place more emphasis on flavor as a breeding criterion. This area of research still lags behind more urgent practical concerns like resistance to the big three among fungal diseases: witches' broom, frosty pod, and black pod rot. But it will definitely be the wave of the future. Part of the training programs for cacao researchers and agronomists now involves learning to recognize the best-tasting specimens and to select them for reproduction with the goal of excellence clearly in mind.

Yet for all the present possibilities and future advances, nothing can ever eliminate the risks, uncertainties, and infinite labor of actual cacao farming. It will always be at least as much an art as a science, and all chocolate lovers should understand what is involved.

ON THE THRESHOLD OF GENETIC BREAKTHROUGHS

From the road outside, the entrance to the Horticulture Research Station of the USDA's Agricultural Research Service (ARS) looks like the manicured approach to another fancy condo complex. But inside, it is home to several tropical plant collections and headquarters for groundbreaking research on cacao genetics.

I spent two days at the station learning about its colorful story with the help of head geneticist Dr. Raymond Schnell, his geneticist colleagues Dr. Stephen Brown and Dr. Juan Carlos Motamayor (a Mars liaison), molecular biologist Dr. David Kuhn, and agricultural science research technician Mike Winterstein.

The Miami facility began as a quarantine station and germplasm bank in the 1950s, when the USDA was seeking to stop the movement of cacao diseases between Old and New World growing regions. It stands on the site of property originally bought by the legendary horticulturist and tropical plant explorer David Fairchild in 1923. At one point, he was able to cannibalize the paving stones of a nearby World War I military airstrip for the imposing gray stone walls that now shelter parts of the station's botanical collections, including cacao. They help retain daytime heat through the night, creating a few extra degrees of warmth that enable cacao and other tender tropical plants to survive this far north.

In 1992, Hurricane Andrew destroyed most of the trees, and it took six years for the station to resume activities. In the interim, the State Department had decided that cacao looked like a good replacement crop for coca and marijuana in the Latin tropics, and invited Schnell, who was already involved in cacao research, to aid the effort.

About a year later, the work moved into another phase, when Mars, Inc. became involved. Having seen the destruction of the cacao industry in Bahia, formerly one of its major supplying regions, the company offered to fund research to develop plants resistant to some rapidly spreading epidemic fungal diseases, especially witches' broom (*Monoliophthora perniciosa*) and another disease called frosty pod (*M. Roreri*). As Schnell explained, the great priority was to protect African cacao, which is the mainstay of the U.S. chocolate industry and rests on a perilous narrow genetic base of Lower Amazon Amelonado and a few strains of Upper Amazon cacao brought as pods from Trinidad by A. F. Posnette in the 1940s. The team first started working in Latin America, then in West Africa, but affiliations with existing centers have since been established in Puerto Rico, Costa Rica, Ecuador, Peru, Brazil, and New Guinea.

One thing is connected with another, and the disease prevention program gave rise to far-reaching attempts to collect and—just as crucial—accurately identify cacao specimens. As Schnell and Winterstein told me, this is no mere academic exercise. DNA testing has made it possible to see that some of the world's great germplasm banks have often been full of mislabeled specimens—a hindrance to any scientific breeding program meant to exploit a particular cultivar's precise qual-

Genome scientists at the USDA's Agricultural Research Center, standing with young cacao trees, within the enclosed stone walls built from the original World War I airstrip. From left to right: Juan Carlos Motamayor, David Kuhn, Stephen Brown, Raymond Schnell, Mike Winterstein.

ities, from subtle flavor nuances to certain kinds of disease or pest resistance.

Everyone from cacao growers to chocolate makers to consumers would benefit if the climate of misinformation could be corrected. Now we have the means for accurately matching tree cuttings or beans with true genetic fingerprints. For the last decade, Schnell's team has been systematically examining germplasm from many collections, trying to set the record straight and make this information accessible. As he says, "If you were a geneticist, you could go to our Web site here in Miami and you could pull out the genetic fingerprint for a given clone. All the important breeding clones are in there," meaning the station's database.

Mapping Cacao

One of the ultimate goals of the USDA/Mars cacao research program is to construct an overall genetic picture of the species itself through two interrelated molecular biology programs: the International Marker System Selection Program and the Genome Sequencing Program, which has gotten the lion's share of publicity.

Dr. Stephen Brown, who showed me some of the results in progress, was able to put the individual efforts into overall perspective. He commented that though cacao has lagged behind genetic research on staple crops like corn or wheat, it actually has some advantages for research purposes. For one thing, the number of chromosomes in the cell nucleus is comparatively small (10 is the haploid number, compared to 23 for human beings), which means that there is less material to analyze. But there is also the fact that because annual plants reproduce once a year or more often, it doesn't take much time for them to start genetically diverging from the original ancestor. Because cacao doesn't have to reseed itself every year, there are fewer intervening generations between the ancestral and modern plant. In other words, he explained, modern cacaos "are not that far from

wild cacaos compared to corn and wheat." The grain crops have been more intensively manipulated for human purposes, resulting in more shuffling around and repositioning of genes on the chromosome. An ancient Old World crop like wheat is surrounded with more overlays due to human intervention than cacao is. This isn't to say that cacao breeding has not resulted in the loss of important germplasm.

I was then shown into the area where scientists are performing different kinds of genetic analysis. Cecile Olano, a support scientist in the International Marker System Selection Program, was using a capillary electrophoresis apparatus (ABI Sequencer) to examine small fragments of cacao DNA that had been extracted from leaves and amplified through polymerase chain reaction. "Electrophoresis" is visualizing the movement of particles in an electrical field; in this case, particles of genetic material move through tiny capillaries and fluoresce because they have been tagged with a fluorescent substance during amplification. A camera records the fluorescence that they emit, and then researchers can view the complete data on an electropherogram through a computer screen to see the size of the fragment that has been amplified.

While waiting for the results of Olano's work, Schnell described the outlines of the Genome Sequencing Program, a pioneering project launched in June 2008 with funding from Mars, Inc., and being carried out at several locations in collaboration with other research organizations. The participants include IBM, the Genome Institute of Clemson University in South Carolina, and an ARS laboratory in Mississippi. (Mars will release the final results in a publicly available database.)

The sequencing program consists of two complementary genetic map projects, to be done on entirely different machines using different sets of chemistries. The "linkage map," broadly speaking, provides information about genes that tend to be "linked," or inherited together in a group, because they occur very close to one another on a chromosome. This work has been done in Miami. Most of the sequencing runs will be done by computational molecular biologist Brian Scheffler at the Mississippi ARS labs. He has a special machine that can read sequences of 300 base pairs faster and with less expense. The more precise "physical map" will reproduce the whole start-to-finish sequence of all the genes on a chromosome. It starts with ordering different limited (short) DNA sequences (like isolated words in a coded sentence) on a chromosome (this is the material provided by Scheffler). The sequences are then "assembled" (like putting together the whole sentence) and the resulting information is "annotated" (sifted through to differentiate actual genes from other bits of DNA occurring along the sequence).

Any bit of data from the linkage map can be used in breeding programs as it emerges. For example, the gene for witches' broom resistance was identified by F.J. Pound in the 1930s and has been used ever since. DNA analysis and other modern methods made it possible to actually locate the specific position of this gene on the chromosome. Genes of known locations can be used as markers. "Using these molecular markers," Stephen Brown says, "we can go out and screen the progeny [offspring of crosses] to see

Venezuelan-born Dr. Juan Carlos Motamayor.

which one contains the correct alleles [members of dominant/recessive gene pairs] for resistance." In consequence, researchers don't have to grow plants all the way to maturity and wait ten years to select the resistant progeny. They can confirm resistance in a year or two and quickly eliminate nonresistant trees, allowing them to concentrate on other qualities like yield.

The physical map is a more complex whole than the linkage map. Its initial stage was finished in early March 2009; Schnell hopes to have a draft genome sequence ready for presentation by the start of 2010, and estimates that the whole project will be completed by about 2012–13.

BREAKING THE CRIOLLO/ FORASTERO PARADIGM

The article "Geographic and Genetic Population Differentiation of the Amazonian Chocolate Tree (*Theobroma cacao L*)" by Juan Carlos Motamayor et al (*PLoS ONE,* Vol. 3, Issue 10 October 2008) was a groundbreaking event in cacao-genetics circles. It did away with the long-accepted paradigm that divided all cacaos into Criollo or Forastero types and substituted a new model based on genetic analysis of 952 different cacao specimens (whittled down from an initial 1,241). By studying DNA patterns, the researchers were able to identify all specimens as belonging to one of ten "genetic clusters," mostly named for place of geographical origin. (And the number will likely grow as research continues.) In alphabetical order they are Amelonado, Contamaná, Criollo, Curaray, Guiana, Iquitos, Marañón, Nacional, Nanay, and Purús.

The cacaos belonging to these clusters are not in themselves necessarily "new" or newly discovered. Of course Criollo, Amelonado, and Nacional are names that have been in use for generations, basically referring to the same cacaos covered by the new designations. Of the rest, many have been part of the commercial cacao gene supply since the 1930s, when they were introduced through clones or seeds of stock brought back from the famous collecting expeditions of the "fruit explorer" F. J. Pound. It is now possible to be more precise about the genetic identity of this material. For instance, we now know that the prolific and disease-resistant cultivars Scavina 6 and Scavina 12, found all over the world, are in fact members of the Contamaná cluster, which originated in northeastern Peru (see page 87).

Motamayor's work also addresses the confusions that arise from what he calls "introgression," or the movement of genes from one original gene pool to another by deliberate or accidental crossings. The Porcelana cacao of Venezuela is one example. People who know cacao types can be fairly sure that the trees on some old plantations are more or less "pure" Porcelana—"pure" meaning that a complex of traits controlled by a very few genes is passed on without dilution. Less-experienced observers may identify anything as pure Porcelana that happens to have the typical white cotyledons, whether or not it also has the right delicate, nutty flavor. There are several possible routes by which genetically determined traits originally belonging to one population may show up in another. But the important fact is that an accurate map of genes and the qualities they control will make it possible to test claims against reality.

Motamayor's research has three crucial dimensions, all bearing on the problem of accurately classifying the plants that growers work with. He studies not only actual cacao genetics in the laboratory but cacao geography—the movement of populations across different regions—and cacao anthropology—the human element involved in distributing the plant to diverse locations. None of these factors can be adequately understood without examining the others.

Essentially, all three "traditional" domesticated cacao types (Amelonado, Criollo, Nacional) have undergone a centuries-long (or even much older) process of losing genetic diversity in the course of migrating to new areas such as Central America, the Amazon regions, and the Pacific coast of Ecuador. The general pattern is the same everywhere: they have become more uniform in makeup while losing the genes that provided ancestral populations with qualities necessary for their survival (for instance, resistance to disease) or for a spectrum of other traits.

A good instance is the white cacao of Tabasco, Mexico, which has attracted attention from chocolate makers all over the world because at a superficial glance it appears to be a Criollo. It has been advertised as having close relationship with the Venezuelan Porcelana. But Motamayor, who has done the genetic fingerprinting, understands more of its actual history. Originally selected in Tabasco by a grower named Echeverría, it is a productive cacao that does have several Criollo characteristics, at least on the surface. But these "phenotypical" qualities, such as the white color of the beans, are controlled by a handful of genes, while the genes responsible for flavor may have been lost. DNA analysis has revealed a large introgression of Amelonado genes in Tabasco white cacao—meaning that it certainly is not a pure Criollo. Chocolate made from it may be light in color like that from Porcelana cacao, but will have a telltale fruitiness, residual astringency, and bitterness that are never part of the true Porcelana flavor profile. Similarly, when Amelonado was taken from its Lower Amazon birthplace to commercial plantations in Central America after growers there turned away from Criollo, it lost much of its original genetic diversity, as breeders concentrated on a relatively few qualities that they considered desirable.

For the first time, modern techniques make the dream of accurately classifying these and all other known cacao specimens look achievable. Motamayor is a key player in the effort. He was instrumental in producing the 2008 report that broke the former paradigm dividing cacao into just "Criollo" and "Forastero" types and identified ten distinct genetic clusters of cacao. Like many other people in the chocolate-cacao world, I was thrilled and bewildered at this breakthrough because it threw some of my own preconceptions in doubt. At one point I said to Motamayor that maybe it was just the beginning—who knows if there are still other genetic clusters waiting to be discovered? His answer was both yes and no. There are possibly two new clusters in store, from expeditions to Bolivia in 2007 and Peru in 2008, which have not been named yet because more analysis is needed. But with unexpected somberness he told me that the time for some discoveries may be growing short, because rapid deforestation of natural cacao habitats may wipe out some populations before anyone has the opportunity to find them.

But still the classification work goes on, at many levels. The materials analyzed come from three sources. Some are in germplasm banks, or are being grown by farmers. Others, however, are wild cacaos that have never undergone breeding. These are collected by field expeditions. The exact location of each specimen was originally established by maps but now is done with GPS. It is then photographed in situ and the collectors gather leaves from each plant to be sent to the Miami ARS laboratory for DNA analysis. They also make cuttings and send slips to be grafted at the major breeding institutes in Ecuador and Peru. Gradually the many separate pieces of the giant puzzle are coming together.

But there's one piece of the puzzle that has not kept pace in the swiftly moving search to unravel the genetic mysteries of cacao: the actual flavor of the beans. I thought of it when Motamayor described to me the legacy he'd like to leave through his work. Of course, he would like to be remembered as the scientist who broke what he calls the "unscientific" old "Criollo" and "Forastero" divide. But most importantly, he would also like to be remembered for helping farmers in particular ways—for instance, making it possible to plant orchards with small, strong, fast-growing cultivars that produce more fruit than yesterday's varieties, are easier to prune and manage, and are more resistant to pests and diseases. The result would be larger harvests with lower labor and maintenance costs, as well as less need for pesticides (meaning less exposure to toxic chemicals for the farmer, a greener future for the industry). Motamayor does appreciate the flavor qualities of the cacaos he's finding and classifying. He's especially excited about the potential of San Miguel 8, an Ecuadorian cacao within the Curaray genetic cluster, with large white cotyledons and an attractive fruity taste. But flavor as such doesn't always get its due.

According to Dr. Raymond Schnell, flavor-testing facilities to make micro-batches of chocolate from cacao breeding samples exist at only two of the world breeding stations with which the USDA has connections (Ecuador, New Guinea, and Puerto Rico). He would like to have this capacity at every station, but as Motamayor frankly put it, "Flavor is not a major objective right now." The majority thinking is that at least for now, the problems faced by cacao farmers are too pressing to divert attention from goals like productivity and disease resistance. The specter of fungus-born plagues and catastrophic shortages is intensely present to all observers.

My own dream is to see cacao research like that of Schnell, Motamayor, and their colleagues lead to improvement in every aspect of the cacao-chocolate endeavor, from life on the plantation to the products of a fine chocolate maker. It saddens me that nearly all the big breeding stations lack facilities to taste the results of what they're growing—in a way, it defeats the whole purpose of cacao growing, which is to enjoy chocolate. Yet I think a more holistic approach will eventually prevail. No one wants something like cacao on steroids with miserable flavor. In the end, I believe that a more accurate knowledge of cacao genetics will mean more respect for chocolate quality.

CACAO: "HEART AND BLOOD"

When Europeans first tasted cacao in the sixteenth century, they promptly began to map the medical powers of chocolate by the light of existing medical theory. Later researchers followed suit with varying results. In the last few years, however, the Aztec proverb that identified cacao with "heart and blood" has turned out to be uncannily prescient. We are now learning that chocolate contains substances offering great promise against cardiovascular disease.

There is an exotic but true Latin American backdrop to this growing realization. In the mid-1990s, Norman K. Hollenberg, a Harvard Medical School nephrologist and cardiologist investigating the genetics of blood pressure levels, came to the San Blas archipelago, which runs along the Caribbean coast of Panama, to study the Cuna (also spelled Kuna) Indians who live on these palm-dotted islands. (Coincidentally, I had known and admired the Cuna since researching an illustrated book on their world-renowned *molas*, the front and back panels of the blouses worn by the women.)

Hollenberg was pursuing a 1940s lead concerning the near-complete absence of hypertension among the Cuna from youth into old age, despite a diet high in salt. His original goal—to demonstrate there is a genetic basis for this people's circulatory health—didn't pan out. Cuna Indians living in Panama City had hypertension rates close to those of the general population. But his inquiries suggested a possible dietary link with cacao. And soon a research proposal that he had submitted to the American Cocoa Association attracted the attention of scientists at Mars, Inc., who had been learning surprising things about the chemistry of cacao.

At this point Mars was starting to take on a leading role in different aspects of chocolate-cacao research. Part of the impetus was the 1980s Brazilian witches' broom epidemic, which underscored the terrible vulnerability of cacao as a crop. By the time Norman Hollenberg became interested in the relationship between cacao and health, Mars was already pursuing several kinds of highly specialized scientific investigation into the plant that had long furnished its livelihood.

One important avenue of research was taking shape in the Mars laboratory in Hackettstown, New Jersey, headed by Harold H. Schmitz. It involved polyphenols, a large family of compounds occurring in many foods that seemed to play a role in cacao-chocolate flavor and to have other physical effects.

Two Mars researchers, Lee Rosanczyk and John Hammerstone, had begun examining a polyphenol class called flavonoids, and more specifically a flavonoid subgroup called flavanols. (Media reports about flavanols often vaguely describe them as "antioxidants," but the Mars researchers quickly recognized that they must trigger some particular circulatory mechanism that went beyond general antioxidant activity.) When I spoke to Schmitz in the spring of 2009, he told me that Rosanczyk had done the initial chemistry sleuthing, analyzing particular flavanol molecules and deducing from their shape that they were likely to have an impact on circulation; Hammerstone worked to "fractionate" cacao flavanols (separate out different kinds) and helped Schmitz refine the overall picture.

At this point, the Mars team had developed an unsurpassed understanding of cacao-chocolate chemistry. They were eager to find clinical researchers with complementary skills. Norman Hollenberg's epidemiological research on the Cuna presented an opportunity to take their findings to another level.

Hollenberg had discovered that Cuna islanders consumed large amounts of chocolate every day (some from locally produced, unfermented and unroasted cacao, some from a Colombian instant cocoa powder). They drank it in several forms: mixed with corn or bananas or dissolved in water. This fact fitted well with the Mars team's embryonic theory that the flavanols in cacao had important vascular effects. Indeed, it looked like promising epidemiological proof. In 1996, Schmitz and Rosanczyk walked into Hollenberg's office at Harvard and showed him their lab's chemical and biological findings. According to Schmitz, Hollenberg's response was: "Wow, that's top-caliber data!"

It was a lucky meeting of complementary approaches. Hollenberg had worked for years with chemists and biologists in the pharmaceutical industry, with which the Mars people had no contacts. Schmitz and Hollenberg began pursuing the cacao-flavanol link with a study of the Cuna on the island of Ailigandi that quickly provoked media headlines like "Chocolate found to fight heart disease in Panama Indians." The facts are much more complex.

The Cuna project did point to a link between cacao consumption and low blood pressure. But it was not intended as definitive proof of any hypothesis, and it didn't attempt to exclude other potentially important variables in a complex food system. (As Schmitz told me, "There's no epidemiologist on earth who can conclusively say that because you're eating a specific thing, that's why something is happening.") But the findings lent momentum to other research on flavanols.

The groundwork was now laid for controlled flavanol studies on human subjects that would be carried out by Hollenberg at Harvard as well as researchers from the University of California at Davis and Heinrich Heine University in Düsseldorf, Germany, in collaboration with Mars. Their ongoing work has made knowledge of flavanols more precise, pointing

attention away from earlier emphasis on cacao as a source of antioxidants and focusing specifically on substances called (-) epicatechin and its procyanidins that seem to mediate improved blood vessel function. The consequences of this research are bound to affect the cacao-chocolate industry from plantation source to retail store.

Young girl from Cartí Yantupo (the Island of the Peccary).

Flavanols: The New Focus

The most promising flavanols are a subgroup containing the comparatively simple compounds catechins and epicatechins, together with others known as procyanidins that are built from catechin and epicatechin units. One particular flavanol, "minus"—written "(-)"—epicatechin, is thought to help a circulatory enzyme, nitric oxide synthase, trigger production of nitric oxide, which in turn has an anti-inflammatory effect on the artery lining and promotes the dilation of blood vessels.

Schmitz is excited by the promise of procyanidins and other flavanols in cacao, but cautions that there are still many unanswered questions about the forms in which flavanols are actually metabolized and released into the bloodstream. (Procyanidins containing more than two units of catechins or epicatechins have been hard to detect in the bloodstream, either because they are broken down at some point in digestion or because they are changed into other bioactive forms, undetectable by current research, that perhaps may produce the crucial ultimate effects.)

But just what consequences will the new focus on cacao flavanols have for the entire cacao-chocolate industry? For one thing, the industry now has a stake in understanding what factors can increase the content of particular flavanols known to improve circulatory function. It is already known that fermentation, roasting, and the widespread industry practice of alkalizing ("dutching") the beans or ground cacao mass to soften harsh flavors destroy or sharply reduce flavanol content. (The Cuna islanders often use their own unfermented and unroasted cacao to make the chocolate that first attracted Norman Hollenberg's attention.) There is a clear implication: we're going to see more marketing emphasis on very intense, unalkalized chocolate from lightly fermented, lightly roasted beans, with only small amounts of sugar (since that has its own undesirable effects). Possibly we will soon see information about flavanol content on chocolate labels. And perhaps bulk beans that otherwise would have never have been dignified with name recognition will now turn up on the labels of flavanol-rich single-origin chocolate bars.

It also seems likely that as specific flavanols are identified and analyzed, they will be used in concentrated form to enrich "functional foods" made with specially formulated chocolate. (And as Harold Schmitz points out, there are equally striking implications for other common flavanol sources, from apples and berries to tea.) Only a thin line separates such dietary enhancements from actual pharmaceuticals that not only may, but probably will, one day be developed to aid diabetics, geriatric patients, heavy smokers, and others with circulatory impairment. In the controlled studies done in recent years, flavanol-rich chocolate drinks have shown distinct benefits for people in these groups.

Then there are the implications for cacao growing, starting with the enhanced value farmers may realize from cacao as a crop if the chocolate made from it can play a role in combating one of the world's great killer diseases. We can see that those who handle cacao at the source may have to rethink their fermenting and roasting practices. But what if it also proves possible to affect flavanols by the management of trees? What if there is a genetic component that creates higher flavanol levels in some cultivars than others? Here we must wonder whether the cacao genome project now being conducted by the USDA and Mars will yield insights into the properties of different strains.

Some people may find irony in the leading role played by a candy company in teasing out the secrets of flavanols. The story has proved larger, more complex, and more important than anyone foresaw twenty (or ten) years ago. Today Mars finds itself not just a company pursuing marketing opportunities but an informational clearinghouse for several kinds of world-class scientific investigations. (A good guide to the state of research can be found in the Web site of Mars Botanical, a new division of the company).

Though different pieces of knowledge are impressively falling into place, so far they have involved only short-term experiments with carefully delimited goals. As Schmitz points out, it would take a larger cast of researchers and coordinators to demonstrate that the effects seen to date "would actually increase life span or somehow improve specific aspects of quality of life." But he thinks the momentum of what's been done already is essentially unstoppable—or in other words, the compelling nature of the chocolate-flavanol data nearly ensures that "funding and intellectual interaction between government, university, and industry will come together and really answer the ultimate questions."

IDENTIFYING CACAO

N O FOOD PLANT IS MORE DIFFICULT TO ARRANGE in logical classifications than cacao. It does not have a large genome (the haploid chromosome number is only 10), but when we start trying to apply such different criteria as the outward appearance of the pod, the color and shape of the beans, and the flavor characteristics passed on from generation to generation, we quickly find ourselves in layer upon layer of confusion.

With some tree fruits, there may be some genetic puzzles, but it is fairly clear how most of the modern cultivars are related to parents. Cacao is another case. Until only a year ago, breeders and agronomists were working with a model that seemed to reflect the best guesses of different cacao varieties' ancestries but turned out to be inconsistent and inadequate. In the fall of 2008, all previous classifications were superseded by a new system of groupings based on rigorous comparative examination of a very large sam-  pling of known germplasm sources. Much of the received wisdom about the relationships of different cacaos is still valid, but some assumptions have had to be revised. The following discussion takes into account the new advances in knowledge while retaining some still-useful older descriptors.

OPPOSITE: Cacao pods display a diversity of sizes, shapes, textures, and colors.
RIGHT: Frances Bekele, an expert in cacao morphology, is currently working on a classification project for the Cocoa Research Unit in Trinidad.

It is still valid to write of "Criollo" cacao, but it is now necessary to distinguish among nine other genetic clusters instead of lumping together all non-Criollos under the convenient umbrella term of "Forastero."

MORPHOLOGICAL TYPES

Morphology is the study of structure and form in living organisms. It gives us a convenient way to classify cacaos by external characteristics. For a long time there were no other tools for distinguishing one kind from another. The various names that sprang up to describe cacao varieties during the colonial period have been superseded by others for purposes of genetic identification, but they are still useful as general descriptors.

Amelonado. Pods have a melonlike shape that has been described as resembling a cantaloupe crossed with a football, with thick, usually smooth skins and occasionally some wartiness. The pod has shallow ridges and furrows and the tip is rounded rather than pointed. At most, it shows a faint hint of a bottleneck. It is now the name of a major genetic cacao cluster.

Angoleta. Pods are long and ridged but less warty and furrowed than Cundeamor, with wide shoulders and little or no bottleneck. The tip is usually somewhat pointed but not curved.

Calabacillo. Reflecting its name, this cacao has the shape of a small pumpkin (*calabaza* is the Spanish name for pumpkin). It is round or oval, with thick and very smooth skin. It has almost no ridges or furrows, and no suggestion of tip or bottleneck. Usually it is on the small side. Unlike most cacaos, it has a characteristic color: grass green changing to a beautiful deep yellow as it matures. Calabacillo is now considered an extreme form of the Amelonado pod.

Cundeamor. The name Cundeamor (also spelled Cundiamor) originally referred to a somewhat similar-looking fruit that is in the same genus as the Chinese bitter melon. These cacaos have long, warty, deeply ridged and furrowed pods, with either a pronounced bottleneck or a suggestion of one at the stem end and a pointed tip ("apex") that is curved in some varieties. The most exaggerated example of the Cundeamor type is Pentagona (*Theobroma cacao* var. *pentagona,* see page 70), a type of Criollo.

THE MANY FACES OF CACAO

Before I introduce you to some important cacao cultivars, let me remind you again that in just the last couple of years there has been a revolution in the genetic classification of basic cacao types. Let's take a look at some important cacao cultivars. Some are old cacaos whose origin is surrounded with some mystery; others are genebank creations engineered by scientists. We are not yet at the point of knowing exactly how the "information" locked within the genes of a cacao plant translates into everything we see in the actual plant. Time and again we find ourselves explaining that Cacao A must have arisen by interbreeding with distant cousin Cacao B or C, leading to a vast tangle of names.

What might seem peculiar is that some of the cacaos pictured in this identification section don't always find their names printed on a bag of beans. Cacao beans are normally sold under the name of the country or—more rarely now—the region of origin or port of shipment. Though Ghana cacao is mostly Amelonado cacao, you will never see it sold as such in the international market. Indiscriminate hybridization has also contributed to muddled distinctions between different strains. The beans produced on a single plantation or in a particular region might literally be a mixed bag of several cultivars that will never receive individual credit. But here you'll get to see some important varieties with their corresponding beans. I have used specimens provided by scientists and progressive growers from some of the world's finest plantations and genebanks.

Carte de Embouchere du Lac de Maracaye jusques a Gibraltar. Exquemelin. Paris, 1686. A fascinating chart from a French edition of Exquemelin's *Buccaneers of America* showing the mouth of Lake Maracaibo in Venezuela and the towns of Maracaibo and Gibraltar, from which cacao was exported, and details like cacao plantations on the top right of the map.

CRIOLLOS

Western Venezuelan Criollos

If there is one place where we are likely to find pure Criollos, it is in the western reaches of Venezuela wandering toward the Colombian border. Broadly speaking, there are two cacao environments here. One is the area called Sur del Lago: the humid, marshy lands south and west of Lake Maracaibo, once the source of the beautiful Maracaibo beans prized by connoisseurs. The other area lies farther westward and is the highest terrain on which cacao has established itself: the foothills of the Venezuelan Andes. The strains that grow here are collectively called Andean Criollos (*Criollos andinos*).

BELOW: Red Porcelana pods. **OPPOSITE:** White Porcelana pods. **OPPOSITE, INSET:** Detail from *Venezuela cum parte Australi Novae Andalusiae* by Henricus Hondius, 1642 (see page 38). The humid flatlands of Lake Maracaibo in Venezuela are the home of Porcelana, the world's most coveted Criollo.

Porcelana: The Holy Grail of Pure Criollos

It seems that the Spaniards found cultivated cacao in western Venezuela upon their arrival. An early sixteenth-century entry in Venezuela's national records describes thousands of cacao trees growing in rows south of Lake Maracaibo. This humid hothouse is home to the holy grail of pure Criollos, the exquisite cacao called Porcelana. It was probably synonymous with most of the old Maracaibo cacao, though it had such unique status that it actually shows up as the most expensive cacao in documents of the nineteenth-century Hamburg cacao exchange.

Scattered Porcelana groves can still be found in the basin of the Escalante River, which drains into Lake Maracaibo. You can also find trees in mixed-variety plantations along with currently more popular cultivars, such as the Amelonado-type cacao called Pajarito. But all local cacao farming is under siege here as more and more farmers are cutting down cacao trees and starting to grow less-demanding crops such as oranges or bananas, or to raise cattle.

Can this lovely cacao be saved? After visiting an experimental farm sponsored by the government of Zulia State and run by a team of state agronomists, I thought the answer might be yes. Estación Experimental Chama, located near the town of El Vigía, about twenty-five miles south of Lake Maracaibo, is a germplasm bank for pure Porcelana. This seven-acre plantation is dedicated to the preservation and propagation of this variety, a vestige of commercial cacao's Golden Age.

The farm, set in the muggy and buggy green flats of Sur del Lago, has the look of a traditional plantation cordoned into tracts by irrigation ditches, the trees planted at generous (by modern standards) 3-by-3-meter intervals. Of course I have walked through many cacao groves, but this was a delicious experience in itself. The big shade trees were mamey sapotes (*Pouteria sapote*)—one

of the most beloved of Latin American fruits. The fruits were ripe when I visited and the beige-brown mameys squashed underfoot as I walked, tempting me to pick them up and munch on their salmon-colored flesh.

When you see Porcelana cacao growing on the tree, you understand where the name came from. Some of the unripe pods are translucent green enamel that makes you think of celadonware or Chinese jade carvings. Some are as red as Snow White's apple, or dappled with a pinkish hue. When fully ripe, they may be orange-red or light yellow shot with green. What astonished me, and must also have completely amazed the first Spanish cacao entrepreneurs to set eyes on it, is that the fruit is completely smooth (when spared by insects), an anomaly among Criollos. The shape can be nearly as ovoid as a typical Amelonado, sometimes with a suggestion of a bottleneck or faint ridges, or it can be long and skinny, almost daggerlike. The giveaway to its identity is the conspicuous nipplelike tip.

LEFT: Red and green Porcelana pods showing the characteristic white and light pink cotyledons and large plump beans of a true Criollo (center). A homespun chocolate bar prepared with Porcelana beans (top, left). RIGHT: A mixed batch of Porcelana pods and other Sur del Lago cacaos—including some specimens of Pajarito, an Amelonado from nearby Colombia—are stored for five days before opening to improve flavor.

Insects such as thrips had carved many pods with miniature moonscapes or huge pockmarks and meandering trails. These invaders can do much worse to the usually fragile Porcelana variety. They can chew the thin-skinned pods badly enough to leave them easy prey for squirrels or deadly fungal diseases. But the trees of the Chama facility seemed healthy and had managed to escape *Moniliasis,* the scourge of this humid region.

This facility has no commercial output but supplies Porcelana seedlings and clones grown in its large nursery to farmers interested in reviving the historic strain. On several occasions I was given laboratory samples of chocolate made with Porcelana by a manufacturer testing the potential of different Venezuelan cacaos. While visiting Chama, the head agronomist gave me a large bar she had made of well-fermented Porcelana beans in all their gritty, homespun glory, using a disposable aluminum container as a mold. If you were to sample it along with chocolates made with other Venezuelan cacaos, it would be the least acidic or fruity—you would find it as neutral and nutty as a buttery macadamia, with low levels of astringency and bitterness. This comes as a surprise to people who are expecting a crowded busload of flavors. What is striking about Porcelana is its pure and powerful lingering chocolate flavor and aroma as well as its delicate notes of nut and spice.

Transplanting shade tree seedlings at Estación Experimental Chama.

Until recently this region produced only a mixed batch of cacaos combining Porcelana with Trinitarios and Colombian Pajaritos. The blending of types was only half the problem. Properly fermented and dried, this natural blend of cacao beans would yield a flavorful chocolate. But postharvest practices in this very humid region are poor and have lagged behind other regions of Venezuela. It is not uncommon to detect musty, hay, and even jute bag off-flavors and smells in a good-looking sample of Sur del Lago Clasificado beans (the premium classification that has come to replace the old Maracaibo label).

When I saw the type of Porcelana grown at Chama, with pure white cotyledons that instantly gave away their unmixed Criollo ancestry, I realized that good Porcelana plantations could be viable in that region of Venezuela. Certainly the market existed among knowledgeable chocolate makers for this rarest of Criollo cacaos. But at the time there was not a single chocolate made with these pure beans. The proof arrived when Valrhona's local farm El Pedregal, which had survived an unpromising start, began producing reliable crops of fine Porcelana followed by an exquisite limited edition Porcelana chocolate named El Pedregal. This has now been superseded by Palmira, named after another Valrhona Porcelana farm. There are now several Porcelana chocolates in the market, by a range of chocolate makers, with varying quality and authenticity.

Guasare

Some years ago, people in the cacao business started hearing tales about a remarkably fine cacao showing up at market in small amounts. It came from the mountainous area of the Sierra de Perijá, close to the Colombian border. Where was it being grown? At last the specific source was identified as one farmer on a small, remote plantation called Tía Locha on the River Guasare in the state of Zulia, where he grew 16 hectares (40 acres)

Venezuelan scientists examine a Guasare pod for signs of disease. Right to left: Gladys Ramos Carranza and Antonio Azócar, of the Campo Experimental San Juan de Lagunillas, and visiting scientists, the late Humberto Reyes and Lilian Capriles de Reyes.

Newly planted Guasare seedlings from San Juan de Lagunillas thrived at the Finca San Joaquín in the Venezuelan plains. Rather than starting the Guasare field from scratch, agronomist Beatriz Escobar opted for the *cultivo de monte*: clearing the underbrush and planting seedlings under the protective shade of existing tall trees. Two years later, the trees were already bearing blossoms. Now the farm has been taken over by squatters and the fields have been abandoned.

of pure Criollo. Agronomists found the Guasare cacao to be one of the purest Criollos they had ever seen—probably an Andean strain that might have traveled north to Central America.

The scientists decided that this "old" cacao deserved to be thoroughly investigated. They collected pods at Tía Locha and brought them back to Campo Experimental San Juan de Lagunillas, the agricultural experimental station headed by Gladys Ramos Carranza close to the Andean city of Mérida, a center of research for various crops. The Guasare cacao was planted and grown out like the Porcelana at Chama (less than a couple of hours away), the only difference being that the climate in Mérida is semidry and the land sandy and rocky. The seedlings were unusually precocious, blossoming at two years and bearing at three— a clear advantage over slower-maturing varieties. Even more tempting for growers was the experts' estimate that at full maturity (about six years), Guasare trees planted at 3-by-3-meter inter-

vals could potentially deliver 1,500 kilos (3,300 pounds) of cacao per hectare (2.5 acres) in a year.

Guasare pods are imposing, some larger than 13 inches. They exhibit the characteristic warty Cundeamor shape, with a discreet bottleneck and slightly curved tip. There are red and green Guasares. The latter range from grass green to deep olive green, turning greenish yellow when fully mature. The red type is a stunning cabernet red when immature, ripening to a burnt

orange. The beans are large, plump, and pure white inside. Their quality is extraordinary. The chocolate I sampled, made from well-fermented Guasare at a manufacturer's lab in 1995, was fantastic—everyone at our tasting panel found it even more flavorful and complex than the even-keeled Porcelana. My judgment was later vindicated in 2002, when I was asked to source Porcelana and Guasare beans and turn them into chocolate for a collaborative project with Mars for a Cocoa Merchants Association Conference. The chocolate with 61 percent cacao content was light caramel and full of exuberant complexities yet delicate flavors.

Soon growers from every cacao region of Venezuela were coming in droves to the nursery at the Mérida station, looking for Guasare pods and stock to plant as their star cacao. Interestingly, so far it seems sturdy and productive in different environments, even at the high-altitude testing area at Mérida (1,066 meters / 3,500 feet). It seems to have appeared on the scene at just the right moment to attract notice from some of the world's top chocolate makers—certainly it will be showing up in premium European and U.S. chocolates.

ABOVE: Red and green Guasare pods at different stages of ripeness next to plump, freshly harvested beans. At San Juan de Lagunillas, Gladys Ramos Carranza fermented the beans in small sweat boxes and dried them in the sun to make chocolate samples.

BELOW: A rain-soaked, immature Guasare pod in the Venezuelan Andes.

Andean Criollos from Mérida

In 1900, a thriving colonial plantation in Mérida State called La Molina had 300 hectares (740 acres) planted with Criollo cacao so pure it required only twenty-four hours for full fermention. The plantation produced an average yield of 200 quintales (about 20,000 pounds) yearly. The area even had its own denomination of origin, "Cacao de Estanquez," and it was taken down to the port of Gibraltar in Sur del Lago to be shipped with Porcelana and other Criollos to the larger international port of Maracaibo. By the 1930s, the plantation had gone over to sugarcane, and little remained of the once-flourishing Criollo trees. Only the tiered drying yards and a practical rail system to transport cacao in wagons speak of its former life. This seems to summarize the commercial history of cacao throughout the Venezuelan Andes.

Today there are only isolated pockets of Criollos of various phenotypes (Cundeamor, Angoleta, Porcelana) in many Andean communities. Some of the most fascinating specimens have been found growing as ornamentals near farmhouses. Scattered Criollos can also be found on most working plantations where Trinitarios and the now ubiquitous Pajarito from Colombia prevail.

For years Gladys Ramos Carranza collected specimens of pure Andean Criollos and planted them in a plot at her experimental station. The trees are thriving. Shown here is a pure Criollo hybrid with the characteristic smooth skin and the telling nipplelike tip imprint of Porcelana and large, plump, white seeds.

RIGHT: This red, warty *Theobroma cacao* var. *pentagona* pod comes from an isolated tree grown as an ornamental at the home of Eulogio Contreras in the town of Hernández in Táchira State, on the Venezuelan-Colombian border. The beans of this cacao are large and plump and show a more pronounced purple hue than would be characteristic of red-skinned Porcelana.

Theobroma Pentagona

The most exotic of the western Venezuelan cacaos, and the one that has caused the most head scratching, is something that people didn't originally know was cacao at all. Decades ago, the literature used to describe it as another species, *Theobroma pentagona,* found growing wild (or semiwild) in Central America. But about ten years ago, specimens growing in a semiwild state were discovered on a few scattered farms in the Criollo Andino territory of Venezuela.

The pods of this odd-looking cacao have five sharply defined ridges that recall the folded angular wings of a fruit bat, and the whole pod seems to erupt with lumpy warts, as if some primeval animal was hatching within and getting ready to burst forth. This cacao has the characteristic thin skin of Criollos and contains fifteen to twenty beans that are large and plump.

Thanks to DNA research, it is now considered to be a true Criollo cacao and has been reclassified as *Theobroma cacao* var. *pentagona.* As for its rare appearance, geneticists explain that it is an extreme form of the Criollo pod. Its thin skin and large beans might prove to be an important genetic resource for the improvement of Criollo. With any crop as fragile and often besieged as Criollo cacao, any rich source of genetic insight is a well-timed miracle.

Central Venezuelan Criollos

The strikingly beautiful river valleys of Venezuela's central coastal highlands in the state of Aragua—Choroní, Chuao, Cata, Ocumare, and Cuyagua—are nestled among tall mountains that plunge abruptly into the Caribbean Sea. The names of some of the most coveted cacaos in the world still resound in these fertile oases, where relics of the Criollo cacao, believed to have been brought to Venezuela from Nicaragua or the Nicoya Peninsula in Costa Rica in the early colonial period, still survive. Here also live the descendants of Africans brought as slaves, most probably from Angola, to work on some of the finest plantations in the world.

During carnival and religious festivities, such as Corpus Christi and Saint John's Eve in June, the valleys explode with the sounds of Africa. For a few frantic days, the sounds of the plantation routine drawing to its second annual peak are replaced by something as old as the Venezuelan cacao trade. Religious rites, songs, and dances that once were an integral part of the life of the African slaves are reenacted in a secular context.

Recurrent outbreaks of cacao disease starting in the nineteenth century meant the introduction of sturdy Trinitarios, which the Venezuelans called *forasteros* ("alien," "non-native") to the confusion of modern observers who think that Forastero refers only to Amazonian cacao. Because of more than a century of hybridization between Criollos and Trinitarios (followed by the ill-advised introduction of Amelonados and other Amazonian cacaos at a later period), the percentage of pure Criollos found in these valleys fluctuates widely. Venezuelan scientists classify these extant Criollos as "modern Criollos," *(Criollos actuales)* to set them apart from the "old Criollos," such as Porcelana and Guasare, native to Venezuela.

RIGHT: On the religious feast of Corpus Christi, masked dancers known as Los Diablitos ("the Little Devils") parade the main road of the town of Chuao to the sound of drums. The dancers are cacao workers belonging to La Sociedad de Corpus, an all-male religious confraternity.

Choroní

A century ago, Choroní meant cacao. Today the name conjures up vacation time and scantily clad German and Canadian tourists getting to know the locals "intimately." This once-thriving cacao region has succumbed to its own tropical charms. Small hostels and hotels have sprung everywhere, and carnival time attracts throngs of beer-drinking revelers who clog the narrow mountain road and fill the streets near the port.

Close to the coast, the mountains are dry, covered with mixed cactus growth. But seen from above, a broad meandering green snake seems to cut its way toward the sea. This is the Choroní River, which runs through a narrow valley lush with cacao and its motherly shade trees.

The dignified old town, Santa Clara de Choroní, with its white houses trimmed in colonial blue and its ancient wooden doors, is a striking contrast to the garish tourist town that has sprung up near the port. Only a few cacao plantations remain—the loveliest of all, La Sabaneta. This restored colonial beauty has hundreds of acres planted with cacao. Walking through its many sectors is like getting lost in a genetic maze where you occasionally find your bearings by spotting an old Criollo tree with red, warty, deeply furrowed red pods sporting a curved pointy tip. This is the heart of old Choroní. The pulp is good to eat and the pods have a high percentage of plump, white beans, betraying their strong Criollo germplasm.

Two factors have contributed to the demise of this wonderful Criollo: tourism, which draws workers to the hotel industry and away from the cacao tree; and disease, which has been a constant threat since at least the nineteenth century. Many pods look healthy, but when you cut them open, you find the seeds ravaged

TOP: A cacao worker examines a Choroní pod.
ABOVE: Ancient shade trees loom like a mantle over the thick cacao groves of the eighteenth-century Hacienda La Sabaneta. Kai Rosenberg, the owner of this colonial beauty, is intent on revitalizing Criollo cacao in Choroní. Together with four other local growers, Rosenberg is collaborating with scientists from FONAIAP (Fondo Nacional de Investigaciones Agropecuarias) to combat cacao diseases and improve productivity.

by disease. The scourge of Choroní is the deadly *Ceratocystis fimbriata,* a fungal disease known as *mal de Choroní* (Choroní disease or cocoa wilt), which can kill cacao overnight.

Chuao

Merchants in France and Spain always spoke of Chuao cacao as one of the finest that could be had for the money, and they paid high premiums for the prestigious beans. Even today European manufacturers jockey to corner the whole production of the area's only farm, meager though it has become in the last decades (ranging from eight or nine metric tons a year to an alleged fourteen metric tons in 1999).

Chuao was always one of the most isolated Venezuelan cacao estates, reachable only by boat from the nearby coastal valley of Choroní. Naturally it has resisted most kinds of visible change. The faces of the people reflect those of residents in the seventeenth century, and the same few surnames (Liendo, Bolívar) testify to the early history of the hacienda.

What has changed is the quality of the cacao. At the beginning of the nineteenth century, Chuao cacao was a pure and delicate Criollo. But the diseases that attacked Criollo cacao elsewhere caught up with even remote Chuao. The threatened groves were replanted first with Trinitario strains that were less vulnerable but had good flavor. Through the years, however, inferior Amelonados were used to replace older or diseased Criollo and Trinitario trees. Just walking through some sectors of the plantation, you see typical long, warty Criollo pods with the characteristic hooked tip of the Cundeamor type alternating with round, shiny specimens that anyone familiar with cacao would recognize at once as Calabacillo, a type of Amelonado. A batch of freshly harvested beans appears large and promising at first glance, but on cutting them open you find that they exhibit every color between pure white and deep purple. This means that the farmers are working with such a mixture of cacaos that one fermentation approach can't do justice to any of them, much less all of them. Still, bring a bunch of dried Chuao beans close to your nose. In this now-natural blend of varying quality cacaos, the perfume of Criollo still flutters like a brightly colored banner.

ABOVE RIGHT: A ripe pod displays the characteristic warty textue and typical Cundeamor shape, a pronounced bottleneck with a slightly curved tip. It contains plump beans with pure white and light pink cotyledons of a true Chuao Criollo.

RIGHT: Boats ferry passengers along the rugged coast of the state of Aragua to inaccessible towns such as Chuao.

LONG LIVE THE CACAO OF CHUAO!

The famous Venezuelan plantation of Chuao on the central Caribbean coast was originally a royal *encomienda* (land grant) given to an aristocratic Spanish family in 1592 and worked by Africans brought as slaves. When the surviving heir, Doña Catalina Mexía de Liendo, died in 1669, she donated the plantation to the Franciscan friars as a charitable gift and stipulated that "my slaves" should go along with the property, enabling them to remain together and to continue forging a bond with the land.

The Franciscans owned Chuao until 1827, by which time Venezuela had won independence from Spain. Simón Bolívar, the "Liberator," donated the hacienda to the University of Caracas, which retained ownership for several generations, eventually handing over the plantation to the Venezuelan government in 1883. First it was sold to the dictator Antonio Guzmán Blanco, then it was shunted from one political racketeer to another for about eighty years. Finally it came under the aegis of the state and the control of the ill-fated Fondo Nacional del Cacao, organized in the 1960s as a government monopoly of all Venezuelan cacao. The Fondo Nacional turned over the management of the farm to the workers, and Chuao became a cooperative of about 300 hectares (740 acres). And so in a rare instance of historical justice, it has come to be governed by the descendants of the same slaves who had been "given" to the Franciscan order by Doña Catalina three centuries before. The women still sing to Catalina while they dry the beans in the courtyard of the church: *El cacao de Chuao, ¡que viva que viva! Que Catalina lo fundó, lo fundó* (Long live the cacao of Chuao that Catalina founded!).

OPPOSITE, INSET: A sample of beans from Chuao's only fermentation facility shows a rainbow of cotyledon colors—from ivory white (after oxidation) to light pink to deep purple—a sign of the genetic diversity of the contemporary cacao plantation.

LEFT: Oliver Bolívar (left, front) and friends.
RIGHT: Pancho Bolívar returns from the fields on the cooperative's tractor.

Ocumare

Ocumare de la Costa is another lovely valley on the central coast of Venezuela. There Criollo cacao has undergone a severe process of hybridization, but cacao still remains viable as a commercial crop. Though yields are very low, cacao from Ocumare and the equally remote neighboring valley Cuyagua (which has similar cacao) often reaches the world market as a single-origin specialty cacao and is sold for a hefty premium.

In the 1940s, a group of Venezuelan scientists made a selection of healthy, productive Criollo trees in Ocumare and numbered them for reference. The marvelous cacao shown here, with classic Cundeamor shape and lovely hues of pink, is the selection Ocumare 61. Select clones such as this have been planted all over Venezuela, because they have proven to be vigorous and flavorful. When you cut open a pod, you find very large and plump beans with cotyledons that range from pure white to light pink to light purple.

Ocumare 61 was the predominant cacao in the San Joaquín Estate chocolate made by El Rey, a gutsy, earthy chocolate with peachy fruitiness and a floral bouquet. Most of these flavor notes plus a very subtle dairy note can be attributed to Ocumare 61.

OPPOSITE: A prime specimen of Ocumare 61 at the Finca San Joaquín.

RIGHT: A pure Ocumare 61 clone grown at the Finca San Joaquín, an experimental farm on the plains of Venezuela, in the state of Barinas. If the trees had been planted from seed, they would grow straight, dividing into jorquettes higher up, but this is the characteristic forked shape of the clonal tree.

CUYAGUA

Cacao has a long history at the spot where the Río Grande flows from the coastal mountain range through the idyllic Cuyagua valley to open on a wide, sandy beach. In the mid-eighteenth century, one of the Venezuelan *grandes cacaos* (literally, "big cacaos," the cacao-growing gentry), Martín Tovar Galindo, is recorded to have had an hacienda of 24,000 trees in the valley. In 1823, during the war of independence, royalists seized the property from a Jeronima de Tovar y Ponte, a supporter of the revolution.

As on other cacao plantations, black ex-slaves eventually acquired rights to the land. Today tourism is the main industry of Cuyagua, and it is hard to get people to work the farm. But a small cooperative still works a remnant of the old farm, carrying out fermentation and drying with rudimentary facilities next to an old colonial house. The day-to-day work falls on only six men and eight women.

The approximately 150 hectares (370 acres) of the original farm run steeply uphill just across the river from the town of Cuyagua (workers and visitors must ford the river and climb the rocky slope). It had fallen into partial neglect when I visited it a decade ago. What cacao was still being produced was very good, and for several years my partners, Silvino Reyes and Ana Karina Flores, had been selling small amounts to Scharffen Berger for blending. We all knew that with painstaking rehabilitation this overgrown mini-jungle could be one of the great Venezuelan cacao farms. In 2003, when Robert Steinberg decided to make a limited-edition Scharffen Berger chocolate with Cuy-

agua cacao, Silvino and Ana Karina began a serious reclamation initiative. They supplied the co-op with much-needed machetes, boots, and a small tractor, and hired a technician, Tulio Pagniani, to come to Cuyagua for eight months and supervise the work of clearing and planting *ahilados* half-buried in shrubs and weeds.

When Robert and I visited in 2006, some 26 hectares (60 acres) on the section of the plantation closest to the river mouth had been cleared and were in beautiful condition. This is where the restoration stands at present; further work will have to wait for better economic and political circumstances. But when the plantation is completely rehabilitated, it may have the potential to surpass the better-known Chuao. Like other farms in the coastal mountain valleys, it contains a mix of Ocumare Criollos, Amelonados and Upper Amazons, and Trinitario hybrids. The Cuyagua stock, however, is somewhat less heterogeneous and richer in superior Trinitarios and very good Criollos, like the selections CPC 3 and 4 (Cuyagua Paso Clarito), CRP 2 and 3 (Cuyagua Remedio de Pobre), and CMR 2 (Cuyagua Mamey Roleado), named after specific *ahilados* that produce large, fruity-flavored beans.

Though Scharffen Berger's Cuyagua bar, actually a blend of Cuyagua and La Concepción beans, was celebrated for several years, Hershey's stopped making it some time after acquiring the company. But today Cuyagua cacao is the foundation of a remarkable single-origin or limited-edition chocolate made by Art Pollard of Amano.

NO LONGER FORASTEROS: The Expanding Cacao Tribes

Geneticists have always been puzzled by anomalies within the group of cacaos that used to be lumped together as Forasteros. Some wrinkles have been straightened out by the new cacao taxonomy of the last couple of years (see page 54). Most of the new groupings bear geographical names that can help us grasp the overall picture. To simplify, the growing non-Criollo groupings fall into three main geographic areas: the Lower Amazon, the Upper Amazon, and the Guyana Plateau. Though one of the clusters—the Nacional of Ecuador—grows along the Pacific coast, its origins have been traced to the Upper Amazon basin.

Guiana: A Wrinkle in Classification

Collection expeditions in French Guiana opened a field of inquiry that led to the current classification of cacao. Philip Lachanaud, a French scientist at Centre de Cooperátion Internationale en Recherche Agronomique pour le Développement (CIRAD), noticed that the area's wild cacao, though shaped like an Amelonado, had little in common genetically with either Upper or Lower Amazon cacaos. Based on this result, he proposed a new system of classification with four major groups: Criollos from Central America, Colombia, and Venezuela; Amazons, including Upper Amazon cacaos; Guaianan, embracing the whole of the Guyana Plateau, which is shared by Venezuela, Suriname, French Guiana, and Brazil; and Ecuadorian Nacional or Arriba. This system was presented as a working hypothesis, but research by Juan Carlos Motamayor has confirmed that Guaianan cacao is indeed a distinct genetic group.

Lower Amazon: Amelonado

One cacao type stands as the emblem of the international cacao boom at the beginning of the twentieth century: the ubiquitous Amelonado, a cacao whose handsome, often smooth-skinned fruits have a typical melonlike shape. Amelonado is the archetypal Lower Amazon cacao, probably native to the area of eastern Brazil that is now the state of Pará. The now-superseded classification system identified it as a Forastero, but it is now known to form a separate genetic cluster in its own right. Amelonados are known for vigor and characteristic flat seeds with deep purple cotyledons.

Amelonado seems to be the uninvited guest at every party, popping up next to pure Criollos and showing up—most likely as a workhorse—in many large commercial plantations. It is the cacao Tabasco farmers carry to church, hanging

An Amelonado pod collected at La Pagerie, a former sugar estate, on the Caribbean island of Martinique.

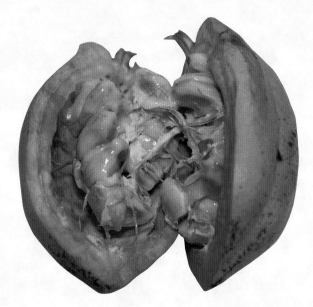

ABOVE LEFT: Unfermented beans drying in the sun on the highway between San Pedro Sula and Tela. Though their external color is light terra-cotta, the cotyledons within remain a deep purple after drying.

ABOVE RIGHT: A Honduran woman of Mayan ancestry holds an Amelonado pod grown on a small farm in the Aldea Toyo, not far from San Pedro Sula. The pulp of this cacao is vinegary and the beans small, flat, and deep purple.

from poles, to be blessed on the feast day of San Isidro. It is also the source of the unfermented flat, tan Tabasco beans that Mexican buyers often prefer to darker fermented beans from Chiapas. You can walk through plantations from the Dominican Republic to Martinique, from Bahia to Nigeria, and recognize the characteristic shape of this Amazonian native. Though most Amelonado pods are green ripening to yellow, there are also red Amelonados.

Amelonado is capable of great finesse when it is properly cared for and fermented for the right number of days. Sun-drying on mats, as is done in West Africa, seems to be a factor in helping to mellow this cacao, which often misbehaves and tastes acrid and acid in its native Amazonian habitat.

Upper Amazon

Every food plant has its Indiana Jones, and for Upper Amazon cacaos the hero was F. J. Pound, a brilliant geneticist who worked at the Imperial College of Tropical Agriculture in Trinidad. Between 1937 and 1938, Pound traveled to Ecuador and through the Amazon River basin to collect pods and budwood of wild cacao showing resistance to witches' broom disease.

Pound paints a dismal picture in the report of his 1938 expedition. He found the disease well established everywhere, from the ornamental cacao growing right next to infected *cupuaçu* trees at the zoological garden of Belém to the wild or semiwild cacao of the headwaters of the Amazon

River. In the end, however, Pound found what he was looking for: pockets of healthy cacao showing vigorous growth amid diseased trees.

From the headwaters of the Amazon to Ecuador and then Colombia, Pound collected important resistant specimens that he sent to Trinidad's quarantine station in Barbados, where more than one thousand rootstocks had been prepared. The collected specimens were planted at Marper Farm, the Manhattan Project of cacao research, where the stock was exposed to witches' broom to test its resistance. The most resilient trees were then crossed with one another or with some chosen Imperial College Selection trees. The stars of the Marper experiment were several lines of IMCs (Iquitos Mixed Calabacillo) from the Iquitos Marañón River area, and the Peruvian Scavina, Nanay, and Parinari selections. (In the new classification, IMCs belong to the Iquitos cluster, Scavina is a member of the Contamaná group, and Parinari is a part of the Marañón cluster, while the old name

Most Upper Amazon cacaos are unprepossessing in appearance. IMC (Iquitos Mixed Calabacillo) pods from the Peruvian Amazon are smallish and nearly monochromatic, a dull green that becomes orange-yellow as it matures.

OPPOSITE BOTTOM: In this picture, taken at Ghana's Cocoa Research Institute, Amelonado (left) is seen with other types of cacao grown at the institute.

BELOW: *Corso del Fiume dell Amazoni* by Vincenzo Coronelli, 1691/1695. This Amazon basin map extends from Panama to Brazil and includes the mythical Lake Parime, the site of El Dorado, between the Guiana coast and the Amazon. Shown in the interior are many curious scenes of Indian life, including a village and farm field, Indians harvesting sugarcane and operating a mill, an Indian battle, and scenes of cannibalism.

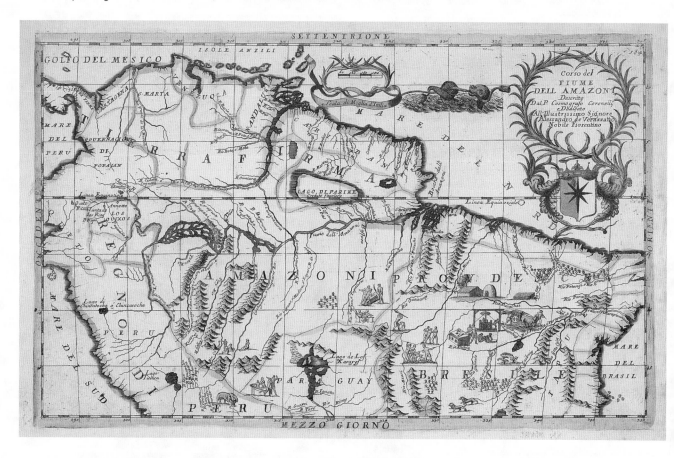

LEFT: The junction of the Río Negro and the Amazon River.

Nanay now applies to a whole group under the new system.)

In later years, new genetic materials from the Peruvian and Ecuadorian Amazon as well as Colombia were obtained by expeditions sponsored by the Imperial College of Tropical Agriculture. These enriched the collection of the Imperial College (later called the University of the West Indies in St. Augustine) in Trinidad, culminating in the creation of the world's largest germplasm bank (ICG, T) with close to three thousand accessions. DNA analysis reveals that Upper Amazon cacaos show more genetic variability than Lower Amazon Amelonado.

Three Upper Amazon selections from the International Cocoa Genebank, Trinidad (ICG, T).

LEFT: London Cacao Trade/Estación Experimental Napo (LCT/EEN), an Ecuadorian cacao collected by the London Cacao Trade Amazonian expedition.

ABOVE: Nanay 399 (name carved by scientist on husk), one of fourteen disease-resistant cacaos collected by Pound in the Peruvian Amazon.

BELOW: Pound 78, a Peruvian cacao collected by Pound in 1943.

THE SCIENCE OF CACAO

Agronomist Julie Reneau, a researcher for Nestlé, prepares leaf samples. Leaf tissue cut from a wide variety of cacao trees at the International Cocoa Genebank of Trinidad will be inoculated with the fungus that causes black pod rot. In two or three days, signs of infection begin to appear on the leaf tissue as dark spots. Unblemished samples reveal resistance to disease. After further testing, these cacaos, mostly selections from the Upper Amazon and select hybrids, will eventually be used for grafting and sent to breeding programs abroad. In the future, such procedures might become obsolete, since a simple genetic test can ascertain resistance or susceptibility to disease.

BOTTOM LEFT: A hand-pollinated cacao flower is protected by a net. The flowers of Criollo cacao are capable of self-pollination, but Upper Amazon Forasteros and some Trinitarios have a condition called self-incompatibility, which can prevent the flowers from being fertilized by their own pollen. In any case, the fruit is more viable when pollinated by another plant. Certain midges are better able than other insects to crawl into the flowers and bring the pollen to the ovary. On some plantations and research institutes, pollination is carried out by hand to ensure that particular crosses between select stock are not ruined by cacao's inherent promiscuity.

FAR RIGHT: Darin Sukha, a researcher at the Cocoa Research Unit in Trinidad, cuts a Nanay 406 pod from the International Cocoa Genebank of Trinidad to study back at CRU.

IMC 67 (Iquitos Cluster)

This sturdy cacao bears the initials IMC, for "Iquitos Mixed Calabacillo," the name originally bestowed as part of a breeding program in Trinidad. You'll find it used in many places where cacao is grown with little shade and where witches' broom or *Ceratocystis fimbriata* (cocoa wilt) are endemic. When crossed with Criollos, IMC 67 lends vigor as well as fruitiness. This Peruvian Amazonian is a good producer (about forty-five flat, dark purple beans per pod) and is often found as a cultivar in commercial plantations across the world from Grenada to Kona Estate in Hawaii.

Scavina 6 (Contamaná Cluster)

If I were to choose only one type of cacao for eating as a fruit, it would be this Peruvian cacao. (The squirrels of Trinidad also prefer it to any other cacao.) The pulp of the Scavina 6 is sweet, fruity, complex, and floral—as perfumed as passion fruit juice. Its robust purple beans contribute a note of bitterness to chocolate, and also add a floral quality and pleasant fruitiness. Of all Upper Amazon cacaos, this is the closest in aroma to the coveted Ecuadorian Arriba.

Scavina 6 can be found all over the world as parent stock in several hybrids or as a cultivar in its own right because of its known resistance to witches' broom. In Bahia, Scavina 6 was crossed with the Trinitario selection ICS 1 from Trinidad to form a cacao known in the trade as Theo-bahia, which has proven resistant to disease.

Scavina 12 (Contamaná Cluster)

A rougher, more pronounced, ridged husk distinguishes this variety from its close relative Scavina 6. The beans are characteristically flat with deep purple cotyledons. The pulp is not as fruity or perfumed as that of Scavina 6.

IMC 67.

Scavina 12.

Scavina 6.

MYSTERIOUS LINEAGE

An aura of mystery surrounds the Scavina, which has often been listed as either a Peruvian or Ecuadorian cacao. Antonio Figuera, a Brazilian scientist, believes it was collected by Pound at the Fundo Monte Blanco, a farm on the left margin of the Ucayali River in Peru that was owned by an Eduardo Scavino. Analysis by the so-called RAPD (randomly amplified polymorphic DNA) technique for detecting genetic "fingerprints" reveals that Scavina is indeed genetically related to other cacaos from northeastern Peru now classified as Contamaná.

A Special Cacao: Arriba

Arriba, now classified as a member of the Nacional cluster, is one of the more coveted cacaos in Ecuador. To reach their potential, the beans need an unusually short fermentation. This makes them unsuitable to throw in as part of a mixed Amazonian cacao batch. Despite fervent efforts by growers, none of Arriba's unique floral fragrance ever develops when it is planted anywhere outside its ecological niche in Ecuador.

Arriba trees are very tall and large, though they are less productive than Trinitarios and other Amazonian cacaos. The thick-husked pods exhibit a mixture of Cundeamor and Amelonado phenotypic features (see page 62), with a suggestion of a bottleneck and a furrowed, often warty surface. The beans range in color from pale to deep purple. Arriba beans are fermented briefly, sometimes less than twenty-four hours, for the optimum development of their characteristic floral perfume.

TRINITARIOS

Trinidad is the Noah's Ark of cacao—a vessel holding the most complete genetic reservoir of the hybrid cacao we know today as Trinitario. Cacao conservation in Trinidad began in the 1920s under the auspices of the Imperial College of Tropical Agriculture. Memories of the genetic catastrophe suffered by the island in the eighteenth century together with the ever-present threat of diseases such as black pod rot and witches' broom prompted geneticists and botanists to begin a systematic classification and selection of the best genetic material available on the island.

Imperial College Selections 1 to 100

In 1933, the geneticist F. J. Pound, under the supervision of the botanist E. E. Cheesman, selected one thousand trees from farms all over the island. The criteria for selection were high productivity and resistance to disease. Further testing narrowed the selection to one hundred clones, which formed the core of the so-called ICS (Imperial College Selections) 1 to 100. The collection and systematic study of these heirloom trees has proven invaluable for cacao researchers at work around the world.

I first encountered ICS trees at the International Cacao Genebank in Trinidad. The trees have been planted over a large area, and I had to traverse rugged terrain, jumping up and down and crossing irrigation ditches to take a closer look at the few trees that were bearing ripe pods that time of the year. After I walked through several lots of Upper Amazon cacao, with their unimpressive smallish yellow pods, ICS 1 came as a refreshing sight. The tree had pods in all stages of growth. The pods, which varied in color from deep crimson to burnt orange, sprang from trunks and branches that sported small tags, pieces of colorful plastic twine, and notes pinned on by the scientists who have done experiments with this accession.

With an estimated production of 106 medium-sized pods a year, enclosing an average of forty-two plump,

A map of Trinidad's cacao growing regions and experimental cacao fields (after a map by Frances Bekele of Trinidad's Cocoa Research Unit).

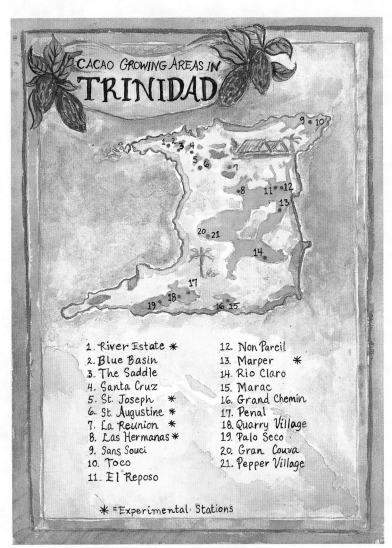

The unripe pod of ICS 1 (right) shows red ridges and green furrows that will later change to the uniform orange of the mature specimen (below).

light-cotyledon beans, ICS 1 is an attractive cultivar. In sensory evaluation tests, ICS 1 liquor is described as having a mild chocolate flavor (in comparison to the West African standard) and a pronounced fruitiness. The cross of ICS 1 with Scavina 6 is found to be both highly productive and resistant to witches' broom.

Clones of the Imperial College Selection were planted in several plantations throughout the island of Trinidad. I first saw the whole collection at San Juan Estate, Philippe Agostini's lovely cacao farm near Gran Couva. The field is located uphill in a rugged section of this old farm. It is really marvelous to see all these heirloom trees together in a single field, many with the original metal identification tags still attached. It is a living document of the enormous range of pod sizes, shapes, and colors possessed by the first Trinitario population of the island. All shades from green to yellow to purple are represented, but the predominant hue is cabernet red ripening to brilliant orange. When cut open, the beans show the full range of possible Trinitario coloring from light pink to dark purple. Some of the pods are long and warty. Others like ICS 82 are huge, round, and smooth skinned, with large, lozenge-shaped purple beans.

ICS 82 (San Juan Estate, Trinidad).

ICS 84, a Criollo hybrid at the International Cocoa Genebank, Trinidad.

ICS 95 (unripe).

ICS 95.

ICS (Imperial College Selection) clones from Trinidad have been planted on cacao farms all over the world. These large pods are specimens of ICS 95, a Trinitario with a strong Criollo germplasm, from Hacienda La Concepción in Barlovento, Venezuela. It has been used there in crossings with the farm's old Criollo selections to produce more flavorful cultivars with plump seeds and thin shells that are also resistant to black pod disease.

TSH (La Reunión, Trinidad).

Ocumare x IMC 67

Hybrids created by Dr. Lilian Reyes between Upper Amazon cacaos and several Criollo selections from Ocumare de la Costa in Venezuela and Upper Amazon cacaos grow on many progressive farms throughout Venezuela, from Barinas to the Paria Peninsula. Technically they are Trinitarios that have proven resistant to several diseases and are tolerant of poor shade. The cross between IMC 67 (Iquitos Mixed Calabacillo; see page 87) and Ocumare 61 (see page 78) yields a full-bodied Trinitario cacao with lots of the fruity qualities of its sturdy Upper Amazon parent and the elegant dairy notes of its Criollo mother. This cacao forms the core of the Río Caribe cacao, the commercial name for the former Carúpano cacao. Before recent events disrupted cacao farming in Venezuela, it was also the most important hybrid in San Joaquín, a progressive plantation in Barinas, in the sun-scorched plains of Venezuela.

TSH (Trinidad Select Hybrids)

Select ICS clones have been further hybridized with the most vigorous and disease-resistant Upper Amazon cacaos collected in Ecuador and Peru by Pound, to produce the so-called Trinidad Select Hybrids, which have been propagated all over the world.

LEFT: Ocumare 61 x IMC 67 (Finca San Joaquín, Barinas State).
RIGHT: A sampling of Trinitario beans from Cuyagua with multicolored cotyledons showing mixed genetic endowment.

VENEZUELA: HERITAGE AND FUTURE

Venezuela is a land that has always offered rare opportunities for cacao growers—but at the price of risky cash investments, struggles with nature, and tensions between the private and public sectors. The first cacao rush, which began in the seventeenth century, created a class of Creole plantation owners so lordly that they were called the *grandes cacaos* (the big cacaos). But even when strains of fine Criollo cacao were winning Venezuela international fame, the Spanish crown and the local entrepreneurs were usually at loggerheads. The *grandes cacaos* did not take kindly to Madrid's efforts to establish a Spanish monopoly on the cacao trade. Much cacao and money surreptitiously found its way between Venezuela, the Dutch and English colonies of the Caribbean, and "New Spain" (Mexico).

Over the years, Venezuela continued to produce more Criollo cacao than any other nation. In the early-nineteenth century, outbreaks of disease prompted the introduction of sturdier Trinitarios. This was followed by much natural hybridization, especially in the forested coastal valleys and the Barlovento area east of Caracas. Today you can still taste a marked distinction between regional cacaos from these places—which are just acid enough to develop a characteristic fruitiness—and the very low-acid, nutty-flavored Porcelana cacao of western Venezuela. But both the Criollos and the Trinitarios of the country remained standards of excellence of their kind for an impressively long time.

Then came the Venezuelan oil boom of the 1920s, which sent cacao cultivation into a decline. There seemed to be faster ways of making a living, or a fortune. Somehow the local cacaos avoided the extreme genetic degradation that took place in parts of Central America, but a lot of Criollo trees were cut down and replaced with very poor Amelonados. Slovenly postharvest treatment practices crept in. The Venezuelan government did not help matters by emulating colonial Spain and taking over the buying and selling of cacao in 1975. The state monopoly, the Fondo Nacional del Cacao, went far toward running the industry into the ground by obliterating any distinctions of quality and buying the best-treated beans at the same price as moldy or unfermented ones.

However, the government monopoly was abolished in 1991, and a handful of growers saw an opportunity to upgrade their operation and sell better cacao at better prices—especially to the up-and-coming Venezuelan chocolate industry and foreign manufacturers of fine couvertures.

These progressive growers drew up an agenda called "Plan Cacao," which if implemented, would have allocated and established, both private and state funds for technical aid to existing cacao farms and established guidelines for certifying quality and origin. Their boldest initiative was the proposed development of an entirely new cacao region, the vast *llanos,* or plains, of Venezuela stretching from the Andes to the Orinoco. This is not only virgin territory for cacao—the *llanos* have historically been home-on-the-range cattle country—but also totally unlike the ecosystem in which cacao has always been raised. The *llanos* are open, shadeless ground that fluctuates between seasons of rain and drought. Farming cacao here means sinking a lot of money into irrigation systems. If the venture had succeeded, the reward would have been an enormous expanse of newly available land, free of the usual forest-bred cacao disease, and a potential source of prosperity for the *llaneros* (plainsmen), who have fallen on hard times.

Unfortunately, these plans were overtaken by political events following the 1998 election of President Hugo Chávez, who has called for the expropriation of productive cacao farms and encouraged violent attacks on farms, such as the beautiful San Joaquín farm co-owned by El Rey and Panaven (the national oil industry). Nearby residents of the countryside have broken into San Joaquín and cut down cacao trees to make room for their own houses. Beatriz Escobar, the main agronomist of the project and born plainswoman, received death threats from the squatters. The thriving cacao fields that I saw Escobar plant with fine clones of Ocumare cacao have now been abandoned.

FROM CACAO
TO CHOCOLATE

Tab 227

IMAGINE WALKING THROUGH AN ORCHARD unlike any other you have ever seen—a jumbled community of trees, vines, and other growth shrouded in the sweltering green chiaroscuro of the South American lowlands. The air is close and humid; the silence is broken only by the hum of insects and the crackle of dead leaves underfoot. The vengeful sunlight of the tropics pierces the great canopy of towering shade trees, slivering into a thousand rays as it hits the leaves of other small, slender trees around you in the dusky understory. These graceful trees, bearing fruit the size of footballs that grow straight out of lichen-spotted, gray-brown trunks, are the real heart of this unlikely orchard. This is cacao, the source of every chocolate bar and truffle ever made. The sight is somehow primeval, atavistic, like something you would expect in a Jurassic jungle. You begin to look for dinosaurs lurking in the dark recesses of this old cacao plantation. No kind of growth seems impossible in the garden of chocolate.

A cacao plantation is a hothouse without glass, a place of wanton promiscuity where slender tree trunks bear weighty fruits like the pendulous breasts of a tropical fertility goddess. The cacao pods thrive in the steamy heat, presenting an incredible wealth of colors, shapes, and surface textures. An evergreen without a distinct harvest season, the cacao

OPPOSITE: Cacao workers in Barlovento, Venezuela.

95

RIGHT: Chocolate in a conche.
BOTTOM LEFT: At the Estación Experimental Chama in the state of Zulia, Venezuela, sectors of pure Porcelana cacao are divided by wide irrigation ditches.

OPPOSITE: Guasare cacao, a pure Criollo, thrives at the experimental farm of San Juan de Lagunillas in the Venezuelan Andes. This precocious three-year-old Guasare tree is being irrigated by the drip method.

tree puts forth flowers continuously. So, at any one moment, you see Lilliputian flowers next to Gulliver-sized fruits, from the tiny gherkin-shaped baby fruits to toddler specimens like small eggplants and adolescent-sized specimens as big as half-grown spaghetti squashes—all in a range of colors that at first seems random.

During peaks of growth, the huge multicolored pods look like parrots and macaws perching on the trees. Even when fully mature, the pods can range from bright green to pale yellow, dark purple to burnt orange or crimson. What makes the sight so amazing is that even at the same stage of growth, two fruits on the same tree may be very different shades. Some seem to be sculpted with ridges, furrows, craters, or warts; others are smooth and shiny as if enameled or rough-skinned and dappled with dark spots. Some have meandering lines over the surface, perhaps traced by insects or other creatures. The shapes are as startling as the colors. A cacao fruit can be as round as a melon or as long as an enormous teardrop. At the stem end, it can have a pronounced bottleneck or none at all. At the other end, it can be pointed, smooth, or indented.

Alongside the luscious ripening fruits hang the remains of others that have withered on the trunk. Cacao fruits refuse to let go of the mother tree even when they have died.

LOGICAL GREEN ANARCHY

To a first-time visitor, a traditional cacao plantation always looks like green anarchy. But for those who work there, it is supremely logical. The skills of the farm workers who maintain the cacao trees and their complex environments are highly developed. This knowledge is usually passed on from generation to generation.

The farms I know most intimately are in the New World. But the same planting and caretaking needs exist wherever cacao is grown and are fulfilled in mostly very similar ways. In traditional farming, the first requirements are shade and water. Shade keeps the leaves from being burned and the soil from being baked and eroded. A good year-round supply of water is also needed, but preferably with adequate soil drainage and no long periods

of flooding. On most new farms today, water for irrigation is piped to the trees from wells or streams and delivered by a drip method. On older farms, the ground on which the trees are planted is often divided into islands by irrigation ditches that workers have to cross to get to their jobs.

But whether or not such visible boundary lines exist, plantations are generally organized into "sectors," which may range in size from a few acres to a hundred acres or more. From Spanish colonial times, the sector (in parts of Venezuela known as *ahilado*) has been the basic unit of responsibility, farmed by a small team of workers—usually a family with roots on the plantation.

At present most of the world's cacao farms have no substitute for the skills of families with deep roots in a plantation; little can be mechanized. The cacao tree does best in a traditional tropical farm setting where a sizable force of highly experienced workers can give constant attention to a complex polyculture every month of the year.

Choreographing Life

A farmer's duties begin not only with planting the cacao trees but also with choreographing their surroundings. Some plots simply make use of existing forest cover, but there comes a time when new tree cover has to be created from scratch. To begin a new plot, the workers must stagger the growth of the shade trees to have them ready at the right time. They plant small leafy trees, such as yuca (cassava) or coffee bushes and plantain or banana trees, so that the first-stage shade will be in place when the cacao starts growing. Meanwhile, they also plant fast-growing upper-story trees that will reach their full growth when the cacao is ready to bear.

The choice of shade trees can be pretty wide. Plantains and bananas are popular everywhere for the early shade. The upper-story trees can be coconut palms (especially in Southeast Asia), kola-nut trees in Africa (though unfortunately they carry cacao diseases), rubber, or mango. Among Latin American favorites are mahogany, or *caoba (Swietenia mahogani); bucare (Erythrina velutina* or *E. poeppigiana);* and the very tall, spectacularly dense and spreading *gran samán* or raintree *(Pithecellobium saman).*

The mix of smaller and larger shade trees, along with many vines and climbing plants springing up in the same space, supports a complex of insect life that helps pollinate the cacao trees and other plants. That is why I consider cacao such a life-giving crop above and beyond the pleasure we take in chocolate—cacao is an intrinsic protector of the environment.

The cacao trees that are planted in each new sector usually are not randomly chosen. The workers already know which of the existing trees in other parts of the farm are the best bearers and try to retain seeds from their pods when the cacao is harvested. The beans will be planted in a nursery area that may also have slips or buds propagated from some desired stock through cloning

Flowering *bucares* tower over a mixed-growth farm in the Venezuelan Andes.

(that is, removing them from the parent tree and grafting them onto other rootstock). The young plants are ready to be transplanted into the prepared ground in a worker's assigned sector when they are slightly bigger than knee high, at about four or five months.

Once established in its sector, a cacao tree usually takes about four years to start bearing, though some varieties are ready at three, or even two. In the meantime, the workers carefully remove any suckers (*chupones* in Spanish) that might drain energy from the main growth. They prune the trees to a compact shape that will concentrate the flowers and fruit on the trunk and lower parts of the main branches, an important advantage for later harvesting. By vigilant pruning, the trees are kept to a standard height of about 20 feet (about 6 meters, half the height of the tallest cacao trees

A typical nursery for cacao seedlings at the Estación Experimental Chama, a propagation center for pure Porcelana cacao in the humid flatlands south of Lake Maracaibo. The nursery workers first loosen the seeds from the mucilaginous pulp of the pods, then plant them, individually enclosed in sturdy polyethylene bags, in rich organic soil. Dark netting protects the delicate seedlings from direct sunlight.

in nature). But the current fashion is for even more severe dwarfing to permit the trees to be planted as densely as 40 inches (about 1 meter) apart.

A cacao seedling will grow fairly straight up to the first branching; a grafted tree generally puts forth spreading boles. While the young trees grow, the workers watch for signs of disease, periodically clear the undergrowth enough to keep the trees accessible, and also manage the edible crops produced by some of the shade trees (*yuca* and plantains).

Blossoming and Bearing

When the tree is between two and four years old, the first diminutive orchidlike cacao blossoms will sprout on tiny stems that stick straight out of scattered cushionlike patches on the trunk (literally down to the ground) and the lowest branches. The flowers are white, varying to whitish pink or whitish yellow (according to individual strain) and not much bigger than tomato blossoms. They have five arrow-shaped petals set around an intricate sheathing of stamens and pistils.

The cacao tree is an indeterminate blossomer, putting forth new flowers year-round with one or two strong peaks per year (according to region), the profligacy of blooms offsetting the amazingly low fertility of cacao flowers. They are so difficult to pollinate successfully that of the many thousand flowers on a mature tree, only about one hundred will survive to become pods in a year.

Once a blossom is successfully pollinated, it takes about five to six months to become a mature fruit. The farmers must keep track of each one as it approaches ripeness. About a month after pollination, a gherkin-sized baby pod, called a *chirel* (in Spanish) or *cherelle* (in French), develops on the short blossom stem. When it is fully grown, it will be from 9 to 13 inches (23 to 33 centimeters) long and can weigh up to about a pound (500 grams). The shape depends on the ancestry of the cacao. Since the colors vary wildly, experienced judgment is needed to know when a green, yellow, or dark purple fruit is ready to be harvested. The harvest season varies from region to region, depending on local rainfall patterns.

BELOW LEFT: On a cacao tree, diminutive orchid-like blossoms and tiny fruits hang right next to mature pods.

Baby cacao pods.

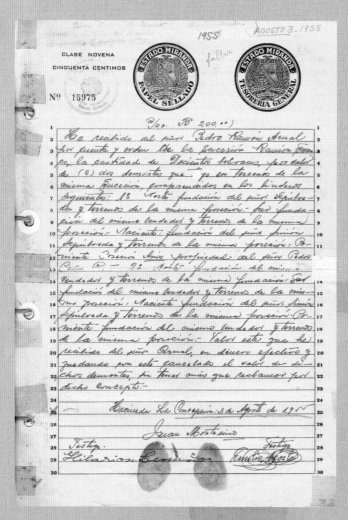

The Arnal and Duarte dispute and hundreds of other plantation minutiae were meticulously recorded in the clear hand
of notaries at the municipal court of neighboring El Clavo.
Looking at the polite formalities of the document, we might
suppose we were observing transactions between social
equals. But then some jarring reminder of the deep divide
between the landowning classes and the people who grew
cacao for them emerges in the form of a thumbprint (in lieu
of a signature) on a lease, or some mention of a farmer's
inability to read and write.

THE BIRTH OF A CACAO PLANTATION

Latin American cacao plantations came into being
over the centuries by varied local paths. The 352-
hectare (870-acre) Hacienda La Concepción in the
northern Venezuelan region of Barlovento typifies a
system that is somewhat like southern sharecrop-
ping in the United States. It probably arose for the
same reason, when many thousands of ex-slaves
were left to fend for themselves after the abolition of
slavery in 1854. The hacienda's records are preserved
to this day and provide a window into the everyday
life of an early modern plantation.

La Concepción's founder was a planter named
Ramón Franco, who started acquiring property in the
area about one generation after emancipation. Franco
then leased the land to an assemblage of tenants,
mostly of African descent, who did the actual farming.
An average initial lease seems to have been for five
years. As in most of the Barlovento plantations, the
agreement was that each tenant was in charge of clearing a designated area or areas at his own expense. In
these parts, such plots were generally called *ahilados*,
a term that roughly translates into "lined-up files"—
that is, rows of trees. They must have varied greatly
in acreage, since the records refer to wildly disparate
numbers of trees in different *ahilados.*

In every *ahilado,* it was the tenant's job to get the
primary and secondary shade trees in place before
planting the cacao. Each *ahilado* had its own nursery,
or *almácigo,* where cacao was grown directly from
seed under the shade of a breadfruit tree. At about
five months, the seedlings were transplanted to their
permanent spots, lined up in the carefully spaced files
to which the term *ahilado* refers.

Most of the early documents concern the rever-
sion of *ahilados* to the landlord, Franco, on the expira-
tion of the initial leases. Up to that point, while the
trees were growing, and probably before they were
bearing, the tenants were allowed to keep and presumably sell any cacao they harvested. The farmers
were then entitled to some compensation for the
addition to the value of the land. What they received

seems to have depended on the number of cacao trees planted in the unit.

Once the trees were producing fully and the first lease was up, another system of arrangement called *medianería* began. The tenant became a *medianero*, who supplied the landlord with a set number of kilos yearly (usually half the cacao crop) or the equivalent monetary value based on the going price of cacao in neighboring towns, and who retained some interest in the cacao trees he or she had originally planted.

That the life of the *medianero* was not an easy one is shown by a series of 1940s documents recording a dispute between Pedro Ramón Arnal, the foreman of La Concepción, and a tenant farmer named Quirino Olegario Duarte. Duarte had failed to come up with the 250 kilos of "good cacao in good condition" stipulated in his contract because his cacao trees still were not bearing. This skirmish between Arnal and Duarte became an ongoing saga. Years later we find Duarte back in court. The dispute was temporarily resolved when Arnal allowed the tenant to remain on his land "two years longer so that he can continue caring for the cacao trees."

After Ramón Franco died in 1921, his children long remained in possession of the farm. Over time, cacao underwent a general decline in Barlovento, and at La Concepción, as at many other plantations, the land was neglected or half abandoned. In some places, the tenant farmers took over or obtained titles to the patches of ground they had been tending for years. This is the origin of the thousands of tiny cacao farms (each one less than about twelve acres) in Barlovento today.

In 1993 new owners bent on revitalization— Silvino Reyes and his wife, Ana Karina Flores—took over La Concepción and started the difficult process of bringing it back to life, *ahilado* by *ahilado*. They succeeded in restoring it to a vigorous plantation of forty-seven *ahilados* laid out with the same spacing of trees that the first farmers established. It was a wonderful union of tradition and technology.

On my many visits to the farm over the course of fifteen years, I found Arsenio Borthomierth, a Venezuelan of Corsican blood who has lived with cacao all his life, studying the phases of the moon to decide how to schedule the pruning of the large shade trees. Silvino Reyes was busy figuring out how to make the fermentation facility more efficient and installing the region's only device for polishing the treated beans, as is sometimes done in Trinidad. And when they discussed their daily routine, they alluded to the names of the original *ahilados,* as if the spirits of the first owners and tenant farmers lived on in these lots of Venezuelan earth.

La Concepción today.

Tending and Harvesting

In all cacao-growing regions, various family members share in the work. In the central coastal valleys of Venezuela, the men do the clearing and heavy cutting in each sector while women tend and harvest the fruit. The worker goes out daily to the assigned sector with a machete and a sharp blade fixed on a long pole. The trick is to sever the stem and retrieve

OPPOSITE: Virgilia Córdoba has spent all of her life working as a cacao harvester in Barlovento, Venezuela.

the heavy pod without disturbing the cushionlike area that it grows from, and without damaging any flowers or immature fruits. The pods are cut open to remove the seeds and the sticky, sweet-tart pulp that surrounds them. On some plantations, the harvester does this on the spot, right under the trees, and then carries the beans in a basket lined with plantain leaves to a central location. There she will dump the cacao beans in a heap, coming back and forth several times over the course of the day until she has checked all her assigned trees. Only then will she start carrying the beans back to the farmhouse to be weighed. On other farms, the unopened pods may be carried on somebody's back or head (or via mules or horses) to a central location. There another woman waits to split the pods open.

Back at the farmhouse, the baskets are weighed. Harvesters are normally paid by the weight of the wet, freshly harvested cacao in its surrounding pulp, technically, *cacao en baba* (from the Spanish *baba*, or "slime"). Once the beans are collected, the cycle of growth and harvest is complete.

Cacao goes on bearing without interruption until it reaches the end of its life. Most trees peak when they about seven years old, but can continue producing well for another fifteen to twenty years. Some are still producing good crops when they reach fifty to seventy-five years of age. But generally the trees of a given sector are replaced long before this. In progressive plantations, a veteran plantation manager or skilled technician usually replaces the older trees with cloned (budded or grafted) stock rather than seedlings. This ensures a high degree of uniformity in the tree's performance. An entire sector may be planted with clones from a single strain that is developed on a specific plantation or at one of the world's great

germplasm banks and is known to possess fine flavor or resistance to a particular disease.

CACAO-TO-CHOCOLATE ALCHEMY

All cacao farming closely follows a similar routine up to the moment when someone cleaves open the pods and disembowels them. This takes great skill and strength; the rind of the fruit in some cacaos, particulaly Amelonados, can be extremely hard to cut through cleanly, and it is easy to slice into the beans.

Fermenting

In the best South American cacao farms, an important role is played by the glistening white fruit pulp, or *baba,* that surrounds the almondlike beans. The sticky mass is first cleaned of foreign objects, pieces of rind, and fibrous placenta. Then workers heap it in wooden bins and cover it with plantain leaves to begin fermentation.

The rich complement of sugars in the sweet-tart *baba* starts fermenting at once, eventually turning into acetic acid (the main component of vinegar). The temperature of the mass rises while the pH goes down, which causes the hulls and the germ tip to soften and allows the acid to penetrate. These factors together kill the germ or embryo within the bean. Meanwhile, the semisolid *baba* spontaneously melts into a liquid vinegar that drains off of its own accord to leave the slightly darkened beans free, though still full of moisture.

The death of the embryo is like turning off an override switch—it allows the bean to rush into another mode, launching a complex sequence of chemical processes like a tiny factory. Some of the sour, bitter, and astringent compounds (organic acids, anthocyanins, tannins, catechins) within the beans pass through the now-permeable skins,

eliminating the harsher flavors. Some begin to transform into mellower substances by the action of enzymes.

The length of the fermentation process depends on the variety of cacao: the best Criollos need as little as forty-eight hours and the other cacaos about six or more days. The beans are rotated from one bin to another to promote the aeration of the fermenting mass. The proper degree of fermentation is determined by cutting some beans open and checking to see if the cotyledons are wrinkled.

Box fermentation at Hacienda La Concepción in Barlovento, Venezuela. A worker arranges plantain leaves over a large "sweating" box filled to capacity with *cacao en baba,* to promote yeast and bacterial activity during fermentation. The beans are mixed and turned from box to box three or four times during the fermentation period.

Drying

When fermentation is completed, the beans are removed from the fermenting bin and spread in the sun to dry on the cement floor of a drying patio or on large, wide wooden shelves or platforms. During this period they are periodically turned with wooden rakes. At night they are pulled into sheds for protection or covered by clear plastic roofing materials. In about five to six days, the chemical changes within the beans gradually slow down and then stop when the moisture content has dropped to less than 8 percent by weight.

Workers then take a sample of one hundred beans and perform a cut test to make sure they are perfectly dried before removing them from the drying yard. Only then are the beans transferred to a storage room, where they are usually heaped against a wall. As the beans accumulate, workers shovel them often to facilitate aeration and to prevent molding. At the peak of the harvest, the pile of beans can easily reach the storage room ceiling.

The beans are now hard, dry, and somewhat shrunken. They have acquired a new name in Spanish-speaking countries: *almendras,* or almonds. Up to this point they have been known as *semillas,* or seeds. For the first-quality Criollo and Trinitario cacaos grown on the premier farms, the interior color, which began as white or very light purple and changed to yellowish brown during fermentation, is now medium brown. An Amazonian cacao like Amelonado will have turned from purple to dark brown. The underpinnings of chocolate flavor are now in place (though you wouldn't find them fully developed if you ate a bean at this stage).

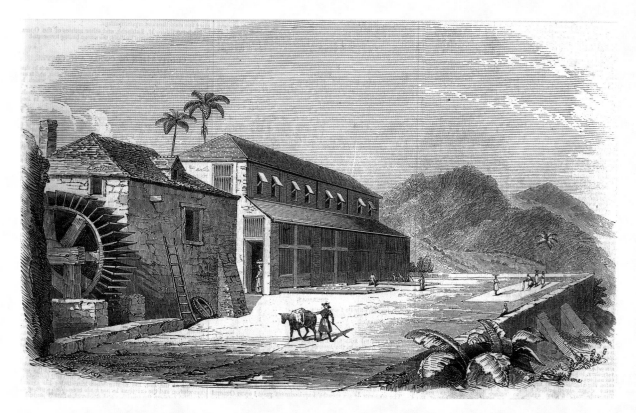

On the island of Grenada, as in parts of Venezuela, coffee and cacao are sun-dried on large paved patios adjacent to the curing (fermentation) houses, as shown in this print, circa 1857.

LEFT: Alexander Fariñas, a worker at Hacienda La Concepción, turns cacao beans with a wooden rake several times a day to ensure that they are evenly sun-dried.
BELOW: A cut test ensures proper drying for the cacao beans.

Yanomami women wash freshly harvested cacao beans to extract the pulp at the Venezuelan community of Washewe on the Mavaca River in the Upper Orinoco Basin.

At least up to the eighteenth century, most Latin American plantations from Mexico to northern South America grew delicately flavored Criollo varieties of cacao, which require only light fermentation to develop a rich chocolate flavor and aroma. When the cacao in commercial plantations became mostly Lower Amazon Amelonado or a mixed batch, the whole equation changed. Those people who choose a short fermentation period or none at all for such cacao are helping to produce bitter, astringent, and overly acid cacao beans. Those who ferment for an extended period can tame the harshness of Forastero. But unfortunately many cacao processors have no choice but to mingle beans of different origins in the fermenting bins—their plantations are a genetic mosaic. Only with constant care of the fermenting mass can they reach a comfortable middle ground to keep the better beans from overfermenting and developing off-flavors, or the cheap ones from being underfermented and acidic. This explains why it is not uncommon to find partially fermented purple beans in a batch of fine Trinitario beans. In some producing countries like Malaysia, it has been found that the flavor of cacao can be improved and high acidity and astringency reduced by the simple postharvest technique of leaving the pods unopened for several days. Also, where a uniform,

fairly homogeneous crop has been grown with care—for example, the sturdy, dependable Amelonado cacao of Ghana—experienced farmers can ferment it for reliable chocolate flavor.

THE CACAO TRADE

After the beans have been fermented and dried, they are classified according to size. For this, most plantations I have seen use creaky turn-of-the-century European sorting machines that look like ancient drums. They still do their job to perfection. In newer cacao-growing regions like Bali with less of a traditional infrastructure, the sorting might be done by hand. This is an important moment in the life of chocolate. The trade classifies beans according to size and quality. Only specialty or high-quality beans are sold at premium prices. The sorted beans are then placed in burlap bags and weighed.

A complex web of buyers and intermediaries is behind every bag of cacao that leaves its place of origin. Because cacao is produced in Third World countries with no tradition of large industrial chocolate production, until recently the best cacao was exported rather than used for local manufacturing or by artisanal producers. This is beginning to change, but the bulk of the cacao is still shipped

BUILDING LAYERS OF FLAVOR AND AROMA

If you were to line up and taste two dozen finished chocolate samples from as many manufacturers, the variations you would find—aside from the innate differences among different cacao strains—would overwhelmingly reflect what had been done during fermentation and drying.

Extensive, well-developed fermentation may well have been a Spanish contribution. Whether the first colonists found the Mexicans fully fermenting cacao beans *en baba*, or simply rinsing the pulp after a very

short sweating, may never be known. Some peoples of Latin America today, like most farmers in Tabasco, Mexico, and some Amazon and Orinoco region Indians, simply rinse the cacao pulp.

Without the help of the sugar-rich pulp, their cacao does not have a chance to ferment even partially when drying. The result is aspirin-bitter beans. In many parts of Latin America, the beans are simply spread to dry on any flat surface after being extracted from the pod. When this is done, the beans experience a partial fermentation, which is better than none at all.

LEFT: At La Reunión, a government-run plantation in Trinidad, dried cacao beans are classified according to size using a nineteenth-century sorting machine.
ABOVE: After being dried and classified, cacao beans are placed in burlap bags and weighed according to each producing country's regulations.

overseas from where it is grown. The rest is used by local manufacturers or by artisanal producers. In Latin America, only Venezuela has a modern European-style chocolate company of world distinction (owned by Venezuelans) that uses 100 percent premium Venezuelan cacao and processes it with state-of-the-art European technology. Other companies are being created or revamped in Ecuador and Colombia that now export finished chocolate to the United States.

Most chocolate companies prefer to use brokers to buy the raw material. From glistening offices in London, New York, and Amsterdam, these brokers act as intermediaries between producers or local brokers and the manufacturers. In a single day, a busy New York cacao broker working for a large international firm will deal by phone, fax, and e-mail with as many as twenty cacao-producing countries around the world to discuss prices, draw contracts, and arrange shipments. Both brokers and chocolate manufacturers require samples of any lot of beans before shipping or upon arrival. Buyers reserve the right to turn down any shipment on the basis of a test of the sample beans.

Cacao prices are futures commodity prices per metric ton set by the New York or London stock exchange. They can fluctuate wildly along with changes in the supply of beans or for other external reasons. In the late 1990s, for example, world prices plummeted to an all-time low, though individual producers or countries were sometimes able to charge a premium for superior-quality beans way above market price. Some countries—for example, Trinidad—have chosen to set their own prices independent of the vagaries of the stock exchange. And individual farms sometimes can set their own prices for special heirloom cacaos, as often happens in Venezuela.

At times an unexpected spike in prices can wreak unintended consequences. This is an era of cutthroat competition for beans, in which no cacao gets to the chocolate shelves of First World shops without a certain amount of behind-the-scenes maneuvering that would make a great plot for a movie.

For instance, ten years ago on the fabled coastal Venezuelan plantation of Chuao (see page 75), the forty-five-member growers' cooperative was selling its cacao to the French firm Valrhona for its "Chuao" chocolate. Enter the young and ambitious Italian company Amedei, then seeking good Venezuelan sources of Criollo with the help of cacao geneticist Juan Carlos Motamayor. Through Motamayor, Amedei learned that the co-op was ready to be courted by a new suitor. Motamayor was able to offer the necessary ballpark figures for Amedei to offer the co-op a seven-year contract, which would enable them to secure financing, implement improvements, expand production (eventually to 20,000 metric tons a year), and emerge with a comfortable profit. In consequence, the price of Chuao cacao increased substantially. Amedei asserted exclusive rights to use the Chuao name, and Valrhona had to put the qualification "vintage" on the labels of chocolate made from its remaining Chuao stock.

The Chuao coup drove up Criollo cacao prices so steeply in the region that brokers and manufacturers throughout the chocolate world reeled. The worst sufferers were local buyers who had been dealing with nearby growers but now saw European competitors rushing in to outbid them. The co-op, far from putting its windfall to use in improvements and maintenance, soon let annual yields decline.

Another recent example of sudden price spikes was a rush on Venezuelan cacao triggered by Japanese companies looking to beat a 2006 deadline for new Japanese regulations barring cacao exposed to certain insecticides. (The cause was the use of anti-tick agents in an area with large livestock farms close to cacao orchards.) Between 2005 and 2006, prices shot up so wildly that Venezuelan cacao became an irresistible target for misrepresentation on the part of sellers and distributors. Japanese buyers were willing to pay literally anything for cacao labeled "Venezuelan" with no opportunity to verify what they were really getting. Good-faith contracts between producers and brokers had to be broken because of sudden price distortions reaching every level of the industry. Price inflation and other repercussions linger to this day. Because the Venezuelan cacao-buying frenzy coincided with surpluses and depressed prices in Ecuador and Colombia, distributors took to surreptitiously mixing inferior beans from these sources with Venezuelan cacao, resulting in loss of quality.

The political backdrop to stories like this is that ten years ago Venezuela appeared poised to become the greatest world supplier of fine-flavor beans to premium chocolate makers. But the campaign for expropriations of property and businesses led by President Hugo Chávez has swelled to include cacao growers and the cacao-exporting trade.

Major plantations have been invaded by squatters, and crops and facilities have been destroyed. The future of the national industry is in grave doubt. But Venezuela's misfortunes have meant opportunities elsewhere in Latin America, as growers in Ecuador, Peru, Bolivia, and the Dominican Republic have moved in to secure a share of the prestigious flavor bean market.

Perilous Journeys

The life of the cacao bean is perilous from beginning to end. Each step cacao takes toward the chocolate factory has a bearing on the ultimate quality of the final product. International trade regulations as well as strict sanitary protection laws by each importing country require that the bags be sprayed against parasites, moths, and other stowaway critters both before being shipped and upon arrival at their destination. (Fans of "organic" chocolate may not want to hear this, but the same regulations apply to organic cacao.) Humidity control during shipping is also essential for quality. Most cacao beans travel around the world for months in the bowels of large ships before reaching the factory. This is an expensive proposition, for long voyages require ventilated storage containers. Upon reception at the factory or broker's warehouse, the bags are fumigated again and ideally stored in temperature-controlled rooms. Other challenges await the beans at the factory.

Passing the Quality Test

Every lot of cacao that makes it to the factory is examined carefully. Technicians take random samples of three hundred beans per metric ton of cacao and separate them into three groups of one hundred each. After weighing one hundred beans to estimate bean size, they cut all the beans lengthwise, revealing the open cotyledons, to look for insect activity, flat beans, clustered beans, and mold, and to determine the degree of fermentation. The trade classifies beans as "slaty" when the cut cotyledons look flat and compact, with none of the

characteristic open kidneylike structure and light break of the well-fermented bean. Each company has a different protocol with regard to the percentage of defects allowed in a single sampling.

The technical staff of any chocolate company makes routine laboratory samples of cacao liquor from each lot for sensory evaluation. Each company appoints a panel of expert tasters whose job is to sample cacao liquors almost on a daily basis. Silvio Crespo, formerly a technical director for several chocolate companies, says that he used to eat a pound of chocolate a day (counting both liquor and finished chocolate).

Liquor tasting is not the same as chocolate tasting. Tasters must concentrate on the intrinsic flavor and aroma of the cacao beans, undistracted by texture or sugar—which enhances desirable flavor and tames off-flavors. Each company has a specific liquor-tasting protocol. When a taster is tasting five or six liquors, it is standard practice to include a West African sample as a basic, neutral flavor reference. The lights of the tasting area are red to mask differences in color, forcing the tasters to focus on flavor.

Once the beans are accepted by the manufacturer and a master recipe for a particular chocolate has been formulated, the cacao beans are ready to be processed into chocolate.

ON TO THE FACTORY:
Chocolate Achieved

Most chocolate manufacturers carry out more or less the same procedures in the same sequence, but the variations among the different cacaos bought by individual firms don't simply disappear at the factory gates. They dictate how the beans will be handled at certain stages. They are also responsible for the wide range of flavors and nuances clearly tasted in the finished chocolates.

When the beans arrive at the manufacturer, they are first run through a machine to remove foreign objects such as jute fibers, stones, or sticks, as well as bits of loose hull or cacao placenta. They are then delivered to giant roasters. The roasting temperature and time depend on the type of bean and the desired effect. Fine, aromatic flavor beans are roasted for twenty to thirty minutes at temperatures between 220° and 240°F, changing the interior color to a richer brown. In general, overroasting is a disservice to high-quality Criollo cacao. Cacaos under the broad Forastero umbrella would ordinarily be roasted for a longer time.

The beans are now brittle, somewhat shrunken, and easier to detach from the hulls. From the roaster, they go to a machine that crushes them just enough to winnow the hulls, or officially "shells," from the broken fragments of beans, or "nibs." The shells, which contain the bitter alkaloid theobromine, at one time were sold to make a cheap cocoa or coffee substitute (sometimes called "miserables" in Ireland); now they furnish theobromine for medical purposes and are sold as mulch for gardens. In Michoacán, Mexico, the roasted shells are further toasted, ground with aniseed, and added to thick atoles. The nibs, now just starting to be available for retail purchase, are prized as a new and valuable ingredient by discerning chefs and home cooks, but still nearly all go into commercial chocolate and cocoa processing.

The nibs are next crushed in high-speed mills and ground to a heavy mixture called "cacao liquor" or "cocoa liquor," which is composed of cacao butter and cacao solids (mostly protein and starch). Despite the name "liquor," it is not alcoholic and would ordinarily be solid at room temperature. The brown gritty mass is further refined to break down the size of the particles. At this point, the liquor is ready to make chocolate. However, since most companies need a supply of cacao butter and cocoa powder, some of the liquor is diverted to hydraulic presses where the solids and butter are separated under pressures of more than six thousand pounds per square inch. Most large manufacturers also subject the cacao butter to a deodorizing process. This ensures that it will have a less emphatic effect when added later to chocolate made from miscellaneous lots of different cacao beans or when combined with milk and sugar to make the so-called white chocolate.

The butter content of the cacao liquor depends on the origin of the bean and fluctuates according to season and harvesting conditions. A Saint Lucia cacao may have barely 46.1 percent cacao butter by weight while the Brazilian Cruzeiro Sol tilts the scale with 61 percent. Venezuelan cacaos contain 51 to 60 percent butter. Normally chocolate manufacturers add additional cacao butter to some of

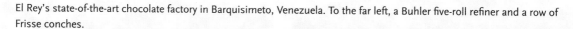

El Rey's state-of-the-art chocolate factory in Barquisimeto, Venezuela. To the far left, a Buhler five-roll refiner and a row of Frisse conches.

their blends during conching to increase fluidity. The total percentage of cacao solids and butter used in a chocolate is called cacao "content." The higher the cacao content, the stronger the flavor, the lower the sugar. Discerning consumers should expect disclosure of this important information, for these percentages do have a bearing on the way chocolate behaves in many preparations—from a simple chocolate drink to an elegant ganache.

It is at this point that crucial ingredients like vanilla, sugar, and often some lecithin (an emulsifier) are mixed with the cacao liquor in specific amounts. For milk chocolate, powdered milk is added at the same time. The mass emerges from the mixer as sticky, gritty blobs of dark chocolate paste. A conveyor belt takes the paste to the refining machine, where it is passed between gigantic steel rollers (set at varying widths) to reduce the particle size to between 14 and 20 microns (about .0005 to .0007 inch). What comes out of the refiner is unrecognizable as chocolate: a light terra-cotta powderlike substance dusting the conveyor belt.

Finally the chocolate is conveyed into the conche, a more powerful and precise descendant

This anonymous print, which originally appeared in the German magazine *Die Gartenlaube*, shows women molding chocolate in a turn-of-the-century factory.

Sticky blobs of dark chocolate paste emerge from the mixer at El Rey's factory.

After being refined, the chocolate takes a powderlike form.

SOME LIKE THEIRS . . . OVERROASTED?

There can be a large element of individual or national penchants in roasting. The eighteenth-century French writer D. de Quelus complained that the French liked a taste and color so burnt that in making chocolate "it would be as worthwhile, coal for coal, to put in the kind from the fire as that from cacao." (The nameless author of the entry titled simply "Chocolate" in the 1873 *Nuevo cocinero americano en forma de diccionario* pointed out that real coal would come a lot cheaper.)

of the one invented by Rodolphe Lindt more than a century ago. Today the purpose of the conche is not so much to break down the cacao particles (which has already been done by other machines) but to knead and agitate the cacao mass until it

undergoes some not-fully-understood chemical changes that seem to mellow, ripen, and round both flavor and texture. Some manufacturers conche only briefly, for four to five hours. The makers of premium chocolates have traditionally conched for about seventy-two hours or longer, though the duration can be cut dramatically with the most efficient new conches. During conching, most manufacturers also adjust the fat content by adding some of the previously separated cacao butter and all or an additional percentage of the emulsifier lecithin, to give a more unctuous, satiny final result.

The mass is sampled at intervals, and when deemed sufficiently conched, it is piped into large storage tanks that keep it warm. When the manufacturer is ready, the chocolate mass is piped into a tempering machine to realign the cacao butter crystals, just as a chef or home cook does it in the kitchen. The tempered chocolate is then poured into molds the size of the finished bar and passed over a conveyor belt that vibrates quickly to expel air bubbles. The molds pass through a cooling tunnel from which the solid, shiny chocolate goes to the wrapping station. The speed of the conveyor

---

FROM LEFT TO RIGHT: At El Rey's factory, a powerful conche heats and kneads milk chocolate to its final texture, flavor, and viscosity. Tempered chocolate is poured into plastic molds, which are then passed over a vibrating conveyor belt to settle the chocolate evenly in the mold and to expel air bubbles before cooling. Workers wrap chocolate bars manually for one of the company's domestic product lines.

belt and the temperature of the tunnel are critical variables. At many factories, the wrapping is done by machine. In others, or for certain lines of chocolate, workers unmold and manually wrap each bar. That would be the end of the perilous journey of our cacao, except that the chocolate still has to get to the store and the consumer. If it is mishandled en route, it can lose temper, absorb obnoxious odors, or become discolored by a surface "bloom."

THE MYSTERIOUS SUBTLETIES OF CHOCOLATE FLAVOR

The lingering fruitiness you detect in a piece of chocolate from one maker, the subtle hint of bitter almonds in another, even such notes as the tealike flavor or odd, faint accent of Swiss cheese or some other dairy product in some dark chocolates are not refinements created at the factory. They come from the latent genetic "messages" inherent in the cacao itself, which are "translated" into detectable characteristics during fermentation. The process mysteriously unleashes the so-called chocolate-flavor precursors in the cacao bean.

But the creation of flavor and aroma does not end with fermentation. When the cacao is spread out to dry, the combined heat of the sun and the chemical reactions going on within the beans can raise the temperature of the mass to as much as 120°F, imparting the sort of warm, subtle suavity that you find in some roasted foods like potatoes.

When it comes to drying, there may be other local differences. Every cacao-growing area of the world must plant for its own climatic conditions. Regions that harvest a lot of their cacao during the rainy season or with cloudy weather—including much of Brazil, Southeast Asia, parts of West Africa, and the Indian Ocean—must use artificial drying methods to decrease the moisture content. None of these is as effective as sun-drying. Much cacao is dried over smoky wood fires on the Indonesian island of Java, giving it a flavor that

reminds most people of smoked ham and me (the Latin cook) of chorizo-type sausage. This is all the more curious because the Java stock has a lot of Criollo ancestry and would otherwise have classic Criollo flavor. In the Bahia region of Brazil, people use gas-fired dryers that can also impart undesirable flavors. Even without such flaws, a common problem with any sort of mechanical drying is that it may not reproduce the smooth sequence of enzymatic and other changes achieved by several days in the sun. The resulting chocolate flavor can be sour, harsh, or flat.

CACAO BUTTER

Cacao butter is one of the most chemically intricate and challenging fats in nature. Like other fats, it consists mostly of triglycerides or compounds formed when three fatty acid molecules hook onto a glycerol molecule. The intricate part is that the three fatty acids on the resulting triglyceride molecule are almost always different kinds and would become solid or liquid at three slightly different temperatures. This is why the sensation of chocolate literally melting in your mouth is so unlike anything else. It is also the reason that people can have so much trouble working with melted chocolate.

During roasting, cacao gains sweetness and a hint of caramel together with floral and earthy notes. Flavors are rounded off when the cacao mass is combined with sugar and vanilla during mixing, and when the mass is reduced in particle size by passing through the refiner. More flavor develops when the cacao mass is conched and heated in the conching machines. While the heated mass achieves that smooth texture we associate with fine-quality chocolate, it also expels volatile acids that contribute to acidity. There is a delicate balance between reducing excess acidity and eliminating the seductive fruitiness that a small amount of acid can contribute to some chocolates.

CACAO:
Flavor Beans and Bulk Beans

Chocolate manufacturers have a world of cacao beans at their disposal. Their choices are as varied and exciting as the colors on a painter's palette—large dabs of basic black and white with a dozen smaller dashes of color, some pure and radiant like the cobalt blue and saturated red of a medieval stained-glass window. The gemlike colors of this palette are the finest cacaos in the world—the precious and glistening remnants of true Criollos that account for less than 1 percent of world production: the perfumed Chuao, the nutty Porcelana, the citrusy and delicate Java. Secondary and tertiary colors, the ones resulting from mixing, are the flavorful Trinitarios with their hybrid vigor and the good bones of their Criollo parents.

Of all Trinitarios, the ones from Trinidad, their reputed birthplace, are among the most coveted. They combine the strength of the Amel-onado parent and its resistance to disease with the flavor and aroma of the more fragile Criollo. Trinitarios are classified as fine-flavor beans and sell way above the international market price for cacao, though production has been on a steady decline in recent years, primarily because of severe labor shortages.

In Trinidad there are two basic grades of beans: plantation grade, which is the finest, with plump, perfect beans, and estate grade, with beans of varying sizes and some imperfections allowed. In Trinidad, beans are polished after drying, which greatly improves their appearance, and as some Trinitarians claim, helps to protect the beans from insect infestation. Today polishing is done by machine, but not so long ago it was done "by foot." East Indian workers danced on the cacao, rubbing the beans between their feet to polish them.

Also a part of this first family of cacao, though of different progeny, is the now-rare Arriba from Ecuador, which until very recently was classified as a Forastero. The trade classifies these beans as "fine cacao" or "flavor beans," and they account for less than 5 percent of the world's estimated 3.5 million metric tons of cacao produced yearly.

Flavor beans dazzle with their complexity. The very best among them, the ones that have been treated wisely, offer an exhilarating ride for the taste buds—not one but many notes of flavor explode in the mouth while the essence of pure deep chocolate lingers softly for a long time.

The essential blacks and whites are "bulk" cacao beans, the reliable West African Amelonado that gives necessary body or bulk to many chocolate blends. Ideally, they provide a solid core of satisfactory—or better—chocolate flavor. In some

Trinidad plantation-grade beans.

Trinidad estate-grade beans.

DOMINICAN REPUBLIC

A surprisingly large Latin producer is the Dominican Republic, with production fluctuating between 30,000 and 43,000 metric tons at the end of the twentieth century. Cacao has been grown commercially on Hispaniola (the large Caribbean island now shared by Haiti and the Dominican Republic) with varying degrees of success since the seventeenth century. The bulk of the island's cacao population is a mixed batch of Lower Amazon Amelonados (similar to cultivars from Costa Rica and Tabasco, like the Matina and Ceylan, respectively), though Trinitarios, and even some Criollos from Venezuela, are also represented.

Dominican cacao is known to the trade by the generic name of Sánchez, after the port from which it was traditionally shipped. Until recently, it was considered poor cacao of astringent, bitter, unfermented character. But in the 1990s, a handful of Dominican producers, inspired by Venezuela's success, began to upgrade their genetic material and their processing facilities and to adopt better postharvest methods (fermentation and drying) in order to compete at a higher level of the export market. The leader of the movement was Nazario Ryzek, the son of Palestinian immigrants to the island. His farm, Los Ancones, in the west of San Francisco de Macorís, became a model operation, supplying cacao to Cluizel, Valrhona, and other European and American manufacturers. Today the single-plantation Los Ancones bar made by Cluizel from Ryzek's beans is a full-bodied, robust chocolate that delivers a burst of flavor. The Finca Elvesia, owned by Brazilian-born Joseph Locandro, is another example of the hope of Dominican cacao.

Map of Hispaniola, the island occupied today by Haiti and the Dominican Republic, from the 1616 edition of Jodocus Hondius's miniature Atlas, in *Tabularun Geographicum Contractarum*.

ASIAN ADVENTURES:
NEW LANDS OF CACAO

Vietnam

Chocolate in Vietnam? Probably it looked like a hilarious fantasy to the original owner of this trade card printed for the German chocolate maker Hartwig & Vogel in 1908, when southern Vietnam was Cochinchina. Today, however, it is fact and not fiction. In 1980 the Vietnamese government decided to encourage the development of cacao as a crop.

Cacao had been experimentally introduced to the region at the end of the nineteenth century, apparently without success. A U.S. Agency for International Development project brought 8,000 trees to South Vietnam in 1959. But following North-South reunification in 1974, the government began seriously weighing the possibilities of cacao—not in terms of small-scale or home enterprises, as in Bali, but as a major commercial crop.

Vietnam was then facing the consequences of overinvestment in coffee as a cash crop. Meanwhile, the Ministry of Agriculture and Rural Development (MARD) saw that a reliable new cacao provider would be highly welcome to First World interests worried about the supply from existing sources (for instance, Indonesia, which has a reputation for variable and often poor cacao quality, or the Ivory Coast, which is a huge producer but has been racked by political instability).

Like Bali (see opposite), Vietnam has no native tradition of cacao growing. But its farmers are known for focused application to goals. The government realized that what was needed was a methodical program of information-gathering from international sources, to be followed by educating farmers in the intricacies of a new crop. In recent years, Vietnam has drawn on input from chocolate industry experts, agronomists, and others to draft plans incorporating informed decisions about what cultivars to plant, how to combat pests and diseases, how to make the most of intercropping, and how to match the best received standards of excellence in fermentation and drying. MARD has been content to start small and go slow, hoping to

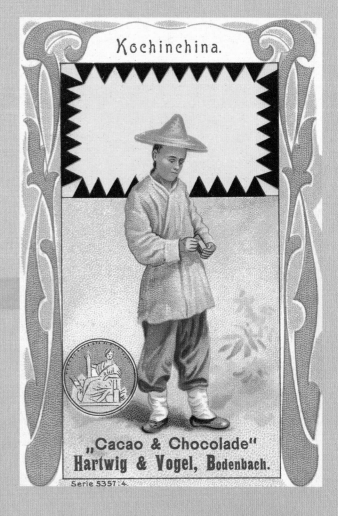

Kochinchina.

„Cacao & Chocolade"
Hartwig & Vogel, Bodenbach.
Serie 5357:4

learn from successes and failures elsewhere. In 2005 the country had a meager 3,000 hectares (about 7,400 acres) under cacao cultivation. As of now the figure stands at roughly 10,000 hectares (24,700 acres), and by 2020 it is projected to reach 80,000 hectares (197,000 acres).

The effort seems likely to be directed toward growing good-quality bulk beans for the major industry players, not fine-flavor beans for the boutique trade. Perhaps Vietnam will come to occupy a position in Southeast Asia similar to that of Ghana in Africa, as a source of sound, well-handled cacao not meant to set the world on fire. Yet I would not be surprised to see the boutique manufacturers experiment with Vietnamese cacao as it comes on the market.

If careful planning can guarantee foolproof results, the country stands poised to become an important international cacao player within a decade. And even granting that there are no such things as foolproof results, Vietnam is likely to be a useful model for other emerging cacao-growing countries that wish to walk into the future with their eyes open.

Bali

In December of 2008, I visited the island of Bali, where I had heard that cacao farming was beginning to flourish, and I was privileged to glimpse a very young cacao scene.

Cacao here does not nestle in the eaves of the rainforest, or occupy great plantations. It is gradually being adopted, on a modest and human-sized scale, in different habitats, including the terraced paddies belonging to one of the world's most beautiful ricelands. Many people grow cacao on their own on very small farms or even in their gardens, and there are about fifty little farming cooperatives, each made up of perhaps a dozen farmers working plots of only about 2 hectares (about 5 acres) apiece. Many farms are of recent date, founded after the government began distributing cacao seedlings to local rice farmers in the late 1980s and 1990s.

This program is no powerhouse campaign meant to turn Bali into a megaproducer. It is a quiet, unimposing effort that has proceeded in little increments, gently integrating cacao trees with their taller shade vegetation into the verdant rice-terrace landscapes of the island. The idea is not to banish the older crop but to soften people's dependence on flooded-paddy rice cultivation—one of the most difficult and labor-intensive forms of farming—by introducing a less-backbreaking tree crop.

Because Bali has no cacao-raising tradition, there was no prior knowledge of practices like fermentation and sun-drying, though the Indonesian government is trying to encourage these methods. With the help of American-born cacao buyer and exporter Chris Hayashi, now living on the island with his Balinese wife, I traveled to Tabana to visit the Koperasi Cacao

Tunjung Sari, a small co-op that ferments and sun-dries cacao. The farmers dry their best cacao in a special solar drying house donated by the government. The rest is spread out on a tarpaulin on the ground, and left to dry under the vagaries of the moist Indonesian climate.

Industrial-scale technology has scarcely touched the cacao enterprise. The co-op ferments beans in large wooden boxes, covering them with banana leaves, as is done in many parts of the world, and sorts them by hand rather than machine. Because it lacks the money for chemical pest control, its members wage war against the virulent Southeast Asian scourge known as the cacao pod borer or cocoa moth (*Conopomorpha cramerella*) by fastening palm fronds laden with hungry black ants—a natural enemy of the insect—on cacao trees. The ants swarm over the surface of the fruit to devour the borer's eggs.

The way things are going, Bali is not likely to become a dominant player on the world cacao stage. But that doesn't seem to be what the islanders want. The best of them are producing a solid basic cacao good enough to appeal to high-end chocolate makers like Amano (which has introduced a Bali bar, Jembrana). Meanwhile, cacao is gradually introducing new possibilities for earning a decent livelihood into people's lives.

I was able to appreciate the real human promise of cacao when I met Gusti Ayu Nyoman Saneh, a sixty-eight-year-old widow whose face and hands showed the toll taken by a lifetime of tending rice paddies in the village of Pangsang. In 1990, a neighbor gave her some seedlings acquired under the government cacao program. Since the trees began to bear in 1994, she has been able to make a living from the 300 cacao trees planted behind her house amid a lovely green welter of coconut trees and other fruit trees, coffee bushes, yuca, and taro. By selling cacao to the local buyer for a distributor in Java, Saneh has a self-sufficient livelihood. But if she could find someone to teach her the skill of fermentation and proper sun-drying, she could get an even better price for her crop.

Today many people on the island are following a similar path, combining a traditional peasant life with small-scale independent cacao farming. In a way, it makes me think of my family's mixed-growth farm in eastern Cuba—but while cacao there is intricately rooted in a long past, here it promises a better future for people who were not born to a knowledge of chocolate. In both cases, the cacao tree is a presence harmoniously woven into the fabric of rural life.

Heaps of lumpy, moldy overfermented cacao beans are laid out to dry. These beans will be sold at a fraction of the price of premium-quality beans and used to manufacture cacao butter.

producing counries this same cacao is poorly fermented and miserably acrid.

The bulk beans account for more than 90 percent of the world's cacao production. West Africa ranks first in world production, with the Ivory Coast taking the lead over Ghana, which not long ago was the continent's premier producer. Indonesia does not lag far behind the Ivory Coast, having surpassed Malaysia in recent years. One of the largest producers of bulk cacao in Indonesia is Sulawesi.

Once the largest cacao producer in Latin America, Brazil has ceased to be an important player. Since the 1950s, production has been on the decline, as witches' broom and black pod rot have decimated the country's most productive regions. In the late 1990s, Brazil had to import cacao from West Africa to satisfy internal demand for chocolate.

There are amazing flavor variations among bulk beans. Nigerian cacao is robust with strong roasted-coffee notes. When Bahia beans are well fermented and sun-dried, they have more of an even-keeled flavor; but when they are machine dried, their acidity varies wildly, from the quirky

DANCING THE CACAO

In this late-nineteenth-century photograph, East Indian workers in Trinidad "dance" over a patch of cacao beans drying in the sun to give the beans a desirable sheen. Nowadays, this process is done by machines. Workers pour the dried beans into a large metal pan fitted with a removable perforated wooden floor and rotating wooden paddles that keep the beans from touching the metal. The beans are wetted slightly and then stirred by the rotating paddles. Electric- or gasoline-generated blowers blow cool air from below. When the polishing is over, the beans are dried with hot air. The friction generated by this process gives premium Trinidad beans their characteristic clean, appealing shine.

squeeze of fresh lime in a *caipirinha* to an overdose of vinegar in your salad. When Dominican Sánchez beans are unfermented, they are nondescript and smell like burnt rubber. Well fermented, they compare favorably with some of the reliable Ivory Coast beans.

Ghana—where the government enforces very stringent standards of quality—produces an especially sought-after bulk cacao of very reliable quality, with a slightly nutty flavor and a suggestion of roast coffee. The beans come mostly from Lower Amelonados—genetically related to the Brazilian "comum"—and some Upper Amazon cacaos brought in the 1940s (see page 52), which have been fully fermented and sun-dried on mats. They deliver clean, good chocolate flavor with no bangs or fanfare. They come with no surprises, lasting just long enough in your mouth to let you know you are eating chocolate and leaving you with neither disappointment nor exhilaration. They are favored by many manufacturers because they are also neutral in acidity; thus cacao liquor made from Ghana beans is often used in sensory evaluation testing as a standard of reference for other liquors.

But in every family there are scoundrels. For them, the trade has an unflattering name: "dogs and cats." These are either cacao beans that have some undesirable characteristic such as extreme acidity, or poor grades of better cacaos that have been rejected for some flaw in processing, such as overfermentation or moldiness. These cacaos are used to provide bulk in some inferior brands of chocolate or are processed into cocoa powder and cacao butter.

Cacao Bean Fashion

Since cacao was first exported to Europe, different regional cacaos have succeeded each other at intervals in general favor or disfavor. By the nineteenth century, the once-prized cacao of Mexico had been so debased that knowledgeable consumers (even in Mexico) often passed it by for the Venezuelan

Caracas, Maracaibo, and Puerto Cabello, and the Colombian Magdalena. In the esteemed Venezuelan producing area of Paria Peninsula, the Trinitario cacao formerly called "Carúpano" (for the port city from which it is still shipped) wore out its welcome when formerly high standards of care declined. The cacao had to be rebaptized "Río Caribe" (the name of another coastal town in Paria) to be accepted when its quality improved. This shows how intensely people identified particular regional origins with definite characteristics. One reason is that the genetic base of cacao used to be less promiscuously mingled; experts tasting cacao beans or chocolate recognized a spectrum of flavors that pointed to origins.

In place of the coveted Caracas, Venezuela now exports a distinct type called "Carenero," which comes from the fertile and humid region of Barlovento, northeast of Caracas. (The name dates from colonial times and comes from the small port from which the cacao was shipped to La Guaira.) The plantations of this area grow a mixed bunch of Trinitarios, Amelonados, and Upper Amazon cacaos brought from Trinidad, but the best growers propagate their cacao by selecting the ones with stronger Criollo germplasm. Select, well-fermented beans from Barlovento are sold as "Carenero Superior" and are prized by manufacturers for their complex lingering chocolate flavor and aroma, spiciness, and characteristic fruitiness. The beans can be recognized immediately for their unique *goût de terroir*. The number of cacaos that retain such a distinctive character has shrunk drastically.

The premium light-colored Java beans (classified as Java A) are getting so expensive and hard to find that manufacturers are switching allegiance to the once-obscure cacao of Madagascar, which has a similar color and a subtle citrus acidity. Plump hybrids from Ecuador are penetrating the market, though the coveted floral Arriba, long a favorite of many American chocolate manufacturers, is now a rarity.

Heirloom beans from particular regions and single plantations represent a minute fraction of the cacao bean trade. Their survival lies in the hands of fine manufacturers and discerning consumers. A few years ago, only a handful of professionals had ever heard of them. Today, however, their names are being eagerly marketed by both boutique manufacturers and the larger established companies. Meanwhile, new makers of premium chocolates are rushing on the scene in such great numbers that there aren't enough of the real heirloom beans to go around.

One result has been a flood of some dubious claims about the pedigree of many chocolates. The terms "Porcelana" and "Criollo" (which are essentially unregulated) tend to get plastered on any light-colored cacao without any attempt on a maker's part to check out other basic clues like the shape of the pods or the presence or absence of the fruity flavors that are foreign to true Porcelana cacao and inconspicuous in Criollo. Advances in DNA analysis may make it easier to distinguish fact from fiction in these cases, and makes it possible to do so at the farm level.

I also think that today's competitive jousting for beans will further spur the best makers to cultivate direct relationships with cacao farmers— not only in the premium lands of Criollo and Porcelana, but wherever interesting cacaos grow around the world, from the Peruvian Amazon and the Alto Beni in Bolivia to Vanuatu in the South Pacific. It may foster the formation of domestically owned chocolate-making businesses in some cacao-growing countries, while perhaps encouraging some European or American manufacturers to establish their own plantations in the same regions or strike exclusive deals with growers.

A RECIPE FOR CHOCOLATE

Cookbooks or culinary encyclopedias used to give suggested custom blends of beans, like this one from *Nuevo cocinero americano en forma de diccionario*, published in Mexico in 1873:

Soconusco	*2 pounds*
Maracaybo	*2 pounds*
Caracas	*2 pounds*

Sugar, 4 to 6 pounds allowing for some preferring it sweeter than others, and an equal number of ounces of cinnamon, making allowance for the irritability of people's stomachs or for each person's taste. Tabasco [cacao] can also be used in place of Maracaybo, but chocolate made with it has less body.

The anonymous contributor also adds optional ingredients like ground biscuits and almonds, but remarks that too much of them makes the chocolate stop being chocolate. Formulas like this show how integral the idea of blending has been to the whole enjoyment of chocolate through the years.

364   *Of Drinkables.*

CHAP. VIII.

Of CHOCOLATE.

YOU are to chuse that which is new made, heavy enough, hard and dry, of a brown reddish Colour, good Smell, and pleasant Taste.

Chocolate is nourishing enough: It is strengthning, restorative, and apt to repair decay'd Strength, and make People strong: It helps Digestion, allays the sharp Humours that fall upon the Lungs: It keeps down the Fumes of Wine, promotes Venery, and resists the Malignity of the Humours.

When Chocolate is taken to Excess, or that you use a great many sharp and pungent Drugs in the making of it, it heats much, and hinders several People from sleep.

The Cocoa, which is the principal Ingredient for making Chocolate, as we shall observe by and by, contains much Oil and essential Salt; as for the other Drugs which are mixt with it, they are all full of exalted Oil and volatile Salt.

Chocolate agrees, especially in cold Weather, with old People, with cold and phlegmatic Persons, and with those that cannot easily digest their Food, because of the Weakness and Nicety of their Stomachs; but young People of a hot and bilious Constitution, whose Humours are already too much in stitution, ought to abstain from it, or use it very Motioately.

From *A Treatise of All Sorts of Foods* by M. L. Lemery, 1745

THE NEW TASTE OF CHOCOLATE

The face of chocolate has changed fantastically in the last few years. Shoppers now find themselves confronted with some bewildering choices between blended chocolates and a newer breed of "exclusive-derivation" chocolates.

The word "blended" is one recurrent source of misunderstanding. What it means is that the cacao beans are of different varieties and/or geographical origins. Do not assume that the result is necessarily an anonymous, homogenized hodgepodge. The practice of blending is very old, indeed pre-Columbian. From the start it was founded on a recognition that the right combinations of different cacaos have a kind of synergy, a total effect greater than the sum of the parts. But to achieve the full potential the maker must treat each variety with regard to its special needs (for example, optimal roasting temperature). This was part of the skill possessed by the older European artisanal chocolate makers.

When the corporate giants came on the scene, they adapted the time-honored tradition of blending to the pursuit of profit more than flavor. But do not imagine that Cadbury, Nestlé, and Hershey's were blind to the distinctions between good and bad cacaos. They never lost sight of a complex calculus between price and quality, enabling them to give cheap, commonplace Forasteros a flavor boost from carefully judged smaller admixtures of better beans.

Depending on the sensory profile they are after, manufacturers might start with a large percentage of a good reliable Amelonado from West Africa. Then they would blend in some of the more popular flavor beans (often suave Venezuelan Criollos with some gutsier, fruitier Trinitarios). The finishing touch might be a small dash of some rare, uniquely scented cacao (the endangered Ecuadorian Arriba or the elite Criollos, such as Porcelana or true Chuao). The sensory profile might also include a certain desired appearance, for example, using Java beans to provide a pale color in milk chocolate.

Sorting out "Exclusive-Derivation" Chocolates

When a new, ambitious generation of bold chocolate makers came along in the 1990s, some took the blending route and others came out with chocolates that identified the origin of the cacao beans or the name of an estate on the label. "Single variety," "single origin" (origen único), "grand cru," "pure origin," and even "estate grown" have become the buzz words in chocolate making today. For the sake of convenience I refer to this cluster of offerings as "exclusive-derivation chocolates." There are parallels between wine making and chocolate making in this respect, though we should remember that wine grapes and cacao are analogous only up to a point.

Chocolate made only from cacao grown in one region (single origin), or even a single plantation (estate grown), will almost invariably turn out to be a blend of botanical varieties, for very few modern plantations grow one cacao strain alone, and any growing region or country is bound to have various hybrids. A bag of Grenada beans, for example, might contain beans from Upper Amazon cacaos such as Scavina 6 or IMC 67 (Iquitos Mixed Calabacillo), Trinitarios like ICS 1 (Imperial College Selection 1 from Trinidad), and Grenada Select Hybrids from the island's original Criollo population. And theoretically—though this is a less likely scenario—you could call a chocolate "single variety" as long as it contained only one specific cacao variety, no matter whether the cacao came from one region or three different countries. What distinguishes one natural blend from the other is a matter of the local soil and environment bringing out inherent genetic characteristics, as well as the way in which particular styles of drying and fermentation have distinct effects on overall flavor and aroma.

LEFT: In 1998, Valrhona added a new vintage estate chocolate to its roster of "grands crus." Chocolat Noir de Domaine Gran Couva is manufactured with Trinitario beans from San Juan Estate, an old Corsican plantation near the town of Gran Couva. This was followed by other single-origin chocolates.

ABOVE RIGHT: Launched in 1999, the first entry in Cacao Barry's Origine Rare line is a dark couverture (70 percent cacao content) manufactured with Cuban beans from the Baracoa region in northeastern Cuba.

ABOVE: El Rey's San Joaquín Estate Grand Cru was Venezuela's first entry in the growing international ranks of estate-grown chocolate. The chocolate was fruity with a pronounced peach flavor, subtle citrus notes, a floral bouquet, and a distinctive earthy accent that calls for the Spanish phrase *sabor a bosque* ("flavor of the woods").

The advantage of the exclusive-derivation approach, when practiced by knowledgeable chocolatiers, is that the individual nuances of a particular bean will register very clearly on the palate. Sometimes you can almost get a cacao education at a single bite—a rare pleasure that few chocolate lovers have had the chance to experience until very recently.

The single-origin approach works beautifully when the beans in question are exceptionally good and noble and have had good postharvest treatment, giving them a well-rounded, complex flavor and aroma. Chocolates El Rey, the Venezuelan chocolate manufacturer and grower that was first in identifying the source of its beans in 1994, buys only fully fermented Carenero Superior beans from Barlovento. The result is a line of single-origin chocolates, ranging from a seductive milk chocolate with 41 percent cacao content (Caoba) to a robust extra bitter dark chocolate with 70 percent cacao content (Gran Samán), which has lately been joined by products that contain higher contents of cacao butter added to the dark chocolate formulas. Though made with the same regional blend of Carenero Superior beans, the varying amounts of sugar and cacao butter in the formulas of the different chocolates play to their distinct notes of fruit, nut, and spice in different keys.

The same is true of single-estate chocolates that blend good-quality, expertly fermented Criollos and Trinitarios raised on one farm, for instance, El Rey's San Joaquín (no longer produced because the farm was taken over by squatters) and Valrhona's Chocolat Noir de Domaine Gran Couva (64 percent cacao content). The latter is made with polished "Plantation Grade" Trinitario beans from San Juan Estate, an old colonial plantation in Trinidad.

But shoppers new to the intricacies of today's chocolate lingo may not understand one loophole in exclusive-derivation terms: if the beans are terrible to begin with, no claim about variety, origin, or *cru* will ever raise the resulting chocolate above the level of the very worst mass-produced blend. Another surprise for novices may be that distinguished Criollo or Trinitario strains aren't the only source of exclusive-derivation chocolates. There are some bulk cacao beans that (when well handled) can yield pleasing chocolate. Some large companies like Callebaut traditionally have gone this route, and other makers are doing it today. The Swiss-owned Barry Callebaut (the offspring of a merger between the Belgian giant Callebaut and France's Cacao Barry) has launched a line of exclusive-derivation chocolates using bulk beans carefully screened for the purpose—from the Dominican Republic, Ecuador, and Indonesia, among others.

Exclusive-Derivation or Blended: Which Is Better?

People new to the appreciation of chocolate often ask which is better, the exclusive-derivation or the blended approach. Both options have equal validity. But as one who thinks the unexamined chocolate is not worth eating, I'd say that the piece of information missing here is the cacao's origin (or origins). This should be on every package, from supermarket candy wrappers to boxes of *luxe* truffles.

Today's boutique chocolatiers have no reason to follow the example of old-style corporate giants who treat their blending formulas as state secrets, and every reason to tell information-hungry aficionados the exact origin and variety of all the cacao in their chocolate. A common argument against disclosure is the manufacturers's need to replace some cacaos from time to time in their blends. Yet this should be a part of the informational literature handed out to consumers.

The labeling issue has another dimension related to the disturbing shifts and disappearances taking place in the global roster of cacao varieties. Truly excellent cacaos currently represent less than 2 percent of the international cacao bean trade, while a few mediocre cultivars have increased their comparative share by leaps and bounds. Who will have any incentive to carry on the demanding task of growing yesterday's rare and exquisite cacaos if today's industry fails to demand fine-flavor beans, pay premium prices for them, and make their names well known to adventurous food lovers? When information about provenance routinely appears on labels, the friends of fine chocolate may be able to strike a few blows for heirloom cacao from particular regions or even particular farms.

The many cacao varieties are a vivid and fascinating array of botanical "personalities." The place to start recognizing the nuts and bolts of the finely tuned construction that you experience as flavor compositions from the likes of El Rey, Guittard, Amano, Bonnat, Amedei, Michel Cluizel, and Valrhona is in the nature of individual cacaos.

CHOCOLATE MISSIONARIES IN AMERICA

No one who loves chocolate needs to be told that today it is experiencing a golden age on all fronts. The theme of chocolate runs through news headlines on everything from archaeological discoveries to front-line research on genetics or chocolate's role in cardiovascular health. Meanwhile, the American public is passionately responding to chocolate that embodies true, vivid cacao flavor and loving artisanship.

As with wine, dedicated amateurs are taking chocolate into their own hands, educating themselves through reading, workshops, classes, and organized tastings. Go to your computer screen

GUITTARD CHOCOLATES: FROM TRADITION TO INNOVATION

In spring 2000, the San Francisco Bay Area's Guittard Chocolates unveiled a new line of couvertures that were a departure from business as usual. These boutique blends featured a high cacao content and a large percentage of heirloom Venezuelan beans deftly combined with other premium beans, such as the aromatic Ecuadorian Arriba. Through such innovations, Gary Guittard pushed his company to the forefront of the new chocolate revolution. Some of these new offerings were inspired by the recipes and labels created in the nineteenth century by Étienne Guittard, the company's founder and Gary Guittard's French-born grandfather—another example of how the past is shaping the new taste of chocolate. But in recent years Guittard has positioned himself as one of the most dynamic premier chocolate makers in the United States and moved full force into the world of "single-origin" chocolates with bars made with excellent beans from Sur del Lago in Venezuela, Colombia, Hawaii, and even Peru.

ROBERT STEINBERG AND CUSTOM-BLEND CHOCOLATE

For many emerging chocolate makers, the advantages of skilled blending were typified by small makers such as the famous chocolatier Maurice Bernachon in Lyon. Together with his son Jean-Jacques, Bernachon made his own chocolate blend using as many as thirteen types of cacao, mostly "flavor" beans from South America, including Chuao from Venezuela, which he regarded as the world's best.

Bernachon's influence shaped the approach of the late Robert Steinberg, who in turn pointed the way for many of today's best small artisanal chocolate makers. Robert had been a practicing family physician for many years when he was diagnosed with chronic lymphoma in the mid-1990s, and began to rethink his life. He traveled to France to apprentice at Bernachon's, joining forces on his return with former Champagne maker John Scharffenberger. In 1996, the two launched the hip Bay Area boutique company Scharffen Berger.

Robert believed in the art of blending—for him, the nuances of cacao beans and the way they were handled became almost a spiritual quest. He had developed a nose for the qualities of fine cacao beans and spent much time and effort in learning the biology, technology, and logistics behind a startup chocolate business.

Using vintage equipment like an old German *mélangeur* with gigantic granite rollers to crush the cacao nibs, sugar, and whole vanilla beans, he and his partner created a high-flavor classic formula composed of 50 percent Venezuelan flavor beans, such as Carenero Superior from Barlovento and Sur del Lago Clasificado from the Lake Maracaibo area, as well as Trinitarios from Trinidad, Madagascar, Java, and occasionally Papua New Guinea. They also used Amelonados such as the reliable Ghana, and occasionally the more acid Bahia—not as bulk beans to add body to the chocolate but as flavor notes in a complex synthesis of elements. Later Robert also developed the fine single-origin El Carmen (named for the single *ahilado*, or sector, on La Concepción farm that furnished the select Carenero Superior beans for the bar) as well as Cuyagua (a blend of Cuyagua and La Concepción beans).

The postscript to the Scharffen Berger story is that in 2005 the company was acquired by Hershey's. It is now being transplanted from its Bay Area roots to new headquarters in Robinson, Illinois.

and you will enter a growing world of online chocolate-heads—bloggers, Web masters, and assorted members of the cyber peanut gallery—circulating a wild, heady mixture of fact and fiction about chocolate, including both useful information and highly personal opinions on the expanding community of chocolate makers.

At the forefront of that community stands a small fraternity of go-for-broke adventurers with ad hoc budgets and fearless palates. Often known as micro-batch chocolate makers, as opposed to medium-sized manufacturers with mainstream approaches, they are infusing irresistible energy into the entire chocolate scene and, in effect, redefining the industry.

The handful of most important American micro-batch makers includes Steve DeVries of DeVries Chocolate in Denver, Colorado; Art Pollard of Amano Artisan Chocolate in Orem, Utah; Alan McClure of Patric in Columbia, Missouri; Sean Askinosie of Askinosie Chocolate in Springfield, Missouri; and Rick and Michael Mast of Mast Brothers Chocolate in Brooklyn, New York. All are self-educated in the craft of chocolate making, and travel where their curiosity about cacao leads them.

They have emphatic ideas about what makes true chocolate flavor, even going so far as to exclude vanilla from their formulas. All work on a comparatively small scale, but some are smaller than others. At one extreme is the Mast Brothers' little Brooklyn facility, with a couple of wet grinders hardly bigger than restaurant-scale stockpots. At the other, Art Pollard at Amano—a hands-on tinkerer since his physics, lab days—has collected and carefully refurbished a whole array of vintage larger-scale equipment from many different sources.

The artisans of this new generation often work with extremely limited amounts of beans—kilos rather than metric tons. Their relationships with growers vary greatly. It is no easy matter to go to, say, the Sur del Lago region of Venezuela and arrange for a few bags of beans to be sent to the United States. There are incredible reams of legal and business paperwork (licenses for export, shipping manifests) to be completed, quite separately from the logistics of getting into the countryside and hauling the beans to the nearest shipping port. Makers who manage to deal directly with farmers and handle their own exports without middlemen are the exceptions.

Where genuinely rare premium beans are concerned, the little guys stand a good chance of being outbid by bigger fish, especially representatives of prestigious European makers, like Amadei.

Art Pollard of Amano Artisan Chocolate inspects for broken beans and nibs. His vintage winnowing machine was constructed of mahogany, maple, and ash in the 1920s or 1930s. Pollard bought it Spain and then fully restored it for his Utah factory.

When they do score a hit, they commonly process and market the beans as "limited edition" bars, to be snapped up by consumers who know that this chocolate might be a once-in-a-lifetime experience.

Despite the hurdles they face, micro-batch makers are shaking up the industry in every way. Even the big players are taking cues from the upstarts, reaching for specialty sales niches. Indeed, the philosophy by which a line of chocolates is made has become an important criterion for consumers and a sales tool for manufacturers.

Today's chocolate makers increasingly realize that the ultimate source of both quality and meaning is the cacao farm. Take the Missouri-based Shawn Askinosie, who left a career as a criminal defense lawyer to open his own micro-batch chocolate company, Askinosie Chocolate, in 2007. He begins by individually meeting every farmer he works with and requesting a commitment to carry out proper fermentation and drying of the cacao harvest. (There are cacao-growing regions where these practices have never been taught.) He makes it his business to stay abreast of conditions in the different orchards, and personally delivers checks for the 10 percent of net profits that he contracts to share with each farmer over and above the agreed-on price per batch of cacao.

AMY SINGH: THE YOUNGEST MICRO-BATCH CHOCOLATE MAKER

In 2002, I was contacted by a nine-year-old reader of my chocolate book: Amy Singh, who had decided to make her own chocolate for a school study project. I gave some advice and some good Venezuelan beans from La Concepción to this serious, collected girl—and was amazed when she went home and produced a chocolate as smooth and complex-flavored as any high-quality commercial bar.

I was impressed enough to call on Amy several times in the next few years for help in making test bars from batches of fine flavor beans, for my own purposes. When I visited her New Jersey home during testing, I found a very smart, pragmatic setup—mostly based on modified home kitchen resources—that she had arrived at with the help of her father's colleague and friend Jim Kopper.

Her roaster was a couple of metal steamer baskets welded together, rotating over the flame of an outdoor gas grill on the rotisserie rod. She winnowed her crushed roasted beans with an electric fan and ground the nibs in a coffee grinder. Her first refiner had been a hand-cranked pasta machine with the rollers sheathed in aluminum foil to make them touch, thus breaking down the particles to nearly the 20-micron fineness of commercial chocolate; from this she graduated to an impressive two-roll refiner designed by Jim. Her conching was done by agitating the cacao mass for ten hours in an electric pasta machine with a lamp on top to warm it to the right temperature.

Amy was the first American micro-batch chocolate maker—and to date is still the youngest. She now has her own Web site, www.amyschocolate.com. At seventeen, she could be in business for herself if school weren't her first priority. Meanwhile, she speaks out against child labor on Ivory Coast cacao farms, an issue of great concern to industrial buyers that depend on beans from this largest of African producers.

Many consumers today share such concerns about cacao farming. They are starting to ask questions about farming methods and the well-being of farmers. There are people who as a matter of principle won't buy anything produced without Fair Trade or organic certification—and though I applaud their altruisim, I am wary. The label "organic" is meant to exclude synthetic fertilizers and pesticides from the farm, but it doesn't guarantee that cacao has been raised without environmentally destructive practices. Similarly, the Fair Trade Federation's price system is meant to ensure just compensation to cacao farmers in developing nations, but it doesn't guarantee substantially higher income for any individual farmer. I feel compelled to point out that organic or Fair Trade cacao can be mediocre (or worse) in quality. Moreover, the certification programs involved in such campaigns introduce layers of bureaucracy between grower and consumer that can cut into a farm's profits.

There are chocolate makers who admire the goals of the reform-minded groups but have chosen to go their own way without enrolling in any certification program, making commitments that hold out more promise for growers' welfare than mechanically complying with checklists of requirements drawn up by a certifying organization. I must also point out that sensitivity to farmers' needs and environmental concerns is increasing even on the part of corporate titans.

A multipronged process of consciousness-raising is unfolding today, touching chocolate makers and chocolate lovers alike. Twenty years ago, who could have predicted the scope of the American love affair with chocolate? Who could have foreseen the range of choices that now confronts shoppers casing the chocolate section of any reasonably well-stocked gourmet shop or the online equivalent? Who could have imagined the many new chapters of the chocolate story being written by very small artisans?

Today you can look for chocolates delicately blended from a combination of different beans, each contributing its own subtleties to the whole. Or you can taste the unmixed effect of beans from a single farm, perhaps a single sector of a single farm. You can look for history in a bar, and find it in some of Shawn Askinosie's different lines based on cacao from places that represent some of the world travels of cacao through Spanish colonial influence—the Philippines and the once-fabled region of Soconusco in southwestern Mexico. You can buy chocolate from cacao produced on legendary plantations like Chuao (Amedei) or Cuyagua (Amano). Even the elusive Porcelana beans that once furnished the finest exports of Venezuela are again being made available to consumers by companies like Valrhona, Amedei, and Bonnat, who use them in single-origin bars, not blended with other cacaos as used to be customary.

You can also search out chocolate made with different cacao percentages, studded with crushed cacao nibs, flavored with anything from curry to bacon to lavender; you can even experience mixtures of "sweet" and "hot" spices like those popular in the seventeenth and eighteenth centuries.

And the range of offerings can only grow. We all have our wish lists, and mine includes the "other" cacao—the wonderfully fragrant and delicious fruit pulp. I have been buying it for years, in frozen form, from Brazilian markets in my region and wish it could be marketed in this country as successfully as the pulp of other tropical fruits like guanábana or passion fruit. Would it not be wonderful to be able to explore chocolate-cacao fruit pairings as easily as we play with partnerships of chocolate and other fruits?

Certainly there are few dull moments in this heady new world of high stakes and daring entrepreneurship, and I love watching an exuberant age of chocolate discovery take shape for an ever-widening public.

TASTING CHOCOLATE

P EOPLE OFTEN ASK ME to tell them what they should look for when tasting chocolate. I can only tell them what I look for. The appreciation of chocolate is always going to be a subjective experience, to which everyone brings a smidgen (or a ton) of personal baggage and cultural or national prejudice. But we can learn to set aside our built-in biases enough to identify important elements with some objectivity.

CHOCOLATE PREFERENCES

Americans in blind tastings instinctively go for blends with especially high West African cacao content. This happens to be a dominant cacao in some of the mass-produced brands most Americans have eaten since childhood. Naturally it is identified with full chocolate flavor (perhaps also because it has an echo of the *robusta*-type coffees that show up on most of our breakfast tables). On the other hand, Germans tend to hate the intense extra bitter chocolate adored in France. Americans gravitate to very light and French people to very dark milk chocolate. The Swiss and the Japanese go hand in hand in their love for buttery, high-fat, slick,

and satiny chocolate. Since the first edition of this book, a rising generation of chocolate connoisseurs has gravitated decisively to new-school versions of chocolate marked by high content of cacao, strong chocolate flavor, decidedly more bitter than sweet—even in milk chocolate.

There are no rights or wrongs with such penchants. We can't necessarily erase the parts of our sensory memory, but to some extent we can separate what we really taste from what we want to taste or imagine we are tasting. Without turning the act of enjoying chocolate into a pretentious ritual, we can sharpen our perceptions enough to take them seriously and to form real judgments. Not all chocolates are born equal, and not all cacaos deserve to be processed into chocolate. Cacao is a noble plant, but some strains are better off back in the jungle or in a germplasm bank helping to preserve the biodiversity of cacao.

HOW TO TEST TASTE

When I taste chocolate for professional purposes, I like to do it as a comparative process with no more than half a dozen chocolates of similar cacao content from several manufacturers. I don't like mixing chocolates with varying degrees of sweetness or milk and dark chocolates in the same sensory evaluation test. The goal is to concentrate on chocolate's intrinsic qualities without being distracted by differing sugar contents or dairy components that mask some flavors and enhance others.

Some companies have developed their own particular language, which they teach their customers, to talk about the flavor and aroma of a chocolate. For the most part, the standard language of chocolate tasting is very much like the language used in wine tasting. I think you will get more from trying to express your sensations in your own words. There is no need to be baroque when describing chocolate flavors. Draw from your experiences. Think of broad categories of flavor: acid, bitter, astringent, sweet. Make connections with everyday flavors: the fruitiness of raisins or prunes, the nutty, buttery flavor of macadamia nuts or the sweeter but more interesting taste of cashews, the tang of cooked cherries, the musky taste of bitter almond in marzipan, the mild astringency of a green fruit or a banana peel. Try to recall the smell of the foods you like (such as freshly baked bread or pungent cheeses) or the aromas of nature itself: flowery, herbal, spicy. Remember the smell of a gush of rain on hot pavement, the tempting scent of ripening fruit, or the disturbing pungency of slightly rotten fruit.

Look for what appeals to you in the chocolates you taste, but also take notes on those elements of flavor and taste that offend you. Here is the way I approach every single chocolate I taste.

Color

I first examine the chocolates visually for color cues that might help me identify the provenance of the beans. But here you need to dismiss the commonly held notion that dark chocolates are best. Some Trinitarios and Criollos, particularly those from the Indian Ocean, have light brown cotyledons that result in light reddish brown chocolate. (Until recently it was very easy to distinguish a chocolate made with a pure Criollos like Porcelana or Guasare by their beautiful rich caramel color. But since Amazonian cacaos and hybrids with white cotyledons have been identified and sourced in Peru and Mexico respectively, these assumptions need to be revisited and conclusions drawn from a flavor perpective.) Some chocolates, such as Valrhona's Manjari, melt with the rich color of copper. African Amelonados are very dark, while others showing an introgression of Criollo genes are a pleasant medium-rich brown. Excellent-quality Trinitarios might range from light brown to dark brown, and some Trinitarios grown in Malaysia are darker in color than West African Amelonados, which are preferred for milk chocolates.

I also look for other external cues such as a "bloom," which is an ashy coating on the surface of the bar. Chocolate bloom is often a sign of poor storage, not poor quality. When cacao is subject to drastic changes of temperature, it loses its "temper," which means that some of the cacao butter crystals have fallen out of alignment and risen to the surface of the bar, forming a bloom.

Aromas

I start tasting by breaking off a small piece of chocolate. To sample chocolate, I first rub it between my thumb and my index finger to warm it up and help release volatile aromatic components. With one hand, I take the chocolate to my nose and sniff it, while cupping the other hand over it. This is your first chance to separate out the different aspects of a complex sensation. Do not underestimate your sense of smell. It is intimately connected with the way we perceive flavors. To prove this point, place a piece of chocolate in your mouth and pinch your nose. You might identify bitter, sweet, salty, or sour sensations, and even get to enjoy the cooling touch of chocolate on your tongue, but you will not be able to explore the manifold nuances of flavor, because you can't smell them.

Undesirable Smells

What does the chocolate smell like? I first check for undesirable odors. These are mostly the result of poor postharvest treatment of the cacao bean or the inherent aroma of certain poor-quality beans. Some unfermented or artificially dried Amelonados and Upper Amazon cacaos smell like burnt rubber or plastic. Cacao has a knack for absorbing odors. When cacao is stored in humid conditions, it can absorb the grassy odor of the burlap bag. Cacao beans dried over wood fires have a smoky scent that the trade characterizes as "hammy." I like to use such beans in cooking and in cacao and spice blends, but when turned into chocolate, they overwhelm other desirable aromas. While overfermented beans give chocolate the smell of rotting fruit, moldy beans impart a disagreeable stale odor.

Desirable Aromas

Next, I fully concentrate on desirable aromas. Your first impression might be just "chocolaty." Keep concentrating and see what other characteristics emerge. Perhaps the basic chocolate aroma is rather dim or very intense. Perhaps it hits you all at once or seems to build. It may be accompanied by a floral sensation, a hint of ripe fruit, a slight suggestion of caramel. Some chocolates smell like freshly baked apple pie, others like luscious caramel toffee.

Taste

Now I taste the chocolate. The natural temptation to judge by texture and mouthfeel is not the same as analyzing flavors, so try to focus on flavor.

Chocolate Flavor

When I first bite into the chocolate, I let a little fragment rest and dissolve on my tongue for about twenty seconds. My initial intent is to measure the length of the chocolate experience. Where does the chocolate bang begin—at the beginning, the middle, or the end? Some brands have a slow start, but the flavor of chocolate blooms and mounts in a crescendo, and then lingers in your mouth. The trade describes this desirable sensation as a long finish. Some chocolates have an overpowering roast coffee flavor, which might be an indication that they have been made with unfermented beans and have been overroasted to compensate for their lack of chocolate flavor. In others, the chocolate flavor is short-lived. It might come in with a roar, but it disappears quickly.

It could be safely generalized that fine "flavor beans" have a long finish. West African cacao is known for an even, monochromatic chocolate flavor experience with a short finish and neither highs nor lows.

Flavor Characterization

In tasting, we experience natural flavors and man-made flavors at once in no fixed order. In something as complex as chocolate, those flavors are bound to merge into one another. I look first for added ingredients: vanilla, salt, malt, cocoa powder, the dairy product in the milk chocolate.

Real vanilla is never overpowering. What vanilla does is both intensify and tame all other flavors, coaxing them to behave in harmony. Vanillin, which tends to be overused in some blends, is too assertive and cloyingly sweet. It always tastes artificial and leaves a bitter aftertaste. It masks other flavors, perhaps undesirable ones—which likely explains its indiscriminate use by some chocolate makers.

Many manufacturers use a pinch of salt to round off the flavor of milk chocolate. Powdered malt cereal is often added to milk chocolates to give a mellower caramel undertone to the blend. The Japanese prefer their milk chocolate with malt. To me, a successful milk chocolate is one in which the milk blends in seamlessly with the chocolate to create one whole integrated flavor. Many manufacturers believe that an even cacao with low acidity is best for a milk chocolate, and therefore they use West African cacao. But I think a fruity cacao with floral notes offers a counterpoint to the inherent sweetness of milk and creates a more exciting contrast. Cocoa powder is sometimes added to a particular blend to add strength to the chocolate and to boost the cacao content, but it often leaves behind a metallic aftertaste.

Natural Flavors

Then I try to get down to the innate qualities of the beans. Again, there may be a more slowly developed general flavor impact. The chocolate flavor of well-handled West African beans is plain and direct, and actually has become the standard against which other singular cacaos are compared. As you taste, try to focus on the natural chocolate flavors: nuttiness, acidity, fruitiness, bitterness, astringency.

Nuttiness is typical of chocolates made with pure Venezuelan Criollos like Porcelana and, to a certain extent, Andean Criollos. An especially crucial variable is acidity. Too much makes a chocolate sour, but without acidity, a chocolate can be monotonous. The right level of acidity enlivens chocolate with a suggestion of fruit or wine, something associated with the best Trinitario varieties and some Upper Amazon cacaos. Of all Venezuelan cacaos, the Carenero from Barlovento is the fruitiest. "Fruity" is one of the adjectives that first comes to mind when tasting exclusive-derivation chocolates made with Carenero beans like El

Rey's Carenero Superior premium couvertures and Amano's Cuyagua or Ocumare from Venezuela's coastal valleys. In Scharffen Berger's original blend we detected a pronounced fruitiness that was reinforced by other equally fruity beans, such as Papua New Guinea or Madagascar beans. The latter have been described as having a fresh citrus flavor as opposed to the more complex flavor of "brown fruit," a trade term for effects reminiscent of raisins, prunes, or dried cherries.

In some chocolates made with a blend of flavor beans, we might detect floral notes of jasmine and roses. Any chocolate made with a small percentage of true Arriba will have a floral component. Dairy flavor can be detected in dark chocolates made with beans from some coastal plantations of Venezuela close to Puerto Cabello. In some blends, there is a subtle but lingering bitter almond undertaste that I find very appealing. This is a flavor developed during fermentation.

PHILIPPE CONTICINI'S FLAVOR EXPERIMENT

Putting together a tasting of many different chocolates is one way to begin schooling yourself in the flavor complexities of chocolate. But what of learning to register interactions between chocolate and other flavors? The Parisian pastry chef Philippe Conticini has devised a brilliant lesson planned around a chocolate mousse and some neutral-tasting prop to put it on, for example bite-sized squares of angel food cake or brioche. These are served with about a dozen small bowls of sweet or savory flavorings to be sprinkled on the mousse, from sea salt to nutmeg. Everyone puts a dollop of the mousse on a piece of cake or brioche and adds a pinch of any preferred "condiment."

Conticini conducts this clever exercise a bit like a "reading," diagnosing some facet of your personality from your choice, perhaps choosing for you depending on the sense he gets of the real you. He uses a mousse made with Valrhona's Manjari chocolate, his favorite. The fruitiness of Manjari does work beautifully, but you may prefer chocolate with some other distinctive quality, or perhaps one with a plainer basic chocolate flavor (from West African or Dominican Republic cacao). The important thing is a mousse with a premium dark bittersweet chocolate.

Round up a collection of interesting little dishes for the "condiments" and use any eight to a dozen that you prefer from the following list of suggestions. It not only makes wonderful party entertainment but provides dazzling insight into the challenge of chocolate to the palate, its capacity to be many things to many people. I suggest using about 1 ounce each of the dried spices, 2 or more ounces of the sugar and coconut.

Cracked black peppercorns (preferably from Sumatra)

Cracked green peppercorns

Cracked pink peppercorns

Ground true Ceylon cinnamon (see page 165)

Ground cassia (sold as "cinnamon" in this country)

Freshly grated nutmeg

Ground allspice

Aniseed

Cumin seeds

Ground cardamom

Ground ginger

Dried lavender blossoms

Grated Indonesian or Indian palm sugar

Grated Latin American brown loaf sugar (also called *piloncillo, panela,* or *papelón*)

Coarse sea salt

Ground piquín chiles

Finely grated fresh coconut or unsweetened flaked coconut

A chocolate can also be described as winy. When you taste some fermented Trinitario beans from Venezuela, the initial sensation is that of having tasted a still tannic cabernet with great promise. Some Venezuelan Criollos, on the other hand, are so low in tannins or astringency that they taste like a hazelnut or macadamia nut.

When I taste chocolate I let my senses guide me, but I also look for memory cues and try to measure the chocolate against the West African standard of flavor. What are the predominant beans in this blend? Amelonados from West Africa, Asia, or Latin America? Criollos or Trinitarios, or a blend of all these beans? I expect that chocolate tasting will become a more holistic experience when cacao beans and nibs that have been identified by origin reach the U.S. retail markets (as has happened with coffee beans). This will enable more people to use the origin as a point of reference in learning to discriminate among the many complex flavors in chocolate.

Texture

A luxuriant "mouthfeel" happens to be one of the first things novices can detect when they begin tasting chocolate. "So smooth!" people will say with approval at tastings. Yes, this can be a pleasurable effect and a mark of excellence when combined with great flavor—but don't let the presence or absence of a satiny texture distract you from the real business of identifying flavors. I tend to think about texture only after I feel I've done justice to the actual flavors. Some chocolates are unbelievably smooth and creamy, some a little gritty. We are often told of the Swiss preference for a supersmooth texture, achieved by conching for days on end. But conching chocolate beyond a certain degree is really meaningless, since any breakdown of the particles during refining to a size smaller than 18 microns is indiscernible to the palate. In addition, overconching can increase the viscosity of a chocolate through evaporation, causing an overall loss of flavor.

APPRECIATING AND CHOOSING CHOCOLATE

When you work with chocolate every day, mediocrity is abhorred.

—BILL YOSSES, WHITE HOUSE PASTRY CHEF, WASHINGTON, D.C.

Which chocolate to choose must always depend on your purpose: fine desserts or truffles, ganaches and sauces, hot chocolate, decorative molding, or artistic chocolate shapes. It is also a matter of personal preference—but preference has to be informed by knowledge.

Your first step must be learning to read labels. Chocolate makers are increasingly aware that people want to know what is in their chocolate. Not all labels are ideally informative, but several companies are starting to provide data on some crucial matters. One of these is the origin of the beans. Whereas labels used to say "chocolate" with no reference to provenance, today even the largest commercial makers have hopped on the bandwagon for boutique-type labeling with identification of national origin. This information is helpful up to a point, but it is not an infallible clue to quality. The fact that the cacao was grown in an exotic-sounding country says very little about the cacao itself—for instance, the variety or the particular region of origin within a country. Though the genetic baseline may be pretty uniform for some countries like Ghana or Ivory Coast, this is not at all true for Venezuela or Ecuador. (I can't tell much from just the name Venezuela, since I know that characteristically assertive Trinitario beans from Paria have nothing in common with the more predominantly, subtle-tasting Criollos of Western Venezuela. Likewise, the rare and coveted floral Arriba of coastal Ecuador cannot be compared with the commonplace hybrid CNN51 that has come to dominate Ecuador's commercial plantations.)

The most important facts, besides the origin of the beans, are total cacao content and cacao butter content. Standards vary widely, but in this country only chocolates with more than 35 percent cacao content can be labeled bittersweet chocolate or couverture (the French require only a minimum of 32 percent cacao content).

The point is important because cacao content is what makes chocolate taste like chocolate, no matter what its intended purpose. Standard supermarket candy bars typically have extremely low cacao content (perhaps only the legal minimum of 15 percent for a milk chocolate) and are beefed up with fillers and sugar. Good eating bittersweet chocolates will have at least the basic 35 percent cacao content. Premium chocolates (for both eating and cooking) will usually have much more, from 41 percent for a first-class milk chocolate to 70 or 75 percent cacao content for an especially intense dark chocolate.

Chocolate for decorative purposes may be another case. Because cacao butter is expensive and can be difficult to work with, special compound chocolates have been devised with partly hydrogenated fats that require no tempering and that mimic the qualities of cacao butter. However, their flavor is invariably inferior.

The only way to familiarize yourself with the range of possibilities is to buy and taste different chocolates, taking into account the amount of cacao listed. You can begin by looking at what is available in stores near you, even supermarkets. If the cacao content is not on the label, call the company and ask for the information. You will soon start to recognize the different intensities and sense the difference between synthetic and real vanilla. You will be able to detect chocolates made with alkalized cacao by their slightly chalky sensation and bland, uneventful flavor profile with no hint of acidity or bitterness aside from that conferred by overroasting. Unfortunately this applies to nearly all the inexpensive chocolates in the market today. They are almost uniformly made with acrid, tannic, low-grade beans that require huge doses of alkalization.

It would be easy to think that the best chocolate is the one with the highest cacao content, but it is not that simple. You must take into account factors such as the original beans and the handling they have received, as well as your intended purpose. For example, if you are making hot chocolate, the richest product available may yield a disappointing result with an unsightly film of melted fat on top. This is the result of extra cacao butter added to some premium chocolates to decrease viscosity. The same too-rich chocolate might be perfect for "enrobing" (coating) truffles, where fluidity and smoothness are everything. A not-so-smooth industrial chocolate with great flavor and no added cacao butter might be great for hot chocolate. Even better are the grainy, powdery-looking, wonderfully spiced artisanal Latin American cacao balls.

The couverture-quality chocolates used in these recipes are also ideal eating chocolates. I consider them to be among the finest fruits of human art and science. What lifts a chocolate into the realm of the superlative? It is a matter of noble flavor beans in the hands of the right people making the right choices as they oversee a battery of powerful, sophisticated machinery, from five-roller mills to open conches. Skilled chocolatiers must judge the chemical and physical attributes of the cacao liquor as it is transformed from a gritty mass into something ineffably silky, fragrant, and tantalizing. For me an exceptional couverture is one that seamlessly blends complex flavor and aroma together with full, velvety mouthfeel.

My idea of the ultimate chocolate dessert—and the ultimate education in the subtleties of chocolate—is a large sampling platter with at least a dozen chocolates made by different manufacturers and representing a wide gamut of flavors, textures, and cacao contents. It's a wonderful way to hone your tasting skills with company.

RECIPES

THE FOLLOWING RECIPES have one quality in common: they showcase the wide-ranging possibilities of chocolate and imaginatively explore its capacity to absorb flavors and harmonize with other flavorings and spices.

Some of these recipes are my own. Others are culled from contemporary chefs who have learned how to work with a new generation of high cacao–content chocolates, and from traditional Latin American cooks who know cacao intimately. The chefs build their recipes around particular brands of chocolate, drawing on their distinctive characters and cacao contents to create subtle variations of flavor and aroma. They use chocolate as they would a spice, highlighting its nuances and pairing it with a spectrum of exciting flavorings. This approach is, of course, nothing new; it was practiced by colonial cooks, and it can be traced back to the Maya and Aztecs.

These recipes range from the modest and simple to the grand and complex. There are traditional Latin American recipes such as homemade cacao balls, which are grated and used to make hot chocolate, and modern creations such as Harold McGee's unusual cheese and chocolate truffles. There are classics such as the Viennese Sachertorte, and playful new inventions such as chocolate soup. There are also recipes from the sixteenth and seventeenth centuries, whose sophisticated blend of spices can inspire the contemporary chef.

Don't think of these recipes as culinary straitjackets. Though each recipe calls for particular brands of chocolate with specific percentages of cacao content, substitutions are always possible. Given the range of chocolates available today, cooks have more choices than ever before.

Candied Cacao Beans Dipped in Chocolate

During my trips to Venezuela with top American and European pastry chefs in the 1990s, chef Laurent Tourondel taught me to roast whole, unshelled cacao beans in caramelized white sugar and then coat them in melted chocolate like truffles. I will never forget how he spent a whole day in my kitchen in Weehawken showing me this and other chocolate recipes. Little did I know that by 2008, commercial versions of the same idea would be approaching the popularity of chocolate-covered almonds. (Those confections have a slick, manufactured look unlike the rougher surface of mine.)

I have adapted his recipe to my taste, using a flavorful Latin brown loaf sugar instead of white sugar. I prefer to use excellent Trinitario beans from Venezuela, but I have also had good results with beans available through mail-order sources. It is important to use a flavorful chocolate with a high cacao content and an excellent-quality cocoa powder (preferably nonalkalized) for the coating. If you want a deeper terra-cotta red color, use Guittard's Dutched Cocoa Rouge. For the chocolate I prefer a mixture of Valrhona Araguani (72% cacao) and Cluizel Los Ancones (67% cacao), a mixture of Cluizel Concepción (66% cacao) and Cluizel Los Ancones (67% cacao), or the deep terracotta-colored Cocoa Rouge by Guittard. Before starting the recipe you should have on hand a candy thermometer, a double-boiler arrangement, one or two sturdy wooden spoons, a rubber spatula, one or two nonstick baking sheets (including one that fits in the freezer), and two plates for the final dusting. If you wish, leave some of the caramelized beans uncoated to offer a trip of contrasts.

MAKES ABOUT 4 CUPS (2 CUPS OF EACH COLOR)

12 ounces (about 3 cups) whole, unroasted cacao beans (see page 235)

2 cups grated brown loaf sugar (preferably a light Colombian *panela*) or Demerara sugar

³/₄ cup water

10 ounces dark chocolate

FOR DUSTING

1 cup cocoa powder, preferably a nonalkalized brand such as Scharffen Berger or Askinosie Single Origin Natural Cocoa Powder—San José del Tambo, Ecuador

1 cup sifted confectioners' sugar

Preheat the oven to 250°F. Spread the beans on a baking sheet and place in the oven until just warmed. (This will avoid crystalization when the temperature of the caramel is lowered later.)

Dissolve the brown sugar in the water in a heavy 4-quart saucepan. Over high heat, cook the syrup to 310°F, or slightly below light caramel stage (it should be just starting to color a little). Immediately lower the heat to medium and add the cacao beans, stirring them rapidly with a slotted spoon,

continued

for about 4 minutes, to coat them all over with the caramel. Not only are you coating the beans with a delicious crunchy armor, you are roasting them as well. During the roasting you will hear the beans making popping sounds, like popcorn.

Working quickly, remove the caramel-coated beans with the slotted spoon and place them on a nonstick baking sheet, spreading them out as flat as possible with the spoon. Try to keep the beans apart from each other and avoid transferring any excess caramel coating. If the sugar hardens too fast, put the baking sheet with the beans in a 300°F oven for 2 minutes to soften the caramel. As soon as the beans are cool enough to touch, pull apart any beans that have clustered together with tongs, a spoon, or scissors. The sugar might be really hot, but there is a narrow window of opportunity before it hardens and the beans can't be pulled apart. Slide the baking sheet with the beans into the freezer and chill for 20 to 30 minutes.

Meanwhile, line a baking sheet with parchment paper and set aside.

Break the chocolate into 8 or 10 pieces and put in the top of a double-boiler or heatproof bowl over simmering water. Heat until evenly melted; remove from the heat and work with a rubber spatula to keep the chocolate smooth while it cools slightly. It should be just above room temperature but still liquid.

Remove the caramel-coated beans from the freezer and pour into a large mixing bowl. Drizzle with about half the melted chocolate and turn with the rubber spatula to start coating the beans. Add the remaining chocolate; stir and toss with the spatula to distribute the chocolate evenly over the beans before the chocolate hardens too much to work.

Again separate the mass into individual coated beans. Spread the cocoa over a large deep plate and the confectioners' sugar over another. Drop the beans, in small batches, directly into the cocoa powder or sugar, as if they were truffles, while shaking the plates. Remove them with a fork, place on the prepared baking sheet, and place in the refrigerator. Once hard, remove the excess powder by shaking them vigorously in a container or paper bag.

To serve, arrange the different-colored beans in alternating rows in a small candy dish or individual dishes. Serve as a sweet snack or as a garnish for any dessert or ice cream. Allow 4 per person if using as garnish, more for a snack. Store the white and brown beans in separate airtight containers, packed in additional cocoa or confectioners' sugar. They will keep in the refrigerator for 2 to 3 months.

Cacao-Chile Salt
Sal de Cacao y Chile

The *ululte* chile and its sibling, the equally fiery *cobanero*, are cultivars of *Capsicum annuum* and close descendants of a minute wild pepper (*C. annuum* var. *aviculare*) from which all *C. annuum* sprang. Although Guatemalan cooks also season their foods with meatier chiles that are closely associated with Mexican cooking, they have a soft spot for these tiny chiles, which they often gather from the wild or grow in their own backyards.

Every year, I grow several types of these wonderful tiny peppers to use fresh in table salsas. I also buy them dried in Mexican markets where they are sold by various names (*chiltepe, chiltepín, piquín, pequín*) derived from Nahuatl, the language of the Aztecs. Toasting them briefly, just to char them a little, gives them a wonderful smoky edge. Ground with cacao and some salt, they make a simple yet terrific condiment for any food, from quick seafood stir-fries to long-simmering stews. Store in a lidded jar and keep in a cool place.

MAKES ABOUT 1 CUP

2 tablespoons dried *piquín* chiles (see above)	1 teaspoon coarse sea salt, or to taste
1 cup (about 4¹/₂ ounces) cacao nibs	

Heat a heavy-bottomed skillet, griddle, or *comal* over medium-high heat. Add the chiles and toast for a couple of seconds to char a little. Transfer to a small bowl.

Add the cacao nibs to the pan and toast, stirring, until fragrant, about 10 seconds. Transfer the toasted cacao nibs to the bowl with the chiles and toss with the salt. Let cool slightly. Working in batches, grind the mixture to a fine powder in a coffee or spice mill. Pass through a medium-mesh strainer or sieve while stirring with a wooden spoon to break up any lumps.

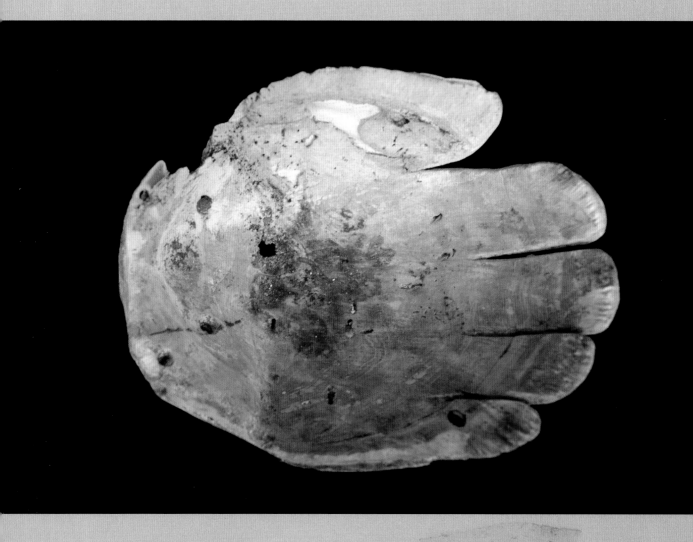

This rare early-Classic Maya hand-shaped scoop, fashioned of spondylous shell, was discovered by archeologist Robert J. Sharer, who found it embedded in cacao residue in a King's tomb in Copan, Honduras. Cameron McNeil, who sent it to W. Jeffrey Hurst for chemical analysis, believes it was probably used to scoop out a spiced caccao powder mixture like *pinole*.

Aromatic Spice and Corn Blend for Hot Chocolate
Pinole o Polvos de Soconusco

Pinole is the name for both a form of ground toasted corn and a flavorful mixture that also includes spices like vanilla, achiote, and cinnamon. It became a well-known flavoring ingredient in Spain and many parts of the colonies. Toasted barley flour, or *máchica*, plays a similar role in Ecuador. Both go into aromatic chocolate porridgelike drinks that would have been familiar to the sixteenth-century observer Juan de Cárdenas, who diligently reported the obsession of budding colonial society with chocolate and the countless new chocolate recipes that seemed to spring from the woodwork. The *pinole* mix makes about 1^1/$_4$ cups, so you'll have extra to keep on hand.

MAKES 1^1/$_4$ CUPS SPICED *PINOLE* MIX

SPICED *PINOLE* MIX

2 plump vanilla beans, preferably Mexican, cut into ^{1}/$_4$-inch lengths

1 cup *pinole* (toasted ground corn; available at Hispanic markets and online sources)

1 tablespoon achiote (annatto) seeds

1 tablespoon small allspice berries

2 (3-inch) sticks true cinnamon (soft Ceylon cinnamon, sold as *canela* in Hispanic markets), coarsely chopped with a knife

1 teaspoon aniseed

SINGLE SERVING OF HOT CHOCOLATE

1 cup whole milk

1 ounce dark chocolate, preferably Askinosie Soconusco (75% cacao), El Rey Gran Samán (70% cacao), or Guittard Quevedo (65% cacao), finely chopped

Pinch of salt

1 tablespoon sugar, or to taste

To make the mix, grind the vanilla to a sticky powder in a mini-chopper or spice mill. Combine with the *pinole* in a small bowl; set aside. Grind the achiote in a spice mill. When it is fairly fine, add the allspice, cinnamon, and aniseed. Grind to a powder. Combine well with the *pinole*-vanilla mixture. (You should have 1^1/$_4$ cups.) Store at room temperature in a tightly sealed jar.

To make the hot chocolate, bring the milk to a simmer in a small saucepan over medium heat. Add the chocolate and stir constantly with a wooden spoon until it dissolves, about 1 minute. Stir in 1 tablespoon of the spiced pinole mix and the salt, then taste and, sweeten with a little sugar. Stir until thickened to the consistency of a light porridge or chocolate sauce, 2 to 3 minutes. Serve at once.

Chocolate-Garlic Mojo with Toasted Cuban Bread
Tostadas de Pan Cubano con Mojo de Chocolate

A sensuous variation on the theme of bread and chocolate is a silky ganache flavored with a garlicky Cuban-style olive oil *mojo*, smeared over slices of Cuban bread. Because the ingredients are so few and basic, it is important to use a not-too-bitter premium chocolate. I also like the effect of a mellow Spanish extra-virgin olive oil made with Arbequina olives, with their slight accent of apple peel. Sea salt sprinkled on the bread right at the moment of serving brings out all the flavors.

SERVES 6

MOJO GANACHE

9 ounces dark chocolate, preferably Cluizel Concepción (66% cacao) or Cluizel Los Ancones (67% cacao), or a combination of the two, finely chopped

4 large garlic cloves, ground to a fine paste with mortar and pestle

1/2 cup extra-virgin olive oil

Coarse sea salt

1 tablespoon freshly squeezed lime juice

TO FINISH

1 loaf Cuban bread (about 10 ounces), thinly sliced on the diagonal

Coarse sea salt

To prepare the ganache, put the chocolate in a double-boiler or a heatproof bowl over simmering water. When the chocolate is almost melted, remove from the heat and stir from the center out with a rubber spatula until smooth.

Combine the garlic and olive oil in a small skillet and just heat it through over low heat. Pour in a stream over the melted chocolate while stirring gently with the spatula, again from the center out. Season with salt to taste. Add the lime juice and stir gently to blend smoothly. The mixture will thicken like mayonnaise. Keep at room temperature.

When you are ready to serve, warm the sauce over simmering water if it has become too stiff. Toast the bread on both sides on a grill or under the broiler. Arrange the toasted slices on a large platter or flat basket lined with a plantain-leaf square. Accompany with the sauce in a bowl or cruet, the coarse salt, and a couple of decorative butter knives. ¡*Delicioso!*

Deep Chocolate Torte

This rich, flourless torte, a cross between an eggy pudding and nonpuffy soufflé, comes from Fran Bigelow, the grande dame of American chocolate confection. Her shop in Seattle is a mecca for chocolate aficionados. She is famous for deluxe versions of popular standbys, like candy bars made with pure Venezuelan chocolate and enhanced with cacao nibs, coffee beans, and candied orange peel. She also has a reputation for using the best sweet ingredients and delivering the deepest chocolate flavor. If you like, serve with unsweetened whipped cream or a raspberry sauce.

MAKES ONE 9-INCH TORTE (ABOUT 8 SERVINGS)

1 pound dark chocolate, preferably El Rey Bucare (58.5% cacao), Callebaut (56% cacao), or Cacao Barry Equateur (60% cacao), finely chopped

6 large eggs

1/4 cup sugar

2 tablespoons Grand Marnier or other liqueur

1 cup heavy cream

Cocoa, for dusting

Put the chocolate in a heatproof bowl or the top of a double boiler over barely simmering water and allow to melt completely.

Preheat the oven to 350°F. Generously butter a 9-inch round regular or springform cake pan. Cut a 9-inch round of waxed paper and press it over the bottom of the pan.

Beat the eggs, sugar, and liqueur in a large heatproof mixing bowl. Place the bowl over a saucepan of simmering water and stir with a wooden spoon until warm but not hot. Remove from the heat and transfer to the bowl of an electric mixer. Beat with the whisk attachment for 5 minutes. Slowly stir in the melted chocolate.

Whip the cream to soft peaks and gently fold into the chocolate mixture. Carefully transfer the batter to the prepared pan.

Bake for 40 minutes, or until a straw or cake tester inserted into the torte at least 2 to 4 inches from the side comes out clean. The center should be just set; do not overbake.

Let cool to room temperature, remove from the pan, and peel off the liner. Dust with cocoa before serving. If necessary, you can refrigerate the torte for up to 1 day, covered with plastic wrap, but bring to room temperature before serving.

Soft Chocolate Cake with Banana-Raisin Sauce and Lime Cream

Rich, moist, all-but-flourless chocolate cakes are now almost standard in modern patisserie. This version, enriched with a fruity sauce and a dollop of cream, was developed by renowned pastry chef Bill Yosses, whom I first knew as pastry chef at New York's Bouley Bakery but who went on to become White House pastry chef under the Bush and Obama administrations. It has especially clean, well-defined flavors, rather than an overwhelming mélange of effects. For the chocolate, Bill prefers Valrhona Manjari or Pur Caraïbe; other possible choices are Callebaut bittersweet or Lindt Excellence. He likes to serve the cake with Champagne, a sweet moscato, or Sauternes (Bill's in-your-dreams suggestion is a 1945 Chateau D'Yquem!). But a Canadian or German ice wine would also make a spectacular combination.

MAKES 6 SERVINGS

CAKE

8 ounces dark chocolate, preferably Valrhona Manjari (64% cacao) or Valrhona Pur Caraïbe (66% cacao), chopped into quarter-sized pieces

1 cup (2 sticks) unsalted butter, cut into cubes

4 large eggs

1/2 cup sugar

1/2 cup all-purpose flour

GARNISH

1/4 cup water

1/4 teaspoon ground cinnamon or 2 blackberry or mint tea bags

1/4 cup golden raisins

2 ripe bananas

1 tablespoon dark rum

1 tablespoon granulated sugar

Juice and grated zest of 1 lime

1/2 cup heavy cream

2 tablespoons confectioners' sugar

To make the cake, preheat the oven to 350°F. Generously butter a 10-inch round cake pan and line the bottom with a 10-inch circle of parchment paper.

Combine the chopped chocolate and butter in the top of a double boiler or heatproof bowl over boiling water. Remove from the heat and let it sit until melted, stirring occasionally. Keep warm, off the heat, while you work.

Whisk the eggs and sugar together in a mixing bowl until light and foamy, about 3 minutes. Sift the flour over the mixture, whisking to incorporate smoothly. With a rubber spatula, fold the batter into the warm chocolate mixture.

Pour the batter into the prepared pan and bake for 35 minutes. Let the cake cool in the pan for about 30 minutes.

Select a serving plate or platter an inch or two larger than the cake pan. Place it firmly over the top and invert the cake onto the platter, tapping it firmly to help loosen it. Peel off the parchment layer. Let sit at room temperature until you are ready to serve.

To prepare the garnish, first make the raisin-banana sauce. Heat the water in a small pan with the cinnamon or tea bags. When it comes to a boil, stir in the raisins and set aside to cool. Peel the bananas and cut into $1/4$-inch-thick slices.

Combine the rum and the granulated sugar in a sauté pan over medium heat and add the lime juice, reserving the grated zest. When the sugar melts, add the bananas and cook over low heat for 3 to 4 minutes, gently turning to coat the pieces evenly. Set aside in the pan until you are ready to serve.

Whip the cream with 1 tablespoon of the confectioners' sugar; when it forms stiff peaks, fold in the reserved lime zest. Refrigerate until you are ready to serve.

At serving time, combine the raisin and banana mixtures in the sauté pan and reheat to boiling. Cut the cake into 6 wedges with a long sharp knife, wiping the blade clean after each cut. Place each piece on a serving plate and spoon some of the hot banana-raisin mixture next to it. With a soup-spoon dipped in hot water, spoon some of the lime-flavored whipped cream over each piece. Sift a little of the remaining 1 tablespoon confectioners' sugar over each portion and serve.

Earl Grey and Orange-Chocolate Roulade

This jelly roll for grown-ups comes from the irrepressible Elizabeth Falkner, a former film-student-turned-pâtissière who makes showstopping desserts at her pastry shop and cafe, Citizen Cake, in San Francisco. Elizabeth fills a delicately textured chocolate sponge with an Earl Grey tea-infused ganache and orange marmalade, then repeats the Earl Grey accent in the whipped cream. Elizabeth recommends using a quality tea with a fine bergamot fragrance. The secret to the cake is the rice flour, which adds a subtle crunch to the texture. You can find it in natural foods stores and Asian markets. Make the ganache a day ahead and refrigerate overnight. Remove from the refrigerator and allow it to return to room temperature for about 2 to 3 hours before using.

SERVES 8

GANACHE FILLING

8 ounces dark chocolate, preferably Scharffen Berger (70% cacao), finely chopped

1 cup heavy cream

2 tablespoons corn syrup

1 tablespoon loose Earl Grey tea leaves

EARL GREY WHIPPED CREAM

2 cups heavy cream

2 tablespoons sugar

2 teaspoons loose Earl Grey tea leaves

CAKE

$1/2$ cup nonalkalized cocoa powder

$1/2$ cup sweet rice flour (Falkner prefers Guisto's)

$1/4$ teaspoon baking soda (omit if using Dutch alkalized cocoa powder)

4 large eggs, separated

$1/3$ cup plus $3/4$ cup sugar

$1/2$ cup cold water

$1/2$ teaspoon cream of tartar

$1/2$ teaspoon salt

1 cup bitter (Seville) orange marmalade

Confectioners' sugar, for dusting

To make the ganache filling, put the chopped chocolate in a small mixing bowl and set aside. Combine the cream, corn syrup, and tea in a nonreactive saucepan and bring just to a boil over medium-high heat. Remove from the heat and let steep for 15 minutes. Return to a simmer, then immediately pour the mixture through a fine-mesh strainer into the bowl of chocolate. Press with a spoon to extract as much liquid as possible from the tea leaves. Whisk to melt the chocolate into the steeped cream. Pour into a shallow container and cover the surface with plastic wrap. Refrigerate overnight. Let sit at room temperature for 2 to 3 hours before using.

To steep the cream for whipping, combine 1 cup of the cream, the sugar, and tea in a small saucepan. Bring just to a boil; remove from the heat and let steep for 15 minutes. Strain through a fine-mesh strainer. Add the remaining cup of cream. Refrigerate until very cold, at least 3 hours.

To make the cake, preheat the oven to 350°F. Coat a 17 x 12-inch sheet cake pan with shortening or spray with nonstick cooking spray. Line the bottom of the pan with parchment paper and coat lightly with shortening or oil. Dust the surface with flour and tap out the excess.

Sift the cocoa, rice flour, and baking soda (if using) into a small mixing bowl and set aside. In a large mixing bowl, whisk the egg yolks together with the 1/3 cup sugar, vigorously whipping until they are pale yellow, about 45 seconds. Add the water and stir until smooth. Add the sifted cocoa mixture and whisk until smooth.

In the clean bowl of a mixer fitted with the whisk attachment, whip the egg whites, cream of tartar, and salt until foamy, about 30 seconds. Increase the speed to medium-high and slowly add the 3/4 cup sugar, beating until the whites are glossy and hold stiff peaks, about 2 minutes.

Spoon about one-quarter of the whites into the bowl with the chocolate mixture. With a whisk, stir the whites into the chocolate mixture to lighten it. Using a rubber spatula, fold in the remaining whites, folding just until no streaks remain.

Pour the batter into the prepared pan. Using an offset spatula, quickly smooth the surface. Bake for 10 to 12 minutes, or until the edges start to pull away from the sides of the pan and the surface is dry and doesn't stick to your fingertip when lightly touched.

Have ready a piece of parchment paper slightly larger than the cake pan. Remove the cake from the oven and cool in the pan on a rack for 5 minutes. Run a small knife along the perimeter of the pan to loosen the cake. Sift the confectioners' sugar over the surface of the cake. Cover with the parchment. Invert the cake onto the work surface, being careful not to dislodge the parchment sheet that lined the pan. Gently peel away the parchment. Let the cake cool.

To fill the cake, soften the room-temperature ganache to a spreadable consistency by beating it with the whisk attachment until smooth, lighter in color, and increased in volume, about 45 seconds. Dot the marmalade evenly over the surface of the cooled cake. Gently spread the marmalade evenly over the cake with an icing spatula. Spread the ganache over the layer of marmalade.

Starting with a short end, gently fold over 2 inches of the cake. Carefully peel off the sugar-dusted parchment. Continue to roll the cake, using the parchment to lift and roll it. Wrap the cake in plastic wrap, and place seamside down on a tray. Chill for at least 2 hours.

To serve, unwrap the roulade and bring to room temperature. Whip the cream to soft peaks. Dust the cake with confectioners' sugar. With a serrated knife dipped in hot water, cut the cake into 1-inch slices, wiping the knife clean between cuts. Spoon a dollop of the whipped cream over each slice.

Classic Sachertorte

The classic Sachertorte is a chocolate layer cake with an apricot marmalade filling and a luscious, shiny chocolate glaze. This version comes from Markus Farbinger, who grew up working at his parents' fourth-generation bread bakery in the Austrian village of Taxenbach, and who also worked at the Hotel Sacher in Vienna, said to have been the original home of the famous Sachertorte.

I met Markus on one of my earliest Venezuelan cacao tours when he was dean of the baking and pastry curriculum at the Culinary Institute of America at Hyde Park. He went on to other adventures, making beautiful chocolate as a managing partner at Larry Burdick's shop in Walpole, New Hampshire, before ending up in South Africa, where he is an artisanal bread maker at his own shop, Ile de Pain, in Knysna. Farbinger's roots are solidly Austrian. Unlike some takeoffs that borrow the Sacher name, his recipe has the classic simplicity of the original. It is very close to an old-fashioned pound cake, but spongier and drier. Farbinger loves Sachertorte with a generous dollop of very lightly sweetened, vanilla-flavored whipped cream on the side. (Purists, he acknowledges, frown on such embellishments.) If possible, follow the weight measurements as given by Farbinger for the truest replication of his recipe.

More difficult to make than the cake itself, the fondant-type icing is a sine qua non for a true Sachertorte. It should have an almost mirrorlike sheen. You will need a clean, nonporous work surface (marble is best; otherwise polished granite, stainless steel, or Formica). Be sure to work in a draft-free room. Warm the work surface by placing a bowl of hot water on it; remove it when you are ready to work the glaze with a spatula. Have ready a quick-reading thermometer and a small pastry brush dipped in water.

MAKES ONE 10-INCH CAKE

TORTE

4³/₄ ounces dark chocolate, preferably Valrhona Pur Caraïbe (66% cacao) or Valrhona Taïnori (64% cacao), finely chopped

9 tablespoons (1 stick plus 1 tablespoon, 4³/₄ ounces) unsalted butter

1 cup plus 2 tablespoons (4 ounces) confectioners' sugar

6 large eggs, separated

1 cup plus 2 tablespoons (4 ounces) granulated sugar

1 cup (4¹/₂ ounces) all-purpose flour

1 cup (8 ounces) apricot jam, preferably Darbo brand (available online)

SACHER CHOCOLATE GLAZE

1 cup (7 ounces) granulated sugar

3 tablespoons water

6 ounces dark chocolate, preferably El Rey Gran Samán (70% cacao), finely chopped

VANILLA-SCENTED WHIPPED CREAM (OPTIONAL)

1 cup heavy cream

2 tablespoons granulated sugar

1 teaspoon pure vanilla extract

continued

To make the torte, in the top of a double boiler, melt the chocolate over simmering water. Set aside.

Preheat the oven to 350°F. Butter and flour a 10-inch round cake pan with 2-inch sides.

In the mixing bowl of a standing mixer fitted with the whisk attachment, cream the butter with the confectioners' sugar. Beat in the melted chocolate. Add the egg yolks one at a time. Scrape down the sides of the bowl as necessary.

In a separate bowl, beat the egg whites until foamy. Gradually add the granulated sugar, beating continuously until the mixture forms glossy, moderately firm peaks. Gently fold the egg whites into the butter-chocolate mixture. Fold in the flour gently but completely.

Pour the batter into the cake pan and level the surface with a spatula. Bake for 70 minutes. Cool slightly in the pan, then turn out onto a cloth and cool completely, upside down.

With a long, thin knife, slice the cake horizontally into two thin layers. Spread about half of the apricot jam over the bottom layer. Replace the top layer, warm the rest of the jam, and spread it evenly over the top. Let stand until the jam has cooled enough to lose its shininess and looks slightly congealed.

To make the glaze, in a small, heavy saucepan, bring the sugar and water to a boil over medium heat and add the chocolate. Heat to 250°F, frequently washing down the sides of the pan with a wet pastry brush. When the mixture reaches 250°F, a small amount dropped from a spoon will form a thin thread.

Remove the pan from the heat. Pour a small amount of the glaze onto a nonporous surface (preferably marble) and quickly work it with a pastry knife until it begins to look a little pale and opaque. Immediately scrape it back into the pan and stir to combine with the rest. Repeat the process, each time working a little of the mixture until it looks light and milky and quickly recombining with the rest. Do not overwork. When the glaze is ready, it will have good body but still be fluid; the temperature should be about 80°F.

To ice the torte, slowly pour the glaze over it, evenly covering the top and sides with a few strokes of an icing spatula. Immediately lift the cake off the rack and onto a baking sheet or serving plate and let stand until the icing is thoroughly set, at least 2 hours.

To prepare the whipped cream, in a chilled mixing bowl, whip the cream, sugar, and vanilla just until the mixture holds soft peaks.

To serve, cut the torte with a knife dipped in water and wiped clean before each new cut. Add a dollop of whipped cream, if desired. The torte should never be refrigerated. It will last 2 to 3 days at room temperature.

Caramelized Chocolate Bread Pudding with Coffee-Rum Sauce

Bread pudding is usually loved as a placid and undemanding comfort food. But my version has the solid, grown-up kind of comfort that wakes you up instead of snuggling you off to nursery dreamland. It is as real as bread, as elegant as Venezuelan chocolate, as bracing as strong coffee, to say nothing of all the subtly blended aromas of rum and spices and of the unexpected crunch contributed by a good dollop of cashews.

MAKES 8 TO 10 SERVINGS

BREAD PUDDING

2 cups sugar

$^1/_3$ cup water

$^1/_2$ cup aged Venezuelan dark rum or Bacardi Premium Black rum

$3^1/_2$ ounces (about $^1/_2$ cup) dark raisins

$2^1/_2$ cups whole milk

1 (14-ounce) can sweetened condensed milk

1 tablespoon aniseed

4 (3-inch) sticks true cinnamon (soft Ceylon cinnamon, sold as *canela* in Hispanic markets)

6 allspice berries

12 ounces dark chocolate, preferably El Rey Bucare (58.5% cacao) or Amano Montanya (70% cacao), finely chopped

6 tablespoons ($^3/_4$ stick) unsalted butter, cut into bits

2 cups freshly brewed Cuban-style espresso coffee (see Note) or other strong black coffee

$^1/_4$ teaspoon salt

5 whole large eggs

2 large egg yolks

1 tablespoon pure vanilla extract, preferably Mexican

1 teaspoon almond extract

1 medium-sized loaf (about 7 ounces) day-old Cuban, French, or Italian bread, cut into 1- to $1^1/_2$-inch cubes (about 7 cups)

3 ounces (about $^3/_4$ cup) unsalted roasted cashews, coarsely chopped

COFFEE-RUM SAUCE

1 cup heavy cream

1 (14-ounce) can sweetened condensed milk

$1^1/_4$ cups freshly brewed Cuban-style espresso (see Note on page 162) or other strong black coffee

$^1/_4$ cup aged dark Venezuelan rum or Bacardi Premium Black rum

TO GARNISH

Cacao nibs

continued

To make the caramel, have ready a 9 x 13-inch heatproof glass or ceramic baking dish. Combine the sugar and water in a small saucepan and cook over medium-low heat until the sugar is a golden caramel color. Immediately pour the hot caramel into the dish and swirl quickly to cover the bottom and sides evenly. Set aside.

To make the pudding, Preheat the oven to 350°F. In a small bowl, pour the rum over the raisins and let stand for 30 minutes.

Meanwhile, heat the whole milk and condensed milk in a small saucepan with the aniseed, cinnamon, and allspice. Bring to a boil, reduce the heat to low, and simmer for about 10 minutes until the milk is infused with the spices.

Combine the chocolate and butter in a large mixing bowl. Strain the hot milk into the bowl through a fine-mesh strainer and stir to dissolve the chocolate and butter. Stir in the coffee and salt until well combined.

In a medium-sized mixing bowl, whisk the whole eggs and egg yolks with the vanilla and almond extracts. Stir into the warm chocolate mixture. Add the cubed bread, rum-soaked raisins, and cashews and toss to distribute evenly. Let stand for 1 hour, until the bread has absorbed the liquid. Mash with a fork or potato masher to break up large pieces of crust.

Pour the bread mixture into the caramel-coated baking dish. Bake for 40 to 45 minutes, or until just set but still slightly loose (the internal temperature should be 175° to 180°F). Turn out onto a platter. At this point, the pudding may be tightly covered in plastic wrap and refrigerated for 2 to 3 days, then brought to room temperature before serving.

To make the sauce, bring the cream to a boil in a small saucepan and cook over medium heat, watching carefully, until reduced by half. Stir in the condensed milk, coffee, and rum and heat just until the mixture almost boils. Remove from the heat and let cool to room temperature. The sauce will keep in the refrigerator for 2 to 3 days but should be brought to room temperature before serving.

To serve, cut the pudding into squares while still warm. Serve in a pool of warm sauce, garnished with cacao nibs.

Note: For the coffee, you can use a regular drip coffee maker and any good coffee, doubling the amount to obtain a very dark brew that will be close enough to what Cubans call espresso.

CACAO NIBS

Cacao nibs are roasted, shelled, and crushed cacao beans. They are the raw material of chocolate, and also a convenient, practical ingredient that allows cooks to experience the true nature of the cacao bean, its deep complex aroma, and bitter edge. Chocolates El Rey and Scharffen Berger were among the first chocolate companies to sell nibs, and they have been followed by many others. Now you have the choice of buying raw or roasted cacao nibs that are either single origin or a blend. You can roast them further to your liking and mix them with sugar and spices to make your own chocolate or use them for a variety of purposes—as a crunchy garnish for savories and sweets or as the main ingredient in delicious spice mixes.

Creamy Chocolate–Cheese Flan with Hibiscus Sauce

I love how the fruitiness of Cluizel Concepción chocolate, mellowed by a little cream cheese, plays against the caramel and the flowery, slightly musky acidity of the blossoms (actually, calyces) called "Jamaica flowers" in Mexico and red hibiscus in this country. (They are what gives Red Zinger tea its color.) When I first developed this recipe, I used hibiscus to flavor the caramel, but now I include it in a separate sauce where its red color makes a gorgeous contrast with the dark flan.

You will find that this flan is reminiscent of the classic cream cheese–fruit paste pairing that Latin Americans like in other contexts. For this recipe, do not use the spice marketed as "cinnamon" in American stores (it's really cassia). Look for the soft, flaky true cinnamon from Ceylon (Sri Lanka), which has a much subtler and more delicate flavor. You can find it in Hispanic markets under the name *canela*.

MAKES ABOUT 12 SERVINGS

CARAMEL

1 cup sugar

1/4 cup water

FLAN

4 1/2 cups fresh whole milk

1 (14-ounce) can sweetened condensed milk

1/4 cup aged dark rum

6 star anise pods

2 (3-inch) sticks true cinnamon (see above)

1 teaspoon aniseed

1 teaspoon pure vanilla extract, preferably Mexican

1 teaspoon bitter almond extract

2 plump Mexican vanilla beans, split lengthwise, seeds scraped and reserved

Pinch of freshly grated nutmeg

1/8 teaspoon salt

6 ounces dark chocolate, preferably Cluizel Concepción (66% cacao), finely chopped

6 ounces cream cheese, warmed to room temperature

6 large egg yolks

2 whole large eggs

Hibiscus Sauce (page 166)

Preheat the oven to 350°F. Set aside an 8 x 4-inch loaf pan (4-cup capacity), 10-inch round cake pan, or twelve 4-ounce ramekins. Have ready a heatproof dish or pan at least 3 inches deep that is large enough to hold the pan or ramekins comfortably.

To make the caramel, combine the sugar in a small pan with the water and bring to a boil over medium heat, watching carefully until the mixture thickens to look like a syrup, bubbles quickly,

continued

and turns a rich caramel color. Quickly pour the hot caramel into the cake pan (or ramekins) and swirl to coat the bottom(s) and sides evenly before the mixture hardens. Set aside and let cool while you make the flan.

To make the flan, combine the whole milk and condensed milk in a saucepan. Add the rum, star anise, cinnamon sticks, aniseed, vanilla and almond extracts, vanilla beans and the seeds, nutmeg, and salt. Bring barely to a boil, reduce the heat to low, and simmer gently for 2 to 3 minutes. Add the chocolate, stirring with a wooden spoon to help it melt and blend. Remove from the heat and let the spiced chocolate mixture cool to room temperature. When the mixture is cool, remove the vanilla bean, cinnamon sticks, and star anise with a fork or slotted spoon.

Meanwhile, preheat the oven to 335°F. Set up a hot water bath by having ready a kettle of boiling water and a baking dish large enough to hold the cake pan (or ramekins).

With a wooden spoon, beat the cream cheese in a large mixing bowl until softened. Beat in the yolks and whole eggs, one at a time, using a whisk or electric mixer. Slowly add the cooled chocolate mixture, whisking to blend completely. Strain the mixture through a medium-mesh strainer into the caramel-coated cake pan or ramekins. Place the pan or ramekins in the reserved larger baking dish, slide into the oven, and carefully pour in enough hot water to come halfway up the outside of the cake pan or ramekins.

Bake the large flan for about 1 hour; bake the ramekins for 30 to 40 minutes. Don't expect the custard to be completely set in the center. Remove from the oven, lift from the water bath, and let cool to room temperature. Refrigerate in the pan for at least 3 hours before turning the flan out onto a platter (or individual dishes). Serve with the Hibiscus Sauce.

VARIATION: For a creamy, rich chocolate ice cream, proceed with the same recipe. Cool the flan overnight. The following day, scoop the flan and the melted caramel into the container of an ice cream machine and process according to manufacturer's instructions. Freeze for about 1 hour for optimum flavor and a creamy texture. Makes about 4^1/$_2$ cups ice cream.

HIBISCUS SAUCE
Sirope de Flor de Jamaica

MAKES 1^2/$_3$ CUPS

4 ounces (about 4 cups) dried hibiscus flowers (*flor de Jamaica*)	2 cups sugar
	8 cups water

Combine the hibiscus flowers, sugar, and water in a medium saucepan over medium heat and cook for 30 minutes, stirring occasionally, until the syrup coats the back of a spoon.

Strain through a fine-mesh sieve, and pour the liquid back into the pot. Bring to a boil and simmer over medium-low heat until the liquid is reduced to the consistency of a thick syrup, about 20 minutes. Cool to room temperature and store refrigerated in a glass or plastic container.

Tropical Night Brownies

My favorite photograph of the Venezuelan tours on which I introduced chefs and food writers to the home territory of chocolate shows cookbook author Flo Braker joyously coated in glistening chocolate from stem to stern like a swamp creature emerging from a mud bath. Another memory I cherish is of a wondrous tropical night at the secluded beach of Playa Medina in the Paria Peninsula and Flo making brownies in the humble kitchen of our hotel, with waves lapping almost to the doorstep and the mingled aromas of salt sea and Venezuelan chocolate filling the tropical night. She used just the ingredients that we could get our hands on there, including fresh coconut, cashews, Venezuelan rum, the local brown loaf sugar (*papelón*), and of course cacao nibs and chocolate. Here is Flo's re-creation of that memorable recipe.

MAKES 16 BROWNIES

10 tablespoons (1 1/4 sticks) unsalted butter

2 ounces dark chocolate, preferably El Rey Gran Samán (70% cacao) or Scharffen Berger (70% cacao), finely chopped

3 ounces dark chocolate, preferably El Rey Bucare (58.5% cacao), finely chopped

1 cup grated brown loaf sugar (preferably a light Colombian *panela*), Demerara sugar, or packed light brown sugar

1/2 cup granulated sugar

3 large eggs, lightly beaten

1 tablespoon dark rum, preferably Venezuelan

1 teaspoon pure vanilla extract

1/2 cup plus 1 tablespoon unsifted all-purpose flour

1/4 teaspoon salt

1/4 cup unsweetened medium flaked coconut or 1 cup fresh coconut, grated on the medium side of a box grater

1/2 cup (1 1/2 ounces) unsalted roasted cashews, coarsely chopped

1/4 cup finely chopped cacao nibs

Place a rack in the lower third of the oven and preheat to 350°F. Grease a 9 x 9-inch baking pan.

In a small saucepan over low heat, melt the butter with the chocolate. Remove from the heat and stir in both sugars. Pour into a large mixing bowl and set aside to cool for about 5 minutes.

Add the eggs, rum, and vanilla, stirring just until blended. Stir in the flour and salt, then the coconut, cashews, and cacao nibs.

Spread the batter in the prepared baking pan. Bake for 22 minutes. Cool thoroughly before cutting into sixteen 2 1/4-inch-squares.

Onyx Chocolate–Coconut Soup with Fresh Bananas and Honey-Cocoa Wafers

This inventive dessert soup comes from the experienced pastry chef Mary Cech, who taught at the Napa Valley branch of the Culinary Institute of America and was one of the pastry chefs who accompanied me on one of my cacao tours to Venezuela. Like many chefs now experimenting with chocolate, she plays up its affinity for other tropical treats, such as coconut and banana.

Hot soups, like hot chocolate, allow the full bouquet of the chocolate to emerge. Mary chose to use the dark bittersweet Onyx from the long-established San Francisco manufacturer Guittard. This chocolate was a historical departure for the company: their first chocolate made with high cacao content and a carefully calibrated blend of different beans—Ivory Coast cacao for clean chocolate flavor, Ecuadorian cacao for flowery notes, and Carenero Superior beans from Venezuela for an intense fruity, lingering finish. Nonalkalized cocoa powder will produce tan wafers, and Dutch-process cocoa will make darker ones.

MAKES 4 SERVINGS

HONEY-COCOA WAFERS

1 cup all-purpose flour

2 tablespoons cocoa powder

9 tablespoons (1 stick plus 1 tablespoon) unsalted butter, softened to room temperature

1/2 cup granulated sugar

1/4 cup confectioners' sugar, plus more for dusting

1/2 cup honey

5 large or 6 medium egg whites, separated individually

SOUP

4 ounces Guittard Onyx dark chocolate (70% cacao) or Guittard Complexité (72% cacao), finely chopped

1 cup canned unsweetened coconut milk

2 tablespoons coconut syrup, preferably Monin brand (available online)

2/3 cup sweet dessert wine, such as Beaumes-de-Venise, vin santo, or sweet sherry

4 tablespoons (1/2 stick) salted butter

2 tablespoons sugar

1 banana, sliced

To make the wafers, preheat the oven to 325°F. Have ready two 17 x 12-inch sheet pans. Cut out five 17 x 12-inch parchment paper rectangles, butter lightly, and set aside.

Sift the flour and cocoa powder together and set aside. In the bowl of an electric mixer fitted with the paddle attachment, cream the butter, granulated sugar, confectioners' sugar, and honey at medium speed until smooth, scraping down the bowl as needed. Decrease the speed to low and gradually add the egg whites, incorporating each well before adding the next. Mix until the egg whites are completely blended in. The mixture will look slightly curdled. Add the sifted flour and cocoa mixture. Mix on low speed, scraping the bowl as needed, until the mixture is smooth and homogeneous, about 45 seconds.

Place 1 parchment sheet flat on the work surface. Using a small offset spatula, spread 1 cup of batter thinly and evenly into a 11 x 16-inch rectangle. Pick up the ends of the batter-coated parchment and transfer it to a baking sheet. Bake for 7 to 9 minutes, or until the wafer batter is firm to the touch, shiny, and slightly brown at the edges. Remove from the oven and slide the parchment from the baking sheet onto the work surface. Run a spatula under the edge of the wafer to loosen it, but do not remove from the parchment. Cool on a flat surface. Let the baking sheet cool before proceeding.

Repeat the process four times, each time spreading the batter onto a fresh parchment sheet, until you have 5 rectangles of wafers. When cool enough to handle, break the wafers into irregular pieces and dust lightly with confectioners' sugar. The batter may be prepared up to 3 days ahead, and the wafers may be baked up to 6 hours before serving.

To make the soup, combine the chocolate and coconut milk in the top of a double boiler or heat-proof bowl over simmering water and stir until the chocolate is melted. Add the coconut syrup, wine, butter, and sugar. Stir until the butter and sugar are smoothly dissolved.

To serve, ladle the soup into soup bowls, allowing $1^1/_2$ cups per serving. Add a few slices of banana to each bowl. Serve with the Honey-Cocoa Wafers.

VARIATIONS: For a variation on the wafers, try curling them or, as one tester did, try baking them in a smaller pan to create a spongy brownie. For curls, follow the instructions as given, but after 3 minutes of baking, remove from the oven and cut the wafers into 3-inch-wide ribbons with a pizza cutter. Return the pan to the oven and continue baking until firm. To shape, quickly lift each ribbon from the parchment and roll it around a jar or rolling pin while still hot. When the ribbons are cool, dust lightly with confectioners' sugar. To make brownies, spread the batter in a 9 x 13-inch pan and bake for 10 minutes, or until no longer sticky when pressed with a fingertip. Cool for at least 20 minutes before cutting.

Cacao Nib Wafers

Years ago I fell in love with a wonderful dessert created by chef Laurent Tourondel, a complex pairing that involved thin, lacy wafer-like cookies made from pure cacao nibs (a new spin on the idea of the classic *tuiles*) and a very rich, super-creamy frozen egg custard with lavender accents. The cacao wafers were spectacular. They are one of those simple things that make you wonder why nobody invented them earlier. They can be served by themselves or as an accompaniment to any dessert from fresh fruit to ice cream.

MAKES 6 SERVINGS

1 cup roasted cacao nibs, preferably El Rey, Valrhona, or Scharffen Berger (see page 237)

²/₃ cup sugar

2 tablespoons glucose syrup, Lyle's Golden Syrup, or light corn syrup

3 tablespoons milk

¹/₂ cup (1 stick) unsalted butter

2 tablespoons cocoa powder, preferably Valrhona

Chop the cacao nibs with a heavy sharp knife or by pulsing in a food processor until they are the consistency of coarse bread crumbs.

Combine the sugar, syrup, milk, and butter in a small saucepan and heat over medium heat, stirring constantly, until the sugar is completely dissolved. The mixture should be hot but not near boiling (about 190°F). Whisk in the cocoa powder until smooth, then stir in the cacao nibs.

Quickly turn out the mixture onto the center of a baking sheet lined with parchment paper. Place another layer of parchment on top of the mass and, using a rolling pin, roll out the mixture between the parchment layers until it is as thin as possible, forming a rectangle a little more than 9 x 12 inches. If the sides of the pan make it too difficult to use a rolling pin, roll and/or press the mixture with a plain glass tumbler. Slide the baking sheet into the freezer and chill for 1 hour.

Preheat the oven to 330°F. Remove the baking sheet from the freezer and peel off the top layer of parchment. Bake the cacao nib mixture for 18 to 20 minutes. (It will start bubbling after 10 minutes, then the bubbling will subside.)

Let the mixture cool slightly. With a small sharp knife, or a pizza cutter, cut the still-warm rectangle into twelve 3-inch squares. Carefully peel off the remaining parchment paper. Let the wafers cool to room temperature. They can be made as much as 2 days ahead and stored in an airtight container, but they are best used the same day.

VARIATION: Replace half the chopped cacao nibs with ¹/₄ cup blanched, toasted almonds. (You can toast the almonds on a baking sheet in a preheated 325°F oven for 15 to 20 minutes, or until golden brown.) Chop to the same consistency as the cacao nibs and proceed with the recipe as directed.

Chocolate-Covered Plantain Chips
Mariquitas Cubiertas de Chocolate

If you are fond of the flavor and texture of chocolate-covered cookies, you will fall in love with these unusual and crunchy chocolate-covered chips, a surprising new twist on a classic Caribbean snack. Serve them like cookies or as a garnish for ice cream or any other dessert of your choice. It is important to use firm, unripe cooking plantains, not bananas or dark, sweet ripe plantains.

MAKES ABOUT 30 CHIPS

3 large very green plantains

4 cups corn oil, for deep-frying

28 ounces dark chocolate, preferably El Rey Bucare (5.5 % cacao), Cluizel Concepción (66% cacao), Cluizel Los Ancones (67% cacao), or Valrhona Araguani (72% cacao) or a combination of chocolates like Cluizel Los Ancones and Valrhona Araguani (72% cacao), coarsely chopped

$^1/_3$ cup coarsely crushed unsalted cashews

$^1/_3$ cup toasted unsweetened grated coconut, store-bought or homemade (see Note on page 176)

To prepare the plantains, peel by cutting off both tips, making a lengthwise incision through the peel with a sharp paring knife, and working the skin free from the flesh with your fingertips. Cut the plantains into very thin ($^1/_8$- to $^1/_{16}$-inch-thick) lengthwise slices, using either the slicing side of a standing grater, a mandoline-type slicer, the slicing disk of a food processor equipped with a large feed tube, or a meat slicer. If you are using a food processor, trim the plantain to fit the tube. If you are not frying immediately, put the slices in a bowl of cold water to avoid discoloration; be sure to drain thoroughly and pat dry with paper towels before proceeding.

In a heavy-bottomed saucepan or deep-fryer, heat the oil to 350°F. Drop the plantain slices into the hot oil, a handful at a time, and fry until golden. Stir frequently so the slices do not stick to one another. As they are done, lift out onto paper towels to drain and continue with the remaining plantains. They should be firm and crunchy.

To prepare the dipping chocolate, have a candy thermometer ready and line a baking sheet with parchment paper. Set aside about 1 cup of the chopped chocolate. Use a double boiler or a heatproof bowl over a pot of water set over medium heat. When the water comes to a boil, add the chopped chocolate to the top of the double-boiler. Check the temperature as the chocolate begins to melt. When it is close to 120°F, lift the double-boiler top from the bottom and set it on the counter. Add the reserved unmelted chocolate to temper it. (For an explanation of tempering methods, see pages

continued

214 to 215.) Stir with a wooden spoon until all the chocolate has melted but still feels warm to the touch.

Holding the plantain chips with your fingertips, dip them, one at a time, in the melted chocolate to coat as desired. Or slide the chips lengthwise through the chocolate to coat only one side. Smooth off the excess chocolate with a metal spatula and place the chips on the prepared baking sheet. While the chocolate is still soft to the touch, sprinkle some with the crushed nuts and the rest with the toasted coconut. Let stand until the chocolate sets before serving.

Note: To toast the grated coconut, put it in a large nonstick skillet and heat over medium heat, stirring with a wooden spoon, until evenly colored, 10 to 15 minutes. You can also toast the coconut in the oven: preheat oven to 325°F. Spread grated coconut in a thin layer on a nonstick baking sheet. Bake for 10 to 15 minutes, until golden.

SANTO DOMINGO PRODUCTS.

THE WORLD IN CHOCOLATE: MICHEL CLUIZEL'S LE PREMIER CRU LINE

A selection of Michel Cluizel's single-origin and estate couvertures (Les Premiers Crus de Plantation), with their respective beans. From left to right: Los Ancones (Dominican Republic), Mangaro (Madagascar), Maraluni (Papua New Guinea), Concepción (Venezuela), Vila Gracinda (São Tomé).

Maya-Mediterranean Chocolate Rice Pudding

In a hole-in-the-wall bookstore in Mérida, Yucatán, I once found a curious little cookbook written long ago by a town historian. It was a gold mine of traditional recipes from another era. My favorite was a simple rice pudding with achiote seeds (also called "annatto") and chocolate. "This is history in a pudding," I said to myself as I read the recipe. Someone in colonial times had the brilliant idea of uniting a homespun Mediterranean sweet and an ancient Maya chocolate drink dyed with the classic coloring of the New World tropics.

It has been a part of my repertoire for many years, but I'm not sure the town historian would recognize what I have done with his quiet, simple model. The original had no spices, except for cinnamon, while my version is rich with spices to suit my mood. But no matter what I do with this rich, sultry, red-tawny dish, I always pledge my Latin American allegiance with a can of our indispensable condensed milk. And I always follow my own idea of what a good rice pudding should taste and feel like—perfumed and sensuous, with the grains of rice almost melting into the matrix of the scented milk. For this, I start by cooking the rice in achiote-infused water so that it will soften nicely and take up the orange color of the seeds before I add the milk. My final touch is another bit of New World culinary history: the irresistible note of pure vanilla bean. This is a generous recipe, ideal for entertaining a crowd.

MAKES 8 TO 12 SERVINGS

1 cup whole achiote (annatto) seeds

10 cups water

1 cup short-grain rice, preferably Spanish

1 tablespoon aniseed

12 allspice berries

4 (3-inch) sticks true cinnamon (soft Ceylon cinnamon, sold as *canela* in Hispanic markets)

1 dried árbol or cayenne chile

2 teaspoons salt

4 cups whole milk

2 (14-ounce) cans sweetened condensed milk

3 ounces fruity dark chocolate, preferably El Rey Bucare (58.5% cacao), Cluizel Concepción (66% cacao), Amano Cuyagua (70% cacao), finely chopped, plus more for shaving (optional)

2 plump Mexican vanilla beans

Ground true cinnamon, for dusting

Put the achiote in a medium-sized saucepan and cover with the water. Bring to a gentle boil and simmer, uncovered, for 5 minutes. Strain through a fine-mesh sieve into a bowl and set aside. (You can save the achiote seeds and reuse them for another purpose by again steeping in hot liquid.)

Meanwhile, rinse the rice under cold running water until the water runs clear. Set aside to drain well in a sieve or colander. Tie the aniseed, allspice, cinnamon sticks, and dried chile in a piece of cheesecloth.

Pour the reserved achiote water into a heavy-bottomed 5- or 6-quart saucepan. Add the drained rice, spice bouquet, and salt. Bring to a boil, reduce the heat to medium, and cook, uncovered, until the rice is soft, 20 to 25 minutes.

Stir in the whole milk and condensed milk. Reduce the heat to low and cook for 5 minutes. Add the chocolate, stirring with a wooden spoon to mix evenly as it melts. Cook, uncovered, for another 40 minutes, stirring occasionally; it should be very creamy but not dry. Halfway through the cooking, split the vanilla beans lengthwise with a small sharp knife and scrape the seeds into the mixture. Add the scraped beans and stir to combine. When the pudding is done but still a little loose textured, remove and discard the spice bouquet and vanilla beans.

Pour into a serving dish, dust lightly with the ground cinnamon, and serve warm or at room temperature. Cacao Nib Wafers (see page 173) are a good accompaniment or garnish with shaved chocolate.

TRADITIONAL HANDMADE CHOCOLATE

Throughout Latin America, cacao is the basis of a small cottage industry controlled by women—the making of rustic cacao balls and bars for hot chocolate. The technique of grinding the roasted cacao beans on a *metate*, perfected in Mesoamerica by the Maya and Aztecs, traveled everywhere that cacao was turned into chocolate for drinking, starting some time in the sixteenth century. Today, not everyone in Latin America subscribes to the back breaking *metate*. In Chuao, an isolated town on Venezuela's central Aragua coast, the children in the family help their mother grind the roasted cacao nibs in a sturdy corn grinder. When I suggested to one of the women that she add some spices to her cacao bars and balls as the women of the Paria Peninsula do, she said that flavorings would spoil the taste of Chuao's cacao, which, she added, "is the best in the world."

LEFT: Ana Rodríguez grinds cacao nibs and half a dozen spices in a motorized corn grinder in Yaguaraparo, Venezuela.
CENTER: The women of Chuao mix freshly roasted cacao nibs with sugar to manufacture cacao balls and chocolate bars.
RIGHT: Women sell rustic homemade chocolate bars at a market in Pointe-à-Pitre, the capital of the French Caribbean island of Guadeloupe.

The New Taste of Chocolate

Homemade Cacao Balls in the Style of the Paria Peninsula

The best artisanal chocolate I know is made by Ana Rodríguez in the dusty northern Venezuelan town of Yaguaraparo in the Paria Peninsula, a hilly finger of land running nearly to the coast of Trinidad. Ana grinds her mixture in enormous quantities, using a motorized grinder perched on the stand of an old sewing machine, and rolls it into grainy-textured balls. Ana starts with the strong-flavored Río Caribe cacao beans that she dries herself on the street in front of her house. Because the cacao is unfermented, she compensates by roasting the beans very deeply. She uses an adventurous range of spices common in Paria. Eight years ago I had to leave out the seed of the mamey sapote fruit, which adds a lovely fragrance like bitter almond. Now that mamey sapote fruits are available year-round in Latin markets, you need only buy one, crack open the pit, and extract the flesh-colored *almendra* (almond) inside. Unfortunately the vanilla-scented tonka bean in Ana's recipe still is not sold in this country for food purposes. (It is a powerful anticoagulant.) But I substitute vanilla to capture the delicate equilibrium of spices in the original. No one flavor dominates; all mingle in harmonious balance.

To make something like Ana's cacao balls, you need a food processor or heavy mortar and pestle, preferably marble, and a hand-cranked rotary grinder for refining the texture of the cacao nibs. The only type of grinder I have found satisfactory is a Corona aluminumized cast-iron plate mill from Colombia, ordinarily used for grinding corn and available in many Latin American neighborhood stores (see Sources). I also recommend a mini-chopper, a spice mill or coffee grinder, and a scale accurate enough to register fractions of ounces or gradations of a few grams.

MAKES 23 OR 24 (1.2-OUNCE) BALLS

1 1/2 pounds whole cacao beans (makes about 1 pound roasted and shelled nibs) or 1 pound (about 4 cups) roasted, shelled cacao nibs

1 pound (2 1/4 cups) sugar, or to taste

1 quarter-sized slice fresh ginger (1/2 ounce), peeled and minced

1 mamey sapote (see above) or 1/2 teaspoon almond extract

2 plump vanilla beans

1 (3-inch) stick true cinnamon (soft Ceylon cinnamon, sold as *canela* in Hispanic markets), coarsely chopped with a knife, or 2 tablespoons ground true cinnamon

1 teaspoon aniseed

1 teaspoon allspice berries

6 whole cloves

1/8 teaspoon freshly grated nutmeg

continued

If you are using whole cacao beans, heat a large (12-inch) griddle, *comal,* or heavy-bottomed skillet over medium heat. Add the cacao beans and roast, stirring constantly, until they develop a deep roasted flavor and a rich brown color. The roasting time will vary according to the size and quality of the beans. Large Criollo beans of an even size will take about 30 minutes; Forastero or Trinitario beans of uneven sizes, 35 to 40 minutes. For even-sized Trinitarios, allow 20 to 25 minutes. In any case, it is advisable to test the beans every 5 minutes or so by breaking one open and tasting it to determine the degree of roasting. It's all a matter of taste.

Place the roasted beans in a tray or bowl and allow to cool. When they are cool enough to handle, shell them one at a time, trying to keep the nibs as whole as possible to avoid waste. From 1 1/2 pounds of Trinitario cacao of uneven size, you can expect to end up with 18 ounces or less of cacao nibs.

If you are using commercial cacao nibs, taste one to see if they have been roasted enough. If you feel your nibs are underroasted, place them on a heated *comal,* griddle, or heavy-bottomed skillet and roast over medium heat, stirring, for about 5 minutes, or until roasted to your liking.

Place the roasted nibs, sugar, and ginger in a food processor and process for about 10 minutes, stopping every 2 minutes and letting the machine rest for a few seconds to prevent overheating the motor. The idea is to grind the nibs finely into a thick, warm paste.

Meanwhile, cut open the mamey sapote and remove the shiny black seed. (Reserve the flesh for another use; it is delicious eaten simply as is. If using the almond extract, add later.) Crack open the pit with a mallet and remove the flesh-colored kernel inside; set aside.

Grind the vanilla beans and mamey sapote pit to a sticky mass in a mini-chopper. Set aside. Next grind the cinnamon to a fine powder in a spice mill or coffee grinder. Then follow with the aniseed, allspice, and cloves. Add the almond extract, if using, vanilla, nutmeg, and the other ground spices to the cacao-sugar mixture and continue processing for 2 to 3 minutes, or until all the ingredients are well integrated into a sticky paste.

At this point the cacao mass needs further refining. It must be put through a grinder like a plate corn mill. Add the warm cacao paste in batches through the machine's feed tube while pushing it down with a pestle. Cranking takes some elbow grease, and the machine must be very firmly clamped to a countertop or table. Put the paste through the machine once more to refine further. The cacao mass will still feel coarse (but that's fine for hot chocolate). You'll lose some cacao mass and end up with about 1 pound 11 ounces of the mixture.

To shape the cacao balls, divide the sticky paste into 23 or 24 equal portions of about 1.2 ounces each. If you have warm hands like me, it might help to chill your palms periodically by rubbing them with ice cubes and drying them well. Roll each portion between the palms of your hands to form a ball or a slightly rhomboid shape. (Don't worry if they do not look perfect.) Place the balls on a tray or baking sheet lined with parchment paper. Allow to dry for a couple of hours or more before storing in an airtight container, either in a cool place or in the refrigerator.

WORLD'S BEST HOT CHOCOLATE

To make Ana Rodríguez's hot chocolate, all you need to do is dissolve 1 cacao ball in 2/3 cup hot milk or water. To obtain a rich head of foam, blend the two with a Mexican *molinillo* (wooden chocolate "mill") or, better still, a handheld electric immersion blender.

Chocolate-Jasmine Ice Cream

In a much-celebrated Italian recipe from the Renaissance, created in honor of the Duke of Tuscany, alternating layers of fresh jasmine blossoms and crushed cacao nibs were allowed to sit for 24 hours until the flavors were fused. This is a lovely idea—cacao and chocolate, with their high fat content, are known for an amazing capacity to absorb taste and fragrance. I've adopted the same combination for another purpose, a smooth and creamy ice cream based on Venezuelan milk chocolate and jasmine tea. To me this is an all-time magical union of tropical perfumes. It deserves to become a classic.

MAKES ABOUT 5 1/2 CUPS

3 1/2 cups whole milk

1/2 cup heavy cream

1 vanilla bean, preferably Mexican,
split lengthwise, seeds scraped and reserved

1/8 teaspoon salt

1/2 cup loose jasmine tea leaves, preferably high-quality pearl jasmine

6 large egg yolks

1 cup finely grated Latin American brown loaf sugar (*piloncillo* or *panela*), muscovado sugar, or packed dark brown sugar

7 ounces milk chocolate, preferably El Rey Caoba (41% cacao), Valrhona Jivara (40% cacao), or Amano Jembrana (30% cacao), finely chopped

In a 3-quart heavy-bottomed saucepan, combine the milk, cream, the vanilla bean, scraped seeds, and salt. Bring to a boil, reduce the heat to low, add the jasmine tea, simmer for 2 to 3 minutes, and remove from the heat. Allow the mixture to stand for 15 minutes, to steep. When the cream mixture has cooled, strain through a fine-mesh strainer into a spouted container. Using the back of a spoon, press the tea leaves to remove as much of the liquid as possible. Rinse and dry the pot.

To make the ice cream custard, beat the egg yolks with the brown sugar until thick and fluffy, about 5 minutes, using a standing mixer or a hand mixer. Reduce the speed to low and pour the cream mixture gradually into the egg mixture while beating. Pour the mixture back into the pot and simmer over very low heat, stirring, until it thickens and coats the back of the spoon, 4 to 5 minutes.

Place the chopped chocolate in a bowl and pour the hot custard over it. Allow it to stand for 1 minute, then mix it thoroughly with a spatula until smooth and creamy. Strain through a fine-mesh strainer into a bowl. Set the bowl in a larger bowl filled with cracked ice and water to cool the custard, stirring often.

When the custard is at room temperature, pour into the bowl of an ice cream maker and process according to the manufacturer's instructions until fully frozen. Scoop into a stainless steel or plastic container and place in the freezer to harden for 2 to 4 hours for optimum texture.

Note: An important ingredient is the richly flavored unrefined loaf sugar known in Latin America as *panela, piloncillo,* or *papelón.* It is available at Hispanic markets. Use a box grater to grate off as much as you need. You can substitute regular brown sugar, but you'll lose something. A good-quality dark muscovado natural cane sugar is a better idea.

The celebrated seventeenth-century formula for drinking chocolate mixed with jasmine was attributed to Francesco Redi, a medical attendant for one of the last ruling Medicis, the Grand Duke of Tuscany, Cosimo III. For the original version, dubbed "The Renowned Jasmine Chocolate of the Grand Duke of Tuscany," see the authoritative *The True History of Chocolate* by Sophie and Michael Coe.

MEXICO'S GIFT TO THE WORLD

ABOVE: The 1940s were a time of prosperity for the vanilla growers of the town of Papantla, in the state of Veracruz, and photographers were called in to record the curing houses (*beneficios*) bursting with shiny, perfectly shaped one-pound vanilla bundles ready to be shipped.

LEFT: Vanilla flowers have a brief life span. They open at dawn, and if they are not pollinated by noon, they wither. Using his fingernail, this Totonac indian worker from Papantla, (circa 1930), hand pollinates this hard-to-reach vanilla blossoms with a fingernail by bending aside a tiny flap of membrane so that pollen can be transferred from the anther to the stigma.

"Age of Discovery" Vanilla-Scented Hot Chocolate

The first European treatise on chocolate, written about 125 years after the Spaniards had encountered the fabulous pairing of vanilla and chocolate in Mexico, is Antonio Colmenero de Ledesma's *Curioso tratado de la naturaleza y calidad del chocolate* (Curious Treatise on the Nature and Quality of Chocolate, published in 1644).

By the seventeenth century, Spaniards in both Mexico and Spain had put their own stamp on the heady Aztec and Maya beverages. For the sake of Spanish cooks, the author suggests substitutes for three of the New World ingredients most commonly used along with vanilla in both pre-Columbian and colonial Mexican recipes for chocolate: a certain type of chile; an edible flower called *ueinacaztli* (*Cymbopetalum penduliflorum*), known also as "ear flowers"; and *mecaxochitl* (the flower spike of the hoja santa plant), today called hoja santa or acuyo and still indispensable in Veracruzan cooking.

In the original recipe, the whole mass of cacao beans was ground to a paste on a grinding stone (*metate*) with whole vanilla beans, nuts, and other seasonings, then shaped into balls or cakes to be dissolved in hot water (sometimes milk or almond milk). Here is my version of this classic using plump Mexican vanilla beans and modern commercial chocolate made with Venezuelan cacao beans—the ones most likely to have been used in an upscale chocolate drink such as this in seventeenth-century Spain.

MAKES 8 SERVINGS

8 cups milk or water

1/4 cup achiote (annatto) seeds

12 blanched almonds

12 toasted and skinned hazelnuts

2 to 3 vanilla beans (preferably Mexican from Papantla), split lengthwise, seeds scraped out

1/4 ounce dried rosebuds (sold as *rosa de Castilla* in Hispanic markets)

2 (3-inch) sticks true cinnamon (soft Ceylon cinnamon, sold as *canela* in Hispanic markets)

1 tablespoon aniseed

2 dried árbol or serrano chiles

8 ounces dark chocolate, preferably El Rey Gran Samán (70% cacao), Amano Cuyagua (70% cacao), or Cluizel Concepción (66% cacao), finely chopped

Pinch of salt

Sugar

1 tablespoon orange-blossom water (optional)

In a heavy, medium-sized saucepan, heat the milk with the achiote seeds over medium heat. Bring to a low boil, stirring frequently. Reduce the heat to low and let steep for 10 minutes, or until the liquid is brightly dyed with the achiote.

continued

Meanwhile, grind the almonds and hazelnuts to the consistency of fine breadcrumbs, using a mini-chopper or Mouli grater. Set aside.

Strain out the achiote and return the milk to the saucepan. Add the ground nuts along with the vanilla beans and scraped seeds, rosebuds, cinnamon, aniseed, and chiles. Bring to a low boil. Reduce the heat to low and simmer for about 10 minutes. Remove from the heat; stir in the chocolate and salt. Taste for sweetness and add a little sugar, if desired, together with the orange-blossom water. Strain through a fine-mesh strainer.

Transfer the chocolate to a tall narrow pot and whisk vigorously with a Mexican *molinillo* (wooden chocolate mill) or a handheld electric immersion blender. It makes a spectacular frothy head. Serve immediately.

LA MERIENDA EN ESPAÑA

Still life (*Bodegón*) by eighteenth-century Spanish painter Luis Meléndez, showing chocolate service with a copper pot (*chocolatera*), bread, biscuits, and chocolate wafers.

Kekchi Cacao-Chile Balls

In Alta Verapaz, a lush and deeply forested region of Guatemala that was part of the ancient Mesoamerican chocolate empire, the Kekchi (also spelled Q'eqchi) Maya roast cacao beans and grind them with *ululte,* the local name for the tiny but devilish chile piquín. They often shape the resulting sticky paste into balls, which are then air-dried and stored. To add heat and flavor to feast dishes like *chompipe* (turkey) and *pepianes* (stews thickened with pumpkin seeds), they grate a little of this mixture over the food.

I've taken up this exciting idea at home, but I tend to expand on the seasonings. This particular version was inspired by a batch of Papua New Guinea beans that had been dried over wood fires during the rainy season. They were too smoky and hammy for a fine chocolate, but perfect for my purpose. I played up the smokiness with a dash of Spanish smoked paprika and added a little allspice and soft true cinnamon from Mexico.

Experiment with other combinations of spices if you wish, or vary the proportions to taste. Once you discover how this magic seasoning wakes up food, you might enjoy passing the cacao balls around the table with a small cheese grater and letting each person grate his or her own onto the plate. I've used it with lobster stew, slightly sweet cream soups, and different meat stews (lamb, beef, even venison).

A powerful mini–food processor is almost essential for grinding the cacao and chile, unless you have a good big marble mortar and pestle or a Mexican *metate.*

MAKES 12 BALLS

3 ounces (about ²/₃ cup) cacao nibs
(see page 237)

3 ounces (about 1 cup) piquín chiles (also
sold as *chiltepe* or *chiltepín* chiles in Hispanic
markets)

1 (1-inch) stick true cinnamon (soft Ceylon
cinnamon, sold as *canela* in Hispanic markets),
coarsely chopped

¹/₂ teaspoon allspice berries

1 teaspoon salt

1 teaspoon Spanish smoked paprika

Heat a griddle, medium-sized cast-iron skillet, or Mexican *comal* over medium heat. Add the cacao nibs and dry-roast for 2 minutes, or until fragrant, turning constantly with a wooden spoon or spatula. Turn out into another container and set aside.

Add the chiles, cinnamon stick, and allspice berries to the griddle and dry-roast, stirring, for 2 minutes. Scrape into a spice mill or coffee grinder with the salt and paprika; grind to a fine powder.

Combine the spice mixture and roasted cacao in a mini-food processor and process into a warm, sticky paste, 3 to 4 minutes, stopping to scrape down the sides of the bowl. Scrape out onto a work surface and shape into 12 small balls. Let sit until thoroughly dried. Store in a tightly sealed jar. To use, grate over any dish of your choice.

The sixteenth-century *Códice Azoyú* is a pictorial chronicle of the political history and chronology of the small kingdom of Tlachinollan, in today's Guerrero State in Mexico. Folio 21 depicts a stylized cacao field in the tributary town of Totomixtlahuacan.

Xalapa-Style Mole
Mole Xalapeño

Moles are a large and very ancient tribe of dishes whose name derives from the overall word for sauce (*molli*) in Nahuatl, the language of the Aztecs. There is no single ingredient, except perhaps for chiles, that is common to each and every example.

Today's moles are diverse Old World–New World hybrids that marry ingredients from both hemispheres and many historical epochs. Many are made with chocolate (though more are made without it). The following recipe is my interpretation of one I had in Xalapa, the capital of Veracruz State. Here the gentle, patient Estela Pérez, head cook at Raquel Torres's beloved but now defunct Churrería del Recuerdo, made me the mole her mother taught her to make in a small town near the capital. The mole resembles the famous one made in nearby Xico, southeast of Xalapa, but it has no tomato and is less spicy. Like all moles, it is essentially a sauce that can be a vehicle for different foods. The chocolate creates certain aromatic nuances with a dash of bitterness, while adding a little extra body. You can also use a sweeter artisanal Mexican chocolate.

Mexicans use moles by adding any meat—precooked or partly cooked—to a large amount of the sauce thinned with broth, and cooking it for a while to marry the flavors. The possible choices include pork, beef, turkey, duck, or chicken, either shredded or cut into bite-sized pieces. Estela also uses her mole to make *enmoladas*, or tortillas dipped in the sauce, rolled around a chicken or pork filling, and topped with more mole, chopped onions, and grated cheese (the dry queso añejo). In this country, there is no reason we shouldn't serve mole as an accompanying sauce with any roasted or grilled meat.

MAKES ABOUT 6 CUPS UNDILUTED MOLE PASTE

continued

A NOTE ON COOKING FATS

When I opened my first restaurant, Zafra, in 2000, my cooks and I started experimenting with mole recipes using both lard and an extra-virgin olive oil made with Arbequina olives (which have subtle notes of apple peel). My Mexican cooks and I unanimously agreed that the olive oil was a perfect fit with the sweet plantains, nuts, and chocolate in the sauce. We still love the assertive, nutty flavor of the lard, but appreciate the subtle, unobtrusive way in which the olive oil blends with the other ingredients.

9 ancho chiles (4 ounces), stemmed and seeded

11 pasilla chiles (4 ounces), stemmed and seeded

12 mulato chiles (4 ounces), stemmed and seeded

1 large white onion, unpeeled

1 medium head of garlic, unpeeled

1 (1-inch) stick true cinnamon (soft Ceylon cinnamon, sold as *canela* in Hispanic markets)

1 teaspoon black peppercorns

1 tablespoon aniseed

1 medium-sized corn tortilla

$^1/_2$ cup (about 2 ounces) dry-roasted peanuts

$^1/_2$ cup (about 2 ounces) blanched sliced almonds

$^1/_2$ cup (about 2 ounces) hulled green pumpkin seeds

$^1/_2$ cup (about 2 ounces) sesame seeds

$^2/_3$ cup extra-virgin olive oil from Arbequina olives or freshly rendered lard

1 medium-sized ripe plantain, peeled and cut into thick slices

$^1/_3$ cup (about 2 ounces) pitted prunes

$^1/_2$ cup (about 2 ounces) dark raisins

3 ounces dark chocolate, preferably El Rey Bucare (58.5% cacao), Askinosie Soconusco (75% cacao), an artisanal Mexican chocolate, or Ibarra brand table chocolate

$^1/_4$ to $^1/_3$ cup (about 2 ounces) grated Latin American brown loaf sugar (*piloncillo*), muscovado sugar, or packed dark brown sugar, or to taste

1 teaspoon salt

Well-flavored chicken broth

To roast the chiles, wipe them clean with a damp cloth. Heat a large griddle, *comal,* or heavy-bottomed skillet over medium heat. Dry-roast the chiles on the griddle in about 6 batches, allowing about 1 minute on each side and pressing them down with a spatula. Transfer them to a large bowl as they are done; cover with about 4 cups warm water and leave them to soak for about 20 minutes. Drain and reserve 1 cup of the soaking liquid.

Dry-roast the onion and whole head of garlic on the griddle, stirring occasionally, until blackened and blistered, about 8 minutes. Set aside until cool enough to handle.

Lightly dry-roast the cinnamon, black peppercorns, and aniseed (do not scorch). Grind them to a fine powder in a spice mill or coffee mill and set aside.

Lightly toast the tortilla on the griddle, allowing about 30 seconds per side; set aside. Dry-roast the peanuts, almonds, and pumpkin seeds, stirring or shaking the griddle, for about 1 minute. Set aside in a small bowl. Toast the sesame seeds for about 30 seconds, stirring or shaking the griddle; scrape out into the same bowl. When cool, finely grind the nuts, seeds, and tortilla in a food processor.

Heat the lard in a large 12-inch skillet over medium heat until melted. Add the the plantain slices and sauté until golden brown. Scoop out with a slotted spoon and let drain on paper towels; set aside the skillet with the fat.

Peel the cooled onion and garlic, chop the onion coarsely, and set aside. Combine all of the roasted ingredients, plantain slices, prunes, and raisins in a large bowl or pot with the reserved chile soaking liquid. Working in 3 or more batches, process the mixture in a blender or food processor to make a purée, adding more chile soaking liquid as needed if the mixture is too thick to process easily. Repeat until all has been processed.

Heat the reserved olive oil or lard in the skillet over medium heat until fragrant. When it ripples, add the purée and cook, stirring, for about 3 minutes, being careful to dodge splatters. Stir in the chocolate and salt, and taste for sweetness; add brown sugar as needed. (Mexican chocolate will require less sugar.) Cook, stirring, for about 5 minutes.

If you are planning to use the paste immediately, dilute it by stirring in chicken broth until it is the consistency of thin tomato sauce. It isn't absolutely necessary, but the consistency will be much silkier if you force the thinned mixture through a fine-mesh sieve by pushing with a wooden spoon. If you are not using it immediately, cool the mole paste to room temperature, transfer to storage containers, and pour a thin film of melted lard over the surface to help keep it from spoiling. Seal tightly and store it in a cool place or the refrigerator. It will keep well for several months.

LEFT: Estela Pérez warming a small portion of her mole Xalapeño.
RIGHT: Estela assembles the mole ingredients.

Tanchucuá (Tanch'ukwa)
Yucatecan Days of the Dead
Corn-Thickened Hot Chocolate with Allspice

My friend Isabel Aguilar was born in Valladolid, a lovely colonial town on the Yucatán peninsula. On the Days of the Dead, her family always places a cup of this spice-perfumed hot drink on their altar. It is similar to the *champurrado* of Central Mexico (see page 198), but what makes it typically Yucatecan is the fragrant, alluring allspice.

SERVES 8

8 cups water or milk

6 (3-inch) sticks true cinnamon (soft Ceylon cinnamon, sold as *canela* in Hispanic markets)

2 tablespoons allspice berries

3/4 cup sugar

1/8 teaspoon salt

1/2 to 3/4 cup commercial dried masa, preferably Maseca brand

2 cups cold water

6 ounces dark chocolate, preferably Askinosie Soconusco (75% cacao), coarsely chopped

Combine the milk in a medium saucepan with the cinnamon, allspice, sugar, and salt. Bring to a boil, lower the heat, and simmer for 15 minutes.

In a small bowl, combine the masa and water and stir well to dissolve any lumps. Stir the mixture into the milk and simmer, stirring, until it coats the back of a spoon lightly, about 10 minutes. Add the chocolate and simmer, stirring, until it is completely dissolved and the liquid is as thick as a light porridge, about 5 to 10 minutes. Strain the mixture into a serving pitcher. Serve at once, piping hot.

DAYS OF THE DEAD

For Mexicans, the intoxicating fragrance of spiced hot chocolate becomes a special bond between the living and the dead once a year, at the feast of Todos Santos, or All Saints. The celebration hinges on the belief that only on October 31 and November 1 are the souls of the dead allowed to journey back for one yearly visit to the living. The souls of those who died at birth or as children return on October 31, the souls of adults the next day. The two days are the Christian feasts of All Saints and All Souls, but strangely, the season more or less coincides with the months of Ochpanitzli and Teotleco in the pre-Hispanic Aztec calendar, when pre-Hispanic peoples of Mexico used to present food and corn to their dead.

Today people mark the occasion by erecting beautiful altars to loved ones decorated with seasonal flowers like marigolds and cockscomb, photographs of the dead, saints' images, and candies in the shape of skulls. They burn *copal* (incense) and bring offerings of what the deceased most enjoyed during life, such as favorite kinds of cigarettes or liquor. There are also offerings of freshly prepared food, often special tamales or the sweet *pan de muerto* (bread of the dead). The dead are guided back to family and friends by the smell of flowers, *copal,* and familiar foods. When they leave, they take these aromas with them. It is not unusual to hear Mexicans comment that the food left on the altar from one day to the next has lost its fragrance and flavor.

Different foods are offered in different regions, but since it is essential that food offerings be aromatic and familiar, it is no surprise to find cups or jars of hot chocolate prominently displayed on many Mexican altars. (A cup of chocolate is also a customary offering to guests after a funeral.) At the old La Locomotora chocolate factory in Xalapa, the capital of Veracruz State, I found chocolate bars being sold alongside large funeral candles. It makes perfect sense. What could better steer the soul on its eager, once-a-year journey back to family and home than the intoxicating fragrance of frothy, steaming Mexican chocolate?

The link between cacao, death, and revival is ancient in Mesoamerica. In this Maya vessel from the Late Classic period (600–900 AD) now at the Popol Vuh Museum in Guatemala City, the Lords of Xibalba—the Maya underworld—decapitate Hun Hunahpu, one of the main characters of the Quiché Maya myth of creation (often equated with the Maize God), and place his head on a cacao tree (a calabash tree in a post-conquest version of the myth). The head comes to life as a cacao pod and, with a touch of his saliva, he impregnates a maiden who bears the avenging twin heroes of Maya mythology.

Champurrado for Christmas Processions
Champurrado para Posadas

Champurrado comes from the Spanish word *chapurrar*, which applies to either mixing ingredients for drinks or mixing up a couple of languages. It is the usual word for an atole, or gruel of nixtamalized (lime-treated) corn masa, that has been flavored with chocolate. There are many kinds of *champurrados* (some versions are called *chocolateatole*). I like to use Askinosie's Soconusco chocolate, but the *champurrado* can be made with any of the Latin American brands labeled *chocolates para mesa* (table chocolates).

Atole or *champurrado* figures in the *posadas*, or door-to-door re-enactments of Mary and Joseph's search for room at the inn, that take place in Mexico from December 16 until Christmas Eve. Processions of children dressed as angels and accompanied by adults parade noisily through the streets, stopping at the houses of friends and neighbors to ask for shelter. After a ritualized exchange of pleas and threatened refusals, the children are allowed in and greeted with hot atole or *champurrado*.

Champurrado is a welcome change from the too-familiar eggnog for a Christmas Day open house or other holiday party. But I like to spice up the usually simple, unembellished original with a little dried orange rind and aniseed or star anise. For a strictly grown-up version, add some wonderful dark rum.

I prefer to use a premium dark, bitter chocolate, but you can substitute a presweetened flavored Mexican chocolate; just adjust the level of sweetness to balance the chocolate you choose. Note that if you find the finished drink too thick, you can always thin it with more hot milk or water.

SERVES 8

1 to 1^1/$_2$ cups commercial dried masa, preferably Maseca brand

2 cups water

8 cups whole milk, or water

6 (3-inch) sticks of true cinnamon (soft Ceylon cinnamon, sold as *canela* in Hispanic markets)

1 tablespoon aniseed or 8 star anise pods

4 strips dried orange rind, 1 tablespoon finely grated fresh orange zest, or 3 orange-tree leaves

2 teaspoons pure vanilla extract

Pinch of salt

1^1/$_2$ cups finely grated Latin American brown loaf sugar (*piloncillo* or *panela*), muscovado sugar, or packed dark brown sugar

6 ounces dark chocolate, preferably Askinosie Soconusco (75% cacao), El Rey Extra Bitter Gran Samán (70% cacao), or Cluizel Los Ancones (67% cacao), coarsely chopped

Combine the dried masa and water in a bowl. Stir well to break up any lumps.

Combine the milk in a 4-quart saucepan with the cinnamon, aniseed, orange rind, vanilla extract, salt, and sugar. Bring just to a boil, stirring to dissolve the sugar. Reduce the heat to low and let simmer for about 10 minutes to allow the flavors to infuse the milk. Stir in the dissolved masa. Cook, stirring, until it thickens to the consistency of a light porridge. Stir in the chocolate and cook, stirring, until it dissolves. Serve very hot.

REMEMBERING VERACRUZ'S BEST HOT CHOCOLATE

Josefa Ramírez used to make classic Mexican chocolate at the celebrated Churrería del Recuerdo in Xalapa, Mexico. After adding hot milk to the cinnamon-spiced chocolate, she twirls a wooden *molinillo* between her palms to whip the mixture to a rich froth.

Dark Milk Chocolate–Coffee Brûlées
Cortadito de Chocolate como Crema Catalana

This take on the Catalan version of crème brûlée (Crema Catalana) combines several of my favorite flavors: a strong, not-too-sweet milk chocolate; the Cuban-style espresso-milk combination called *cortadito*; and Latin American unrefined brown loaf sugar (preferably Colombian *panela*) for a brûlée crust with deeper flavor than the usual kind. It looks pretty when made in shallow earthenware *cazuelitas*, heatproof demitasse cups, or in ramekins. To caramelize the sugar, it is best to use a salamander (preferably the wider Spanish type, pictured on the opposite page) that you simply heat over an open flame or a brûlée torch. The perfect garnishes are caramelized cacao beans or chocolate-covered plantain chips.

MAKES 6 SMALL (¹/₂ CUP) BRULÉES

1 whole large egg

4 large egg yolks

¹/₄ cup granulated sugar, or to taste, depending on the sweetness of the chocolate (optional)

1 cup heavy cream

1 cup whole milk

2 (3-inch) sticks true cinnamon (soft Ceylon cinnamon sold as *canela* in Hispanic markets)

3 star anise pods

1 vanilla bean, split lengthwise

1 teaspoon pure vanilla extract

¹/₂ cup strong freshly brewed espresso

8 ounces dark milk chocolate, preferably El Rey Caoba (41% cacao), Valrhona Jivara (40% cacao), or Guittard Orinoco (38% cacao), coarsely chopped

1 cup finely grated Latin American brown loaf sugar (*panela* or *piloncillo*), Demerara sugar, muscovado sugar, or packed light brown sugar

Candied Cacao Beans Dipped in Chocolate (page 145) or Chocolate-Covered Plantain Chips (page 174), for garnish

Preheat the oven to 335°F.

In a mixing bowl, whisk the egg and egg yolks together with the ¹/₄ cup granulated sugar; set the mixture aside.

Combine the cream, milk, cinnamon, star anise, vanilla bean and extract, and espresso in a saucepan. Bring just to a boil and simmer, stirring, over low heat for about 10 minutes to dissolve the sugar and let the spices infuse the milk. Strain the milk mixture into a heatproof bowl. Add the chocolate and stir gently until melted. (Do not use a whisking motion, because you want to avoid air bubbles.) Gradually stir the warm chocolate mixture into the egg mixture and whisk to combine thoroughly. Strain into a pitcher.

continued

Pour the mixture into six 4-ounce *cazuelitas*, heatproof demitasse coffee cups, or ramekins. Select a heatproof baking dish large enough to hold any of these arrangements comfortably. Place the filled containers in the pan, place on the center rack of the oven, and carefully pour in enough hot water to fill the pan halfway up the sides of the containers. Bake for 35 minutes, or until set.

Let cool to room temperature. If desired, chill in the refrigerator, covered with plastic wrap.

If you are using a salamander to caramelize the sugar, make sure to heat it on an open flame for at least 10 minutes before using it. At serving time, sprinkle enough of the grated loaf sugar over the surface of the custard to coat it thinly but evenly. Caramelize the sugar with the hot salamander by pressing it gently and quickly over the surface of the custard, or use a brûlée torch. (You can run the *crema*—without the garnish—under the broiler, but it tends to dry it out.) Serve as soon as the caramelized crust cools. If you are using cacao beans as garnish, simply place them on top of the custard after the caramel has cooled slightly.

Persian Poem in a Custard

I wanted to create a creamy, satiny-textured custard that would marry chocolate with fragrant flavors reminiscent of a Persian poem. I thought of rose, cardamom, pistachio—perfumes of the East, to be savored while reading the *Rubaiyat of Omar Khayyam*. But I could not resist a dash of Latin heat from dried árbol chiles to heighten the experience. I recommend using Cluizel Vila Gracinda, a chocolate made with beans from São Tomé, the first European colony in Africa to which cacao was brought in colonial times. With only minor alterations, the mixture also makes excellent truffles (see variation on page 208).

MAKES 15 SMALL SERVINGS

4 large egg yolks

²/₃ cup sugar, or to taste

1 cup heavy cream

1 cup whole milk

2 (3-inch) sticks true cinnamon (soft Ceylon cinnamon, sold as *canela* in Hispanic markets)

¹/₂ ounce dried rosebuds (sold in Asian and Middle Eastern markets and as *rosa de Castilla* in Hispanic markets)

1 tablespoon rose water (available in Middle Eastern markets)

1 tablespoon green cardamom pods, lightly crushed

1 small dried árbol chile

Pinch of salt

4 ounces dark chocolate, preferably Cluizel Vila Gracinda (67% cacao), finely chopped

GARNISH

8 ounces green pistachios, shelled and finely chopped

Dried rosebuds, crushed into small bits

Coarse sea salt

Preheat the oven to 335°F.

Whisk the egg yolks with ¹/₃ cup of the sugar; set the mixture aside.

Combine the heavy cream, milk, and remaining ¹/₃ cup sugar in a saucepan. Add the cinnamon, rosebuds, rose water, cardamom, chile, and salt. Place the saucepan over medium-low heat and simmer for 10 minutes. Remove the saucepan from the heat, add the chocolate, and whisk gently until it melts. Let the mixture cool. Stir the chocolate mixture into the whisked eggs until well blended.

Strain the mixture into a shallow 9-inch square pan. Set the pan in a larger heatproof baking pan. Place on the center rack of the preheated oven and carefully pour in enough very hot water to fill the pan halfway up the sides of the smaller pan. Bake for 25 minutes. It will still be somewhat loose, but will firm up when cooled to room temperature.

To serve, scoop into a pastry bag fitted with a fluted wide tip and pipe into small glasses. Sprinkle a little of the pistachios, rosebuds, and salt over each serving. Serve at room temperature.

Chilled Cacao-Almond Horchata
Horchata de Cacao y Almendras

For this recipe I was inspired by *horchata*, a refreshing cold drink from the Spanish provinces of Valencia and Alicante that calls for a starchy ingredient to give body and flavor to a simple mixture of water and sugar. People use almonds, grains such as barley and rice, and even tubers, particularly *chufa* or tiger-nut (*Cyperus esculentus*). Mediterranean *horchata* traveled to Latin America, where cooks, particularly in Mexico and Central America, seasoned it with spices and local ingredients such as cacao. The famous Ve-racruzan *popo*, a frothy drink made from ground white rice, cacao, cinnamon, and the root of a climbing plant called *chupipi*, is strikingly close to an *horchata*. I would not be surprised if the original inspiration was Mediterranean *horchata* grafted onto a pre-Columbian cacao drink.

For my version I use almond milk. This is a very old ingredient in many European cuisines. It spread from the Mediterranean to all places where traders brought almonds, and throughout the Middle Ages it was an alternative to cow's milk for Lenten or fast-day dishes. It was also considered medically preferable to rice in some conditions. Now we know that almond milk is more nutritious than white rice and cacao is rich in flavanols. I combine the almond milk with cacao nibs, which lend a delicious bitter chocolaty edge to the mixture, and often sweeten it with agave nectar, a wonderful alternative to white sugar that roots the drink more firmly in Mesoamerica. Note that even thorough blending will not eliminate the slight crunch from the nibs; I like this, but if you don't, strain it.

MAKES 6 SERVINGS

1 cup whole or slivered blanched almonds

1 stick (3-inch) true cinnamon (soft Ceylon cinnamon, sold as *canela* in Hispanic markets)

8 cups water

1/2 cup cacao nibs, roasted or raw (see Sources, page 237), or to taste

8 tablespoons agave nectar, Catalan wild oak honey, or sugar

Generous pinch of salt

TO SERVE

6 long Ceylon cinnamon sticks (about 10 inches)

Working in batches as necessary, combine the almonds, cinnamon, and water in a blender and purée until you have a somewhat grainy, milky-looking liquid. Strain through a fine-mesh strainer into a bowl, pressing with a wooden spoon to extract as much liquid as possible from the almonds.

Pour the almond milk back into the blender with the cacao nibs, agave nectar, and salt, and process until well combined and frothy. Pour into a pitcher and chill in the refrigerator. Serve in tall glasses over ice cubes.

TRUFFLE WISDOM

My friend Jim Koper is an aerospace engineer who designs laser gyroscopes for a living, but he is passionate about all things chocolate. He has been making chocolate truffles for twenty-two years and every Christmas he sends them as gifts to friends all over the world (see www.JKChocolateTruffles.com). I can always count on Jim to test my truffle recipes and give me technical advice.

Truffles might seem simple, but they begin with a ganache, a tricky suspension of microscopic drops of fat in water, much like mayonnaise, that requires a careful balance of elements. The water comes from the cream or other liquid, the fat from the cacao butter in the chocolate as well as from the cream. When stirring ganache, Jim has taught me to watch for important clues. When the ganache does not stick to the sides of the bowl, it means that it lacks enough water to suspend the fat, a sign that the cream might have lost too much water during cooking. You can fix the problem, says Jim, by quickly adding a little more cream to the ganache and continuing to stir.

As you experiment with your own ganache recipes, feel free to try new things and observe the different texture and flavor profiles you've created. Also, be aware that you don't have to be limited to the use of cream. Any liquid that contains water is a candidate. The orange truffle recipe (see page 210), for instance, trades butteriness for the clean fresh taste of reduced orange juice. For an interesting variation on the pistachio-crusted truffle recipe (see page 208), you can substitute milk for the cream. Small variations in the amount of liquid you add can greatly affect the firmness or softness of the ganache. You may need to experiment, especially if you use chocolate of different cacao percentages. You can even make a ganache with plain water. But Jim explains that creamless truffles need to be eaten within two days. "High water content liquids like juice make very interesting ganaches, but you never see these truffles commercially because of their limited shelf life. Water activity promotes drying out, crystallization of the sugars, and the growth of molds from the air or from the cacao solids. These truffles need to be enjoyed quickly and since you can't buy them, they are a unique treat."

Jim taught me another variation to keep the truffles from drying out: create a thin layer of chocolate under the coating. To do this, he melts about 3 ounces of chocolate (tempering is not required), coats the palm of his hands with the melted chocolate, and rolls the uncoated truffle between his palms until it is covered with chocolate. He then places all the truffles on a sheet of parchment paper until the chocolate hardens and repeats this operation for a second coating, but this time immediately places the truffle in the dish of coating material and rolls it around.

Harold McGee's Chocolate–Cheese Truffles

Harold McGee, the author of *On Food and Cooking*, is my guru for all kinds of food-chemistry questions. He tells me that a few years ago he heard that a celebrated Parisian chocolatier was making cheese-filled chocolates. Harold was intrigued by the combination because chocolate and cheese both go through fermentation stages that produce a number of flavor notes in common—a potential bridge between two otherwise highly contrasting foods. When he eventually got to sample the chocolates in question, he was less than enchanted. However, his disappointment only spurred him to experiment.

Harold finds that of the three suggested chocolate-cheese pairings, the Camembert provides "a buttery richness, the goat cheese a creamy piquancy, the blue cheese a savory saltiness." Serve the truffles with a complex red wine like a Banyuls or late-harvest Zinfandel.

MAKES 12 TO 18 TRUFFLES

FILLING

4 ounces (weight after trimming) ripe Camembert, fresh goat's milk cheese, or Stilton or Gorgonzola, at room temperature

1 tablespoon superfine sugar

1 to 2 ounces dark chocolate, preferably Scharffen Berger (70% cacao), finely chopped

COATING

6 ounces dark chocolate, preferably Scharffen Berger (70% cacao), finely chopped

To make the filling, trim any rind from the cheese and bring the cheese to room temperature; it should be very soft. If it's too firm, microwave it very briefly to soften. In a mixing bowl, combine the cheese and superfine sugar and beat with a wooden spoon until the sugar has dissolved.

Melt the filling chocolate in the top of a double boiler or heatproof bowl, over simmering water. Use 1 ounce chocolate for Camembert and goat cheese fillings; use 2 ounces for blue cheese fillings. Combine the melted chocolate with the cheese mixture and work together with a wooden spoon or flexible spatula until the mixture is homogeneous. (This may be easier if you add a few drops of water or a little butter.) If the mixture is too soft to shape, refrigerate for 15 to 20 minutes. Roll portions of the mixture into $^1/_2$-inch balls and refrigerate for 15 to 20 minutes.

To make the coating, melt and temper the coating chocolate according to the directions on pages 214 and 215. Dip the cheese balls in the tempered chocolate and use a fork to lift them out, letting the excess drain off, before placing them on a sheet of parchment paper or waxed paper. Allow to set at room temperature. Keep in a cool place and serve on the same day.

Note: Cheese will resume fermentation if left at room temperature, so the truffles should be refrigerated if kept for more than a day. Place on a sheet or tray and wrap snugly in waxed paper, then plastic wrap, before refrigerating. Allow to warm to room temperature before unwrapping.

Pistachio-Crusted Rose-Cardamom Truffles

These lovely truffles, crusted with bud-green pistachios and bits of rose petals, have the same aromatic flavorings as my Persian Poem in a Custard (page 203), but deliver a more emphatic flavor in every bite.

MAKES ABOUT 40 TRUFFLES

GANACHE

10 ounces dark chocolate, preferably Cluizel Vila Gracinda (67% cacao) or Valrhona Araguani (72% cacao)

2 cups heavy cream

2 (3-inch) sticks true cinnamon (soft Ceylon cinnamon, sold as *canela* in Hispanic markets)

1/4 cup dried rosebuds (sold in Asian and Middle Eastern markets and as *rosa de Castilla* in Hispanic markets)

1 tablespoon green cardamom pods, lightly crushed

1 small dried árbol chile

Pinch of salt

1 teaspoon rose water (available in Middle Eastern markets)

COATING

8 ounces green pistachios, shelled and crushed

Dried rosebuds, crushed

Pinch of sea salt (optional)

To prepare the ganache, very finely chop the chocolate with a sharp knife or a few bursts of a food processor. Transfer to a plastic bowl and set aside (plastic is desirable because the cream will not prematurely cool). Combine the cream, cinnamon, rosebuds, cardamom, chile, and salt in a saucepan and bring to a boil over medium heat. Remove from the heat and let steep for 20 minutes. Bring back to a boil and pour enough of the boiling liquid through a strainer to get 1 cup. Quickly pour this over the chocolate. Wait 5 seconds, and then slowly stir the mixture from the center with a rubber spatula until it melts into a shiny puddinglike cream. Add the rose water and continue stirring and scraping the sides of the bowl until the whole mixture is uniformly integrated. Do not overstir. Cover the bowl with plastic wrap and let the chocolate mixture firm up overnight. It is best to do this in a cool place, but not in the refrigerator, as cooling too rapidly could make the ganache slightly grainy.

To prepare the coating, put the pistachios in a plastic bag and crush into smaller particles. Remove the petal portion of the dried rosebuds from the stem section and rub the petals between your hands to make flakes. Mix with the pistachios on a shallow plate. Add the sea salt.

To form the truffles, have ready an 11 x 17-inch piece of parchment paper. Using a measuring tablespoon, scoop up enough ganache for one small truffle. Roll it between your palms to form a ball. Place each ball on a sheet of parchment paper. Next, roll each ball in the coating mixture, pressing down slightly with your hand as you roll to make sure all parts are coated.

You can store the finished truffles in a closed container in the refrigerator, but let them come to room temperature before serving. Since they are made with perishable ingredients, they should be eaten within 2 days.

Morir Soñando Truffles
Dominican Orange–Rum Truffles with Cacao Nibs

I've always found it puzzling that in the cacao-producing regions of Latin America the best-known chocolate dishes are based on European recipes instead of the local cooking traditions. When I started trying to imagine recipes incorporating familiar Latin flavors and showcasing chocolate from locally grown cacao, one of the first things I came up with was this recipe inspired by the popular Dominican drink called *Morir Soñando* ("To Die Dreaming"). It's a simple cold drink made by putting ice in a glass, adding orange juice and sugar, and stirring in a little milk that thickens on reaction with the citrus. Part of the reason I was attracted to the possibilities of *Morir Soñando* as the basis of a truffle was my sense that people take too narrow a view of the liquid element in truffles. Cream may be great, but why not use some more fresh-flavored ingredients like a refreshing tropical fruit juice?

What I eventually came up with marries the orange juice–milk combination with a bit of aged Dominican rum and Cluizel's Los Ancones chocolate made from Dominican cacao. I find that Los Ancones has a wonderful body for truffles, as well as robust cacao flavor and just enough fruit to be interesting without adding an unwanted acidity. Here the acidity comes primarily from the citrus. I also like to reinforce the orange flavor by coating the truffles with a mixture of grated orange zest and crushed cacao nibs for extra depth.

These truffles should be kept refrigerated and eaten within a couple of days. Be sure to bring them to room temperature before serving.

MAKES ABOUT 40 TRUFFLES

GANACHE

10 ounces Cluizel Los Ancones (67% cacao), Valrhona Taïnori (64% cacao), or Felchlin Cru Hacienda Elvesia Organic Couverture (74% cacao)

6 sweet juice oranges (about 2 cups juice)

3 tablespoons sugar

3 tablespoons milk or heavy cream

Pinch of salt

3 tablespoons aged Dominican rum, such as Barceló, Brugal, or Bermúdez

COATING

Zest from 6 oranges

Cacao nibs

To prepare the ganache, finely chop the chocolate with a sharp knife or with a few bursts of a food processor. Transfer to a plastic bowl and set aside (plastic is desirable because it will not prematurely cool down the hot mixture).

Squeeze the oranges into a saucepan, with the seeds and pulp. Scrape the zest from the oranges with a Microplane or box grater; cover and reserve. Add the sugar and milk to the saucepan and bring to a boil. Continue to simmer until the liquid is reduced by about half. Pour enough of the boiling liquid through a strainer into a measuring cup to get a little more than 3/4 cup. Quickly pour this over the chocolate. Wait 5 seconds, then slowly stir the mixture from the center with a plastic spatula. It will start to melt into shiny puddinglike cream. Add the rum and continue stirring and scraping the sides until the whole mixture is uniformly integrated. Don't overstir. Cover with plastic wrap and let the chocolate mixture firm up overnight. It is best to do this in a cool place, but not in a refrigerator, since cooling it too rapidly can make the ganache slightly grainy.

To prepare the coating, preheat the oven to 250°F. Spread the reserved orange zest on a flat pan and put in oven until it dries out (about 10 minutes). Crush the cacao nibs into smaller particles and mix with the orange zest on a shallow plate.

To form the truffles, have ready an 11 x 17-inch piece of parchment paper. Using a measuring tablespoon, scoop up enough ganache for 1 small truffle. Roll into a ball between your palms. Place each ball on a sheet of parchment paper. Next, roll each ball in the coating mixture, pressing down slightly with your hand as you roll to make sure all parts are coated.

You can store the finished truffles in a closed container in the refrigerator, but let them come to room temperature before serving. Since they are made with perishable ingredients, they should be eaten within 2 days.

Dulce de Leche Chocolate Alfajor Truffles with Toasted Coconut

Trufas de Alfajor con Dulce de Leche y Coco Tostado

This truffle was inspired by the popular *alfajores* of the temperate-zone South American countries like Argentina and Chile—essentially, sandwich cookies from a crumbly dough resembling shortbread, with a filling of caramel-like *dulce de leche*. (*Dulce de leche* sold in jars is available at Hispanic markets and many supermarkets.) Sometimes the edges are coated with grated coconut, sometimes the whole "sandwich" is dipped in chocolate.

Combining these ideas, I blended together *dulce de leche* with a simple chocolate ganache and coated the truffles with a mixture of shortbread crumbs and grated coconut. (Do not try to mix the chocolate and *dulce de leche* completely, because the chocolate mass will become rubbery. You want a marbled, partly combined effect in which the truffle base is creamy but the *dulce de leche* is streaked through it almost like a soft taffy.) Since the ganache has no added flavorings other than the milk caramel, I prefer to use a mellow but full-flavored chocolate that provides complexity without sharp contrasts of bitterness or astringency. Cluizel Concepción, made with Venezuelan beans from Barlovento, has everything I need to form a seamless, satisfying marriage with the *dulce de leche*.

These truffles should be kept refrigerated and eaten within 4 or 5 days. Be sure to let them come to room temperature before serving.

MAKES ABOUT 40 TRUFFLES

GANACHE

10 ounces Cluizel Concepción chocolate (66% cacao) or Valrhona Araguani (72% cacao)

2 cups heavy cream

Pinch of salt

2 cups *dulce de leche*

3 ounces shortbread cookies (about 4 cookies), preferably Lorna Doones or Scottish Walkers brand

4 ounces unsweetened shredded coconut

To prepare the ganache, very finely chop the chocolate with a sharp knife or with a few bursts of a food processor. Transfer to a plastic bowl and set aside (plastic is desirable because it will not prematurely cool down the hot mixture).

Pour the cream into a saucepan, add the salt, and bring to a boil over medium heat. Measure out 1 cup (use the remaining cream for other purposes) and quickly pour it over the chocolate. Wait 5 seconds, then slowly stir the mixture from the center with a rubber spatula. It will start to melt into a shiny puddinglike cream. Continue stirring and scraping the sides of the bowl until the whole mixture is uniformly integrated. Do not overstir. Cover with plastic wrap and let firm up overnight. It is best to do this in a cool place, but not in the refrigerator, since cooling it too rapidly can make the ganache slightly grainy.

To prepare the dulce de leche, scoop the *dulce de leche* into a saucepan and bring it to a boil over medium heat while stirring constantly. Let it simmer for 2 minutes more. This will thicken it by evaporating some of the water. Let cool to a taffylike consistency.

To prepare the coating, preheat the oven to 300°F. Spread out the coconut on a baking sheet and bake for about 15 minutes, stirring every 3 minutes, until it is golden brown. Let cool. Roll or crush to make the particles smaller. Crush or chop the shortbread cookies into crumbs. Mix equal amounts of shortbread crumbs and toasted coconut in a shallow dish.

To form the truffles, have ready an 11 x 17-inch piece of parchment paper. Whip the hardened ganache with a fork or rubber spatula until it becomes soft and lighter in color. Using an ordinary spoon, scoop up a half spoonful of ganache. With the same spoon, dip into the *dulce de leche* and pick up a small portion (about one-quarter of a spoonful). Then scoop up another quarter spoonful of ganache. Use your clean finger to push the mixture off of the spoon and on a sheet of parchment paper. Repeat for the entire batch. You will now have many oozing mounds of your truffle material.

Pick up a mound of ganache and *dulce de leche* and roll it between your palms to form a ball. This is a sticky operation. Place each ball on a sheet of parchment paper. Roll each ball in the coating mixture, pressing down slightly with your hand as you roll to make sure all parts are coated.

Store the finished truffles in a closed container in the refrigerator, but let them come to room temperature before serving. Since they are made with perishable ingredients, they should be eaten within 2 days.

HOW TO TEMPER CHOCOLATE

To coat truffles or molded candies evenly and attractively with melted chocolate, you must foil the natural tendency of the cacao butter to separate into several different crystal forms when warmed above and then cooled below some critical temperature points. There are different strategies one can take to temper chocolate—that is, to stabilize the cacao butter into one uniform kind of crystal configuration that will not cause the chocolate to discolor or be grainy when it hardens after melting. The seemingly simplest techniques actually require a great deal of familiarity with chocolate.

The "Mush" Method

Veteran California chocolate technologist Terry Richardson—a respected teacher and consultant to the chocolate industry—has developed a foolproof method of tempering that produces chocolate with a high gloss. He calls it the "mush" method. I have slightly modified it for amateurs who are dedicated enough to carry out a precise scenario.

You must be organized and preferably have a couple of double boilers at the ready along with one quick-reading chocolate thermometer that can register fine differences between 65° and 150°F. You will need a clean, nonporous work surface (marble, polished granite, stainless steel, or Formica), a spatula with a thin flexible blade, a scale with fine gradations, and a small electric fan or a hair dryer set on cool.

This method is particularly useful for dark chocolate couvertures with 100 percent cacao butter and for chocolates aged for over three months. Milk chocolate requires a different temperature range. (Richardson emphasizes the importance of contacting manufacturers for precise instructions on tempering their milk chocolates, since dairy butterfat content varies widely.)

1. Finely chop the chocolate (any amount) and put it in a double boiler or heatproof bowl nested over a bottom pan filled halfway with simmering water. Melt and heat the chocolate until it is between 120° and 130°F. (Richardson goes as high as 140°F, to ensure that all of the fat crystals are properly melted.)

2. Have ready another double-boiler bottom (or similar-sized pan) filled halfway with water at about 70°F; place the melted chocolate over this, off the heat, occasionally stirring gently, until the chocolate cools to about 94°F. Be careful not to create air pockets as you stir.

3. When the chocolate reaches about 94°F, place the bowl over the first double-boiler bottom (the water in the double boiler should be 94° to 95°F by now). Pour about one-fifth of the chocolate onto a clean work surface. Quickly start "mushing" the chocolate on the work surface by scraping it back and forth with a thin flexible spatula. When the "mush" acquires a dull and mattelike surface (about 8 minutes), scrape it off the board back into the rest of the chocolate in the top of double-boiler. Stir in the mush until completely blended into the rest of the chocolate; the temperature of the chocolate after blending should be between 89° and 91°F.

4. Check the tempering by cooling a small sample of the chocolate on a piece of aluminum foil in front of an electric fan or a hair dryer on a cool setting. The chocolate should set relatively quickly and be glossy and smooth, not dull. It is now ready for dipping. If the chocolate becomes too thick for dipping after a while, add some warm chocolate that has been melted until it is between 120° and 130°F°, cooled, and kept warm at 89°F to 91F°. Be careful not to let the temperature of the tempered chocolate rise above 91°F; if it gets too warm, the chocolate might lose its temper.

5. If the chocolate does overheat, retemper as follows: grate a very small amount (2 percent of the weight of the melted dipping chocolate will be enough) from a tempered bar or block on the fine side of a box grater. Add the grated chocolate to the dipping chocolate and mix until the mass is free of lumps.

For the best results, cool your dipped chocolate under a fan in a room at a temperature between 70° and 75°F.

The Seed Method

This popular method consists of heating the chocolate to the point at which all crystal forms are melted and cooling it by adding a small amount of reserved unmelted chocolate. Because the reserved chocolate has not gone "out of temper" through heating, it will "seed" the cacao butter with stable crystals.

1. Weigh the amount of chocolate called for in the recipe, and set aside a chunk that is about 10 percent of the total weight. Finely chop the larger amount; grate the remaining chunk on the fine side of a box grater.

2. Put the chopped chocolate in the top of a double boiler or in a clean, dry stainless steel bowl set over a pot filled halfway with simmering water. Allow the chocolate to begin melting at 120°F. (Chocolate technologist Terry Richardson recommends temperatures between 130° and 140°F for dark chocolates with high cacao content that have been aged for over three months). Then remove it from the heat. Have ready another double-boiler bottom (or similar-sized pan) filled halfway with water at about 70°F. Place the bowl of melted chocolate over this, off the heat, and let sit, occasionally stirring gently, until the chocolate cools to 94°F. Be careful not to create air pockets as you stir.

3. Add the reserved unmelted grated chocolate and stir with a wooden spoon until all the chocolate has melted, all lumps are gone, and the temperature has cooled to between 89°F and 91°F. To test the degree of tempering, cool a small sample of the chocolate on a piece of aluminum foil in front of an electric fan or a hair dryer on a cool setting. The chocolate should be glossy and smooth. Keep the chocolate in the double boiler over warm water (about 94°F) while you are dipping. Do not allow the temperature of the dark chocolate to rise above 91°F; if it gets too warm, the chocolate may lose its temper. If the chocolate becomes too thick for dipping or loses its temper, follow the instructions in Step 5 of the "mush" method.

Jim Graham's Quick Seed Method

Chicago-based master chocolatier and industry consultant Jim Graham has devised a quick and painless seed tempering method for the home cook. It is very similar to the seed method, but in place of Step 1, dark chocolate should be finely chopped and 10 percent of the total weight set aside. Follow Step 2 of the procedure, heating the chocolate to 120°F and cooling it to 94°F. Transfer it to a tall, narrow container. Add the reserved chocolate. Place a handheld immersion blender in the chocolate to submerge the blades completely and turn to high speed, moving the blender in the chocolate with a stirring motion. A variable-speed blender will allow you to reduce the speed if the friction of the blades starts to overheat the chocolate. To test the degree of tempering and for retempering instructions, see Steps 4 and 5 of the "mush" method.

My "Imagined" Maya Turkey Soup-Stew with Cacao and Chiles

I have traveled much in today's Mesoamerica—but I've also vicariously traveled into the Maya past by reading early Spanish chroniclers' accounts and by following the stream of recent archaeological discoveries at Maya sites. I am particularly inspired by the finding of a Maya pot containing turkey bones and traces of cacao and chiles at Copan in western Honduras (see page 15).

As a cook tasting some of today's well-known Maya turkey dishes, I have often wondered what they would be like if stripped of all the Old World elements that they have acquired in the last five centuries. It is my theory that the ancient Maya could have used mixtures of cacao and the very spicy chile *ululte* (*chile piquín*) just as the contemporary Kekchi Maya of Alta Verapaz do today to season their foods, particularly festive foods like turkey.

This is my own admittedly very personal attempt to reimagine a lavishly flavored contemporary dish—a turkey stew that I tasted in versions redolent of cilantro, mint, onions, garlic, cinnamon—in the more austere flavor context of a Maya world that had not yet received these ingredients of the conquerors. The predominant flavors are very simple here: tomatillos for acidity, allspice for flowery fragrance, cacao for intensity and color, chiles for fire, and achiote to gild the whole. I suspect that Maya cooks added either fresh corn masa or something like the ground toasted corn that is used to thicken *pinole* (see page 149). I have tried both with equally good results, but here I suggest the easier-to-find commercial dehydrated corn masa. This is a dish that today's Maya would love to eat with Old World rice or tamales flavored with lard—both post-Colombian additions. Hot corn tortillas are closer to the spirit I'm invoking here.

MAKES 6 TO 8 SERVINGS

5 pounds turkey parts (wings, thighs, drumsticks), whole or cut across the bone into 2- to 3-inch serving pieces, or boneless turkey thighs (skin removed), cut into 2- to 3-inch serving pieces (your butcher can do this for you)

10 cups water

1 tablespoon allspice berries

1 tablespoon salt

1 cup (4 1/2 ounces) cacao nibs

1 tablespoon dried *piquín* chiles (also sold as *chiltepe* or *chiltepín* chiles in Hispanic markets)

2 pounds tomatillos (preferably small Milpa tomatillos—a small, sharp-flavored variety), husks removed, rinsed, and patted dry

2 tablespoons achiote paste (available in Hispanic markets), or 2 tablespoons achiote seeds ground to a fine powder in a spice mill or coffee grinder

1/2 cup commercial dried masa, preferably Maseca brand

continued

Rinse the turkey under cold water and combine in a large saucepan with the 10 cups water, allspice, and salt. Bring to a boil over medium-high heat. Reduce the heat to medium-low and simmer, covered, skimming occasionally, until the turkey is tender, 1 to 1¹/₂ hours.

Remove the turkey pieces. Strain the cooking broth through a fine-mesh strainer and discard the solids; reserve 1 cup of the broth and let cool. Return the turkey and strained broth to the pot and keep warm over low heat.

While the turkey is cooking, heat a dry heavy-bottomed skillet, griddle, or Mexican *comal* over medium-high heat. Add the cacao nibs and dried chiles. Roast, stirring occasionally, until they are fragrant but not scorched, 5 to 10 seconds. Scrape them into a small bowl and let cool briefly. Working in batches, grind the roasted nibs and chile to a fine powder in a spice mill or coffee grinder; set aside.

Working in two batches, add the tomatillos to the hot skillet and roast over medium-high heat, turning occasionally, until they are lightly charred, about 8 minutes. Combine the roasted tomatillos and achiote paste or powder in a food processor or blender and process to a purée. Add the purée to the pot of broth and turkey and increase the heat to medium.

For the final thickening, dissolve the dried masa in the reserved 1 cup broth, mixing well to eliminate lumps. Stir into the broth and simmer, stirring, until it has thickened to the consistency of a light cream soup. Taste for salt and adjust seasoning. Serve hot.

Colombian Cheese Arepas
Arepitas de Queso Colombianas

On the Caribbean coast of Colombia, from Cartagena to Barranquilla, locals enjoy afternoon chocolate drinks flavored with cinnamon and sugar (see recipe, page 221), served alongside thick, succulent cheese arepas piping hot from the grill.

MAKES 24 (1-OUNCE) AREPAS

2 to 2¹/₂ cups warm water

2 tablespoons salted butter, melted

1 teaspoon salt

1 tablespoon sugar

2 cups (about 14 ounces) precooked cracked white corn flour for arepas (preferably the Venezuelan brand P.A.N.)

4 ounces grated Colombian fresh cheese (queso blanco)

4 ounces grated Parmigiano-Reggiano cheese

To make the dough, pour the warm water into a medium bowl. Add the butter, salt, and sugar and stir to mix with a wooden spoon. With one hand, pour in the flour in a thin stream while mixing with the other hand. Then knead in the bowl with both hands until the dough feels smooth. Add the cheese and continue kneading until it is thoroughly incorporated and there are no lumps in the dough. Let rest for 5 to 10 minutes, covered with a damp kitchen towel. (You should have about 1¹/₂ pounds of dough.)

To shape the arepas, divide the dough into 24 equal portions (about 1 ounce each). Roll each into a ball. To keep the dough from sticking to your fingers, wet your hands lightly with cold water from time to time as you work. Flatten the arepas lightly but leave them somewhat convex. Cover the shaped arepas with a kitchen towel to keep the dough from drying as you work.

Heat a lightly greased griddle or *comal* over medium heat. Place the arepas on the griddle and cook, in batches, until there is a golden, crusty patch on the bottom, about 4 minutes. Turn with a spatula and cook on the other side in the same way. Continue cooking, turning occasionally, until they sound slightly hollow when tapped. Serve with Colombian-style hot chocolate (see page 221).

Mint-Flavored Hot Chocolate "Bucaramanga"
Chocolate Caliente al Estilo de Bucaramanaga

In Bucaramanga in the Colombian Andes, I have seen chocolate served at the three o'clock *merienda* with a couple of touches that amazed me the first time I encountered them: small slabs of cheese plunked into the hot chocolate and fished out after they have softened a little, and sometimes a few sprigs of mint. I love that idea so much that I've taken to using a whole bunch of mint instead of a sprig or two. The cheese can be the local fresh queso blanco but people seem to prefer imported Dutch Gouda or Edam. If you want to splurge, buy a good-quality farm or aged Gouda.

MAKES 8 SERVINGS

8 cups whole milk

½ cup sugar, or to taste

Pinch of salt

6 (3-inch) sticks true cinnamon (soft Ceylon cinnamon, sold as *canela* in Hispanic markets)

7 ounces dark chocolate, preferably Guittard Chucuri (65% cacao), Colombian chocolate Santander (70% cacao), or Santander Vintage 2008 (75% cacao), coarsely chopped

4 sprigs spearmint, or a bunch if you want your chocolate to be really minty

8 ounces Gouda, Edam, or Colombian fresh cheese (queso blanco), cut into small slabs or cubes

Combine the milk in a medium saucepan with the sugar, salt, and cinnamon over medium-high heat and simmer for 10 minutes. Lower the heat to medium and add the chopped chocolate. Stir to dissolve with a wooden spoon and add the mint. Let simmer for about 10 minutes. Strain into a tall serving vessel, a chocolate pot if you have one. Stir with a *molinillo* or whisk to raise a good foam.

Arrange the cheese on individual plates and serve the chocolate in individual cups. Provide each guest with a small fork and spoon for dunking the cheese and removing it when it softens.

Shrimp and Ripe Plantains in Vanilla-Chile Chipotle Sauce with Dark Chocolate
Camarones de Papantla y Plátanos en Salsa de Vainilla y Chipotle con Chocolate

This dish was inspired by the unlikely but magical combination of vanilla and chipotle in a shrimp dish that I saw demonstrated by a savvy Veracruzan cook, Nohemi Castro of the Alegría de Vivir chapter of INSEN (National Institute for the Elderly), in the vanilla-growing town of Papantla. I experimented further with the idea when I got home and found that it was even better with dark chocolate playing against the tangy, smoky, perfumed tomato-chipotle-vanilla sauce. It is now a perennial favorite at my restaurant Zafra.

MAKES 6 TO 8 SERVINGS

2 plump Mexican vanilla beans

2 ripe plantains (should be soft with blackened skin or large patches of black)

1 cup safflower or corn oil, for frying plantains

2 pounds plum tomatoes (or canned tomatoes, drained), peeled, seeded, and quartered

2 or more canned chiles chipotles en adobo with some of the sauce that clings to them (available in Hispanic markets and some supermarkets)

1/4 cup fruity extra-virgin olive oil

Salt

1 medium white onion, cut in half lengthwise and thinly julienned

1 tablespoon pure vanilla extract

2 ounces fruity dark chocolate, preferably El Rey Bucare (58.5% cacao) or Guittard Sur del Lago (65% cacao), coarsely chopped

1 1/2 pounds large white Ecuadorian shrimp, peeled and deveined with tails left on

TO SERVE

1/4 cup roasted cacao nibs, to garnish

Hot cooked white rice

Chop the vanilla beans into 1-inch pieces, and process to fine crumbs in a mini-chopper. You should have about 1 tablespoon. Set aside.

To prepare the plantains, cut off the brown ends of the plantains and slit the skin lengthwise from end to end along the ridges, preferably with a table knife. Work off the skin with your fingertips. Slice crosswise on the diagonal into 1/4-inch-thick rounds.

Heat the safflower oil over moderate heat in a medium-sized, heavy-bottomed saucepan or deep skillet until barely rippling (about 350°F). Fry the plantain rounds until golden, 1 to 2 minutes. Remove from the skillet and place on paper towels to drain. Keep warm.

To prepare the sauce, combine the tomatoes and chiles in a blender or food processor and process to a fine purée. Heat the olive oil in a 9-inch skillet or medium saucepan over medium heat until it ripples. Stir in the tomato purée and salt. Sauté, stirring occasionally, for about 20 minutes, or until the sauce thickens and the oil starts to separate from the solids and begins to fry again. Stir in the onion, ground vanilla, vanilla extract, and chocolate and cook, stirring until the chocolate dissolves, about 3 minutes. Add the shrimp and the plantains and cook for 3 more minutes. Garnish with cacao nibs and serve immediately with the freshly cooked rice.

The members of the Alegría de Vivir (Joy of Life) chapter of INSEN in Papantla, the Mexican vanilla capital in Veracruz State. This irrepressible group of women is devoted to finding new uses for vanilla in traditional Papantla cooking.

Catalan Prawns or Lobster with Chocolate and Almonds
Langosta o Langostinos a la Catalana con Chocolate y Almendras

When chocolate was introduced to the Catalan table in the eighteenth century, it quickly enriched a fascinating and very old family of savory dishes flavored with sweet ingredients. Chocolate became nearly indispensable in dishes like Catalan-style spiny lobster (*langosta a la catalana*), stews featuring hare or rabbit as well as partridge, and in braised dishes called *estofats*. In typical Catalan style, chocolate became a part of the *picada*, an essential mixture of chopped nuts and herbs, added to saucy foods almost at the end of cooking for flavor and texture.

My friend Montse Guillén, the inventive chef whose whimsical El International restaurant (the second tapas bar in the United States) delighted Manhattan in the 1980s, taught me this dish many years ago. I've made the dish several ways—with lobster tails in the shells, with extra-colossal intact prawns, and various sizes of shrimp. I have to say, eating prawns or shrimp in the rich chocolate sauce is awfully messy if you don't remove the shells (I use them to flavor the sauté oil). Serve with rice or potatoes.

MAKES 6 SERVINGS

SHELLFISH

18 extra-colossal shrimp or prawns in the shells with heads on; 2 pounds large shrimp, in the shells with head and tail intact; or 4 lobster tails in the shell, cut across into 2-inch sections

Salt and freshly ground black pepper

SAUCE

1 1/4 cups extra-virgin olive oil

1 large yellow onion, coarsely chopped

1 bay leaf

8 sprigs thyme

8 ounces smoked ham (sold as *jamón de cocinar* in Hispanic markets) or serrano ham, coarsely chopped

2 pounds ripe plum tomatoes, peeled, seeded, and cut into chunks

4 cups chicken broth

2 1/2 teaspoons salt, or to taste

Freshly ground black pepper

PICADA

4 garlic cloves

2 ounces (about 1/3 cup) blanched almonds, toasted

2 ounces dark chocolate, preferably Cluizel Los Ancones (67% cacao) or the Catalan-made Chocovic Guaranda (71% cacao), or Chocovic Ocumare (71% cacao) finely chopped

8 sprigs parsley

continued

To prepare the shellfish, rinse the shellfish under running water and pat dry. If using prawns or shrimp, remove the shells, leaving the head and tail intact; reserve the shells. Place in a bowl and season with salt and pepper; set aside.

To make the sauce, heat 2/3 cup of the oil in a 12-inch earthenware *cazuela* or deep skillet over medium heat. Add the onion, bay leaf, thyme, and ham and sauté until the onion becomes translucent and starts to brown, about 10 minutes. Add the tomatoes and sauté for about 10 minutes. Add the broth and season with salt and pepper. Continue cooking, uncovered, until the sauce thickens, about 20 minutes. Transfer the sauce to a blender or food processor and process into a smooth purée. Force through a coarse-mesh sieve and set aside.

Pour the remaining oil into the pan and heat over medium heat. If using prawns or shimp, add the reserved shells and sauté for 2 to 3 minutes, stirring, to perfume the oil. Lift the shells out of the pan, letting as much oil as possible drain back into the pan, and discard the shells. Add the shrimp or prawns and sauté briefly for about 1 minute. Lift out of the pan and transfer to a plate. If using lobster, add to the pan and sauté for 3 minutes. Lift the lobster out of the pan and transfer to a plate. Add the puréed sauce to the *cazuela* and simmer over medium-low heat to thicken.

To make the picada, in a large mortar, pound together the garlic, almonds, chocolate, and parsley. Add to the sauce and cook over medium heat for 5 minutes. Add the shellfish and continue cooking for an additional 5 minutes if using lobster or 3 minutes if using prawns or shrimp. If the sauce gets too thick, thin it with a little hot broth or water. Taste for salt and pepper and correct the seasoning. Serve at once.

Glossary

Alkalization: Treatment of cacao beans (or of chocolate at different stages of the manufacturing process) with an alkali, such as potassium carbonate, in order to remove unwanted harshness or acidity. This practice allows manufacturers to mask some of the inferior qualities of cheap cacao. By law, the addition of alkali must be indicated on the label. See also Dutch-process cocoa.

Allele: Either of a matched pair of genes occurring at specific locations on a chromosome and controlling dominant/recessive traits.

Amelonado: The most ubiquitous type of cacao from the Lower Amazon. Formerly classified as a Forastero, now one of the ten genetic clusters in the new classsification sytem proposed by Juan Carlos Motamayor et al. in 2008.

Arriba: A special Ecuadorian cacao prized for its flowery character.

Baba: Spanish for "slime." It refers to the mucilaginous fruit pulp that clings to cacao beans when they are scooped out of the pod. At this stage, the fresh beans are generally referred to as "*cacao en baba.*"

Bean count: Estimation of bean size, using the weight of one hundred beans as an average.

Bittersweet or semisweet chocolate: Sweetened chocolate containing at least 35 percent cacao liquor (i.e., ground cacao mass) by weight.

Black pod rot: A fungal disease affecting cacao caused by *Phytophthora* spp.

Blended: Of chocolates, made from beans of different provenances and qualities.

Bloom: The gray-white film that sometimes appears on the surface of chocolate. It can reflect imperfect tempering of the chocolate or originate when the chocolate undergoes changes in temperature (cacao butter bloom) or is exposed to excess humidity (sugar bloom, caused by crystallization of sugar).

Bulk beans: Cacao beans of average to poor quality, used to add cacao mass to manufactured chocolate. More than 90 percent of the world's cacao supply is bulk beans. See also Flavor beans.

Cacao beans: The seeds of the cacao pod. In Spanish there is a distinction between *semillas* (the fresh seeds capable of reproducing) and *almendras* (the seeds after the drying process, ready to be made into chocolate).

Cacao (cocoa) butter: The waxy ivory-yellow fat obtained from dried and roasted cacao beans; solid at room temperature. It exhibits not one but several different crystal forms on solidifying after being melted and is the major reason for the great technical difficulties chocolate presents to cooks and confectioners. See also Tempering.

Cacao pods: The large colorful fruits of the cacao tree (*Theobroma cacao*). The thickness and hardness of the husk varies according to type, with Criollo cacao having the most fragile exterior; Amazonian varieties, the thickest and toughest.

Cauliflory: In botany, the growth habit of putting forth flowers and fruits directly from a tree trunk.

Cherelle, chirel: Respectively, French and Spanish for "immature cacao pod."

Chicha: Name for a large family of Latin American fermented beverages usually based on fruits or grains.

Chocolate liquor: In chocolate processing, the ground mass of cacao beans. Also called "cacao liquor" or "cocoa liquor."

Chupón: Spanish for "shoot" or "sucker," a secondary branch that must be pruned from the trunk of a cacao tree to concentrate fruit production in the main trunk.

Clone: Offspring of a plant produced asexually by grafting slips or buds of the desired parent onto a prepared rootstock. All clones are exact genetic copies of the parent plant.

Cocoa powder: The product made by pressing nearly all the cacao butter from chocolate liquor. The remaining solids form a compacted cake ("press cake"), which is then ground to a powder. When untreated with alkali, cocoa powder is light in color and retains much of the flavor of the original beans.

Compound coating: Chocolate substitute or analog used in confectionery to bypass the expense and technical difficulty of using real chocolate as a coating. Some varieties contain at least some cacao liquor combined with hydrogenated soybean and/or cottonseed oil; others have cocoa powder combined with highly saturated fats (valued in this case for their high melting points), such as palm oil or coconut oil.

Conching: A crucial step in the chocolate manufacturing process that consists of agitating the refined, sweetened chocolate mass at a temperature of 120° to 200°F in a mixer-kneader known as a conche. Conching can last from four hours (with cheaper brands) to seventy-two hours, though recent improvements in conche construction have somewhat shortened the time. The process has several complex physical and chemical effects that operate to mellow the flavor and smooth the texture of chocolate. Any extra cacao butter and all or a percentage of the lecithin used as an emulsifier are usually added during conching. The best conches are open on top to allow maximum aeration of the mass and proper evaporation of harsh, acidic volatile components.

Cotyledon: The embryonic first leaf pair of a seed plant, such as cacao. The leaves remain tightly folded within the seed (the cacao bean) until it germinates. The cotyledons of different cacao varieties vary markedly in color; this is a common clue to the ancestry of any cacao. See also "cut test."

Couverture: French for "covering" or "coating." In English, this word is used in a nontechnical sense to indicate any high-quality chocolate for cooking or eating. Originally it referred to fine chocolate primarily used for coating truffles or candies. In France,

the minimum cacao content allowed by law for dark chocolate couvertures is 32 percent.

Criollo cacao: A race of cacao that originated in northern South America and is considered the standard of fine chocolate flavor. The interior of the bean is pure white to very light pink. Criollo commands the highest prices on the international market.

Cut test: Standard method of evaluating the quality of cacao-bean shipments by cutting a sampling of beans (100 to 300) open lengthwise, examining the cotyledons, and noting evidence of underfermentation (purple beans), no fermentation (flat, slaty beans), insect damage, mold, or other flaws.

Deodorization: Vacuum process used to remove the characteristic odors of chocolate from cacao butter by the use of steam, making the fat suitable for more purposes and helping manufacturers to produce a uniform product with cacao butter from various origins and mixed-quality beans. It enables manufacturers to use poor-quality, alkali-treated beans, which would produce virtually unpalatable cacao butter if not deodorized. Butter from quality beans retains some of the pleasant flavor and aroma of the cacao solids without deodorization.

Dipping: Process of coating truffles or other candies by submerging them in melted chocolate or a substitute; also called "enrobing." Because of chocolate's unique melting properties, hand-dipping is one of the most technically demanding steps in confectionery.

Dutch-process cocoa: Cocoa treated with an alkali, such as potassium carbonate, to neutralize some of the harsh acid components of the original cacao. The color of the alkalized cocoa is quite dark, but the flavor is much milder than that of cocoa made by other methods.

Estate chocolate: Chocolate made with cacao beans grown on a single plantation. The term does not necessarily mean that the product is made from only one variety of cacao.

Exclusive-derivation chocolate: A broad category that encompasses a wide range of terms used by manufacturers to emphasize the variety or unique provenance of the cacao beans used in their products. See also Single-origin and single-variety chocolate.

Extra bitter or extra bittersweet chocolate: A designation for strong-flavored dark chocolate with particularly high cacao content.

Fair Trade certification: Certification awarded to food producers and retail products through the Fair Trade Federation. This organization seeks to promote sustainable conditions—including reasonable prices for the harvest, encouragement of co-ops to increase farmers' bargaining power, and restrictions on the use of agrochemicals—for farmers in Third World countries that supply such foods as coffee, cacao, tea, and tropical fruits.

Flavanols: An important subgroup of flavonoids (see next entry) that appear to have wide-ranging effects on the circulatory system.

Flavonoids or bioflavonoids: A group of compounds, usually astringent in flavor, found in many food plants, including tea, citrus fruits, and cacao.

Flavor beans or fine beans: Criollo or Trinitario cacao beans of high quality. Exceptional non-Criollos such as Arriba are also considered flavor beans. The term refers to the practice of using them in blends with bulk beans to improve the flavor of the resulting chocolate. See also Bulk beans.

Forastero cacao: Traditional, unscientific name used to designate cacao varieties, primarily Amelonado, that are characterized by flat beans with medium purple to dark purple cotyledons and that were introduced into regions of earlier Criollo cultivation during the nineteenth-century expansion of the cacao trade. The flavor ranges from acidic and astringent among the poorer varieties to flowery and fruity among certain more desirable kinds.

Frosty pod: A major fungal disease of cacao, caused by *Moniliophthora roreri*.

Ganache: A catchall term for multipurpose mixtures of high-quality chocolate melted with cream, other liquids, or butter and used to create glazes, coatings, cake fillings, or truffle centers.

Genome: Theoretically the full picture of the genetic makeup of an organism: the entire complement of genes and other genetic material on a set of chromosomes, identified in exact sequence.

Genotype: The genetic makeup of any organism (such as a strain of cacao) in terms of the actual genes that may or may not be expressed in visible qualities such as size, color, and shape. See also Phenotype.

Grand cru: Winemaker's term borrowed by the Valrhona company to designate several lines of high-quality chocolate made from select cacao beans of particular geographical origins. The word "cru" is used here in a loose sense since with few exceptions specific crus, or growths, are seldom identified by harvest date on the label.

Kakaw: Maya name for cacao, deciphered from glyphs on Classic-period vessels that have been found to contain cacao residues. The origin of the word is uncertain, but it is believed to be the source for the Spanish "cacao."

Lecithin: A type of lipid (fat-related substance) widely used in food manufacturing as an emulsifier (helping fats, such as cacao butter, form stable suspensions with nonfat components). The lecithin in chocolate is usually derived from soybeans and is legally limited to not more than 1 percent by weight.

Limited edition: Term applied to chocolate made in tiny quantities from extremely small batches of cacao and issued on a one-time basis as a unique product.

Linkage map or genetic linkage map: A map showing parts of a genome, constructed by reproducing segments of the complete sequence that are formed by groups of genes occurring close to each other on a chromosome and tending to be inherited together in clusters, thus providing convenient sequencing clues. See also Physical map.

Mélangeur: French term for a mixing machine that combines chocolate liquor and sugar and grinds the mixture to a desired fineness. Though other devices have superseded *mélangeurs* in the large streamlined modern factories, early-twentieth-century models with granite rollers are still used in small plants here and there. Today it is possible to purchase online small *mélangeurs* for home or artisanal use.

Metate: Pre-Columbian three-legged grinding platform made of rough volcanic stone; a stone cylinder *(mano)* is rolled back and forth over the slightly concave surface of the *metate* to do most of what we expect from a food processor. The device was copied in Spain, France, and other European countries during the first Old World chocolate revolution. It is still widely used in Mexico and Central America.

Micro-batch chocolates: Chocolates made in small batches, according to artisanal methods and usually with small-scale machinery, by a new generation of manufacturers ("micro-chocolate makers") who are redefining the industry through tiny, often unconventional operations.

Milk chocolate: Any chocolate that contains chocolate liquor and sugar (with or without other flavorings and ingredients such as nuts) in combination with some form of milk. The term embraces a bewildering range of variables, mostly related to the processing of the milk, which is almost invariably in dried form when mixed with the chocolate liquor. Different drying methods (spray-drying, ball-drying) yield products of highly divergent qualities, with "milk crumb" (made by a special evaporation and condensing process, with a mixture of cacao liquor, sugar, and condensed milk worked to a crumbly product) being considered the tastiest. Poor-quality milk chocolate contains less chocolate (the legal minimum is 10 percent chocolate liquor by weight) and more fillers than any other chocolate product. Nowadays there are some very fine milk chocolates with high cacao content.

– epicatechin or (minus) epicatechin: A flavanol that has been found to improve blood flow. It occurs in cacao beans in amounts varying according to the variety of beans and methods of postharvest processing.

Molinillo: Spanish for "little mill," a long wooden device for frothing chocolate; see the illustration on page 26.

Nacional: A famed Ecuadorian cacao formerly thought to be a fine quality Forastero and now reclassified as a distinct genetic cluster. Also the current name for Bolivian "Criollo" cacao, meaning native cacao, with no relation to the genetic cluster Criollo.

Nibs: The fragmented pieces of cacao left when the roasted beans are shelled; the basic material of all chocolate.

Organic chocolate: Chocolate from cacao farms that use no synthetic fertilizers or pesticides on their trees. Certified under the provisions of the National Organic Standards Board, which also prohibit the use of any other nonorganic ingredients in chocolate making.

Origen único: Spanish for "single origin."

Particle size: Criterion for measuring the smoothness of chocolate. Modern methods of refining with awesome five-roller machines enable manufacturers to break down the particles of cacao and sugar in the final mixture to literally microscopic dimensions. However, there is a point of diminishing returns, since the human tongue cannot register distinct particles below a certain size (18 microns, according to longtime Suchard chocolatier Roger Thürkauf). For a premium chocolate of today, a particle size of 14 to 18 microns would be considered superfine.

Phenotype: The visible physical expression of an organism's genetic inheritance as modified by nongenetic factors in its environment or, in the case of recessive traits, as masked by dominant genes. Although cacao has a comparatively small number of diploid genes (twenty), it exhibits great phenotypical complexity—which is another way of saying that breeding for desired traits is difficult. See also Genotype.

Physical map: As distinguished from "linkage map," a map that shows the entire physical sequence of genes on a chromosome from beginning to end.

Pinole: Toasted ground corn used to thicken chocolate and other drinks since colonial times in Latin America, especially Mexico.

Polyphenols: A large class of compounds found in many foods like cacao that include flavonoids and flavanols among other substances.

Porcelana: A prized Venezuelan Criollo cacao with white cotyedons and delicate nutlike flavor and little acidity, from the area known as Sur del Lago, south of Lake Maracaibo.

Procyanidins or proanthocyanidins: Compounds built up from recurring units of flavanols such as (-) epicatechin (q.v.).

Semisweet chocolate. See Bittersweet chocolate.

Single-origin and single-variety chocolate: Strictly speaking, "single-origin" should refer to chocolate made only with cacao beans from one country or region, like the Catalan company Chocovic's line of single-origin *(origen único)* chocolate containing only beans grown in Grenada. It does not indicate anything about the type or quality of the beans, which may be either uniform or diverse. "Single variety" literally signifies that only cacao beans of one particular variety (for example, Porcelana) have been used in the chocolate. It is best to remember that the terminology of gourmet chocolates is in the process of evolution.

Tempering: A technique of carefully warming, stirring, and cooling chocolate under controlled conditions so that it will preserve a smooth, glossy appearance (rather than hardening into coarse grayish crystals) when used for dipping or other purposes where cosmetic appearances are important. For three tempering methods used by amateur and professional candy makers, see pages 214 and 215.

Theobroma: The genus including cacao *(T. cacao)*, *pataxte (T. bicolor)*, and *cupuaçu (T. grandiflora.)*

Theobromine: A bitter alkaloid found in cacao. It is the marker by which researchers detect the presence of *Theobroma* spp. in food residues on ancient vessels. When found in conjunction with caffeine, it positively shows the presence of cacao.

Trinitario cacao: Name originally applied to a range of cultivated cacao strains with both Criollo and Amelonado parentage. The greater the share of non-Criollo genes, the less delicate flavor and more hardiness the Trinitario cross shows.

Varietal: In chocolate marketing, a somewhat imprecise term modeled on the concept of varietal wines made from the grapes of particular vine cultivars. No official standards govern the use of "varietal" on chocolate labels.

Viscosity: In a liquid or semiliquid substance, degree of resistance to motion. The more viscous a mixture such as melted chocolate, the less fluid. Chocolate refined to a very small particle size may become too viscous to be easily handled in confectionery; extra cacao butter is often added to increase fluidity.

White chocolate: By the federal standard of identity, this popular ivory-colored product is not legally chocolate because it contains no cacao solids. It is made with cacao butter (with or without other fats), sugar, milk solids, and flavorings. The best varieties, resembling the taste of good-quality milk chocolate, are made with nondeodorized cacao butter, and hence retain the fragrance of chocolate.

Witches' broom: A major fungal disease of cacao, caused by *Moniliophthora perniciosa* (previously known as *Crinipellis perniciosa*).

Sources

Chocolate Companies

Amano Artisan Chocolate
Orem, Utah
www.amanochocolate.com
amano@amanochocolate.com
(801) 655-1996

Art Pollard of Amano is a rising star among small U.S. chocolate makers, producing high-end single-origin couvertures of seductive elegance and complex flavors. His Madagascar, Montanya, and Ocumare bars have won gold and silver medals at London's prestigious Academy of Chocolate annual awards, where he was also named Most Promising New Bean to Bar Chocolate Maker in 2009.

Amedei
Pisa, Italy
www.amedei-us.com
011 39 05 87 48 32 08

Founded by Alessio Tessieri and his sister Cecilia, who is the chocolate maker at their factory in Tuscany, Amedei is best known for fine couvertures made with legendary Venezuelan beans like Chuao and Porcelana.

Askinosie Chocolate
Springfield, Missouri
www.askinosie.com
(417) 862-9900

Drawing on historical cacao sources (Soconusco and the Philippines) largely ignored by U.S. companies, Shawn Askinosie is making news with innovations like a white chocolate using goat's milk, non-deodorized cocoa butter, and a rustic Soconusco (El Rústico) bar with crunchy sugar crystals and vanilla bits sold through Zingermans's.

Barry Callebaut U.S.A, LLC.
Chicago, Illinois
www.barry-callebaut.com
www.callebaut.com
(866) 443-0460 (toll free)

In 1999 this chocolate giant—the offspring of a 1996 Swiss-engineered merger between the French Cacao Barry and the Belgian Callebaut—introduced Cacao Barry's single-origin couvertures made with bulk beans from several sources. The line "Origine rare" soon followed with a single introductory product: a 70 percent couverture made exclusively with beans from the humid Baracoa region in northeastern Cuba.

Bonnat
Voiron, France
www.bonnat-chocolatier.com
stephane.bonnat@bonnat-chocolatier.com

This company, founded in nintenenth-century Voiron, France, still makes superlative couvetures from select single-origin beans like their nutty and addictive Porcelana.

Chocolates El Rey C.A.
Caracas, Venezuela
www.chocolate-elrey.com
011 58 212 242 44 51
U.S. Representative: El Rey America, Inc.
(800) EL-REY-99

Founded in 1929, this respected Venezuelan company pioneered the concept of single-origin couvertures in 1995, under the leadership of Venezuelan-born Jorge Redmond Schlageter. The first modern chocolate plant in a Latin American country, it has created remarkable chocolates marrying the best of the colonial Venezuelan cacao tradition with cutting-edge technology. El Rey now sells cacao nibs and cocoa powder, and has added several new formulations with higher cacao content to its popular Carenero Superior line.

Chocovic S.A.
Barcelona, Spain
www.chocovic.es
011 34 93 658 12 08
U.S. Distributor: IN2FOOD
www.in2food.com • info@in2food.com
(770) 887-0086

Located in Barcelona, the site of Europe's first chocolate factory, Chocovic is a modern reincarnation of the nineteenth-century Catalan Xocolat Arumi. Of its wide range of chocolate products, the ones with the strongest claim on chefs' attention in both Spain and the United States have been fine single-origin couvertures using beans from Grenada, Ecuador, the Barlovento region of Venezuela, and other sources. The company's cooking school, Aula Chocovic, draws some of the top pastry chefs of Catalonia.

Coppeneur Canada

Calgary, Canada
www.coppeneurchocolate.com
(888) 735-1387

A young German company, distributing from a Canadian office, that produces organic couvertures from Ecuador and Madagascar, several single-origin bars from small farms, and a bar made with Amazonian white-bean cacao from Peru.

De Vries Chocolate

Denver, Colorado
www.devrieschocolate.com
steve@devrieschocolate.com
(303) 296-1661

Steve DeVries, a former art-glass blower based in Denver, Colorado, has a cult following for the bold flavor of his minimalist couvertures made with Costa Rican beans. Living up to his motto "one hundred years behind the times," he uses vintage equipment, artisanal methods, and just enough sugar to cull true-to-bean flavor from cacao that he sources himself from small growers.

Domori

None, Italy
www.domori.com
011 39 011 99 04 601

Known for its long list of single-origin couvertures ranging from the assertive and deliciously tannic Peruvian Apurimac to a suave Porcelana, the company was recently bought by the Illycaffé Group.

Guittard Chocolate Company

Burlingame, California
www.guittard.com • sales@guittard.com
(800) 468-2462

A family-owned San Francisco chocolate manufacturer established by French-born Etienne Guittard in 1886, known as a maker of classic chocolate couvertures, confectionery coatings, a beautiful terracotta-hued Dutch-process cocoa powder (Cocoa Rouge), and other chocolate products. Cognoscenti also know that they produce fine boutique-style, single-origin chocolates made from excellent-quality flavor beans from small plantations in half a dozen countries. These and Guittard's Collection Etienne, a line launched in the spring of 2000, are now available to consumers through select specialty stores and mail-order sources.

Mast Brothers Chocolate

Williamsburg, New York
www.mastbrotherschocolate.com
(718) 388-2625

Brothers Rick and Michael Mast have the look of Amish farmers, and they live the part while they hand-churn serious couvertures with small-scale equipment that could be at home in any kitchen. You can see the whole chocolate-making operation during a visit to their welcoming shop.

Max Felchlin AG

Schwyz, Switzerland
www.felchlin.com • export@felchlin.com
011 41 41 819 65 75

This respected Swiss company is better known in the United States for its fine couvertures made with organic cacao from Joseph Locandro's Finca Elvesia in the Dominican Republic and wild cacao from Bolivia.

Michel Cluizel

Damville, France
www.cluizel.com
011 33 (0) 2 32 35 60 00
U.S. Distributor: Noble Ingredients
www.noble-ingredients.com
contact@noble-ingredients.com
(856) 486-9292

Founded in Damville, Normandy in 1947 by pasty manufacturers Marc and Marcelle Cluizel, the company is named after their son Michel who apprenticed for 36 years by his parents's side and is still the company's master chocolate maker. Following tradition, Michel's sons and daughters are now involved in the business. Long known for the fine confections sold at its Paris shop La Boutique Michel Cluizel (a New York Branch is poised to open in 2009), the company started to grind cacao for its own couvertures in 1983. Cluizel has captured the imagination of U.S. consumers with a line of excellent single-origin chocolates. The first, Hacienda Concepción from Venezuela was introduced in 1997 and followed by half a dozen others like the powerful Los Ancones from the Dominican Republic and the citrusy Mangaro from Madagascar; a fruit of the company's close collaboration with cacao growers. Cluizel's chocolates are made without soy lecithin and use select cacao and vanilla. The company has recently launched the L'atelier de la Formation, a cooking school for professional at their Damville location

Pâtisserie Chocolaterie Pralus S.A.

Roanne, France
www.chocolat-pralus.com • praluschoc@aol.com
011 33 4 77 71 24 10

Founded in 1948 by Auguste Pralus, the company has since won accolades under his son François for its roster of potent, finely textured chocolates made in small batches with beans from close to a dozen countries including Madagascar (Pralus's favorite), Colombia, Java, and Trinidad. All formulations include heaping cacao contents.

Patric Chocolate

Columbia, Missouri
www.Patric-Chocolate.com
customer.service@patric-chocolate.com
(573) 814-7520

Patric Chocolate is the creation of Alan McClure, a microbatch chocolate maker with a strong philosophy emphasizing the harmonious synthesis of carefully selected single-origin cacao and all other elements in an expanding selection of fine couvertures that reflect his emphasis on quality.

Pure Origin Chocolate

Honolulu, Hawaii
www.choconatshop.com • www.pureorigin.net
(212) 677-0222

Ethnobotanist Nat Bletter—a specialist on healing plants and Maya chocolate uses—has created a line of artisanal dark chocolate bars infused with tropical flavors.

República del Cacao

Quito, Ecuador
www.republicadelcacao.com
011 593 256 1320 ext. 37
U.S. Contact: Bernard J. Duclos
Long Beach, CA
bjduclos@republicadelcacao.com
(562) 537-3656

A line of Ecuadorian chocolate made with cacao harvested in the provinces of Manabí, Los Ríos, and El Oro.

Scharffen Berger Chocolate

www.scharffen-berger.com

The company's original blends with 70 percent and 60 percent cacao contents are still classics and available all over the United States.

SOMA Chocolatemaker

Toronto, Canada
www.somachocolate.com • info@somachocolate.com
(416) 815-7662

David Castellan is Canada's most famous micro-batch chocolate maker. Customers in his retail shop/café can sip spiced, vanilla-scented Mayan chocolate in winter or eat milk chocolate fudge cake gelato in summer while watching him work with his team. Devoted fans like my friend, Toronto-based television producer Mary Luz Mejía, rave about his "whimsical truffles with essence of Douglas fir."

TCHO

San Francisco, California
www.tcho.com • sales@tcho.com
(415) 981-0189

This hip San Francisco company defines chocolates by their predominant flavors—chocolaty (Ghana), fruity and nutty (Peru), and citrus (Madagascar). TCHO hopes to establish a more dynamic dialogue between cacao growing and chocolate manufacturing, and in 2009 hired Brad Kintzer, formerly of Scharffen Berger, as their senior product developer; which bodes well for the future quality of their products.

Valrhona

Tain-L'Hermitage, France
www.valrhona.com
011 33 475 75 07 90 90
U.S. Division: Valrhona Inc.
Brooklyn, New York
(718) 522-7001

Synonymous with quality and finesse, this French manufacturer introduced the concept of "grands crus" to the world of modern chocolate and set chocolate lovers to talking of goût de terroir and the personality of different chocolates. They were also the first to make a selling point of actual cacao percentage. Following the launch of their Gran Couva in 1989, the company produced a Chuao bar and a very exclusive Porcelana bar from its own estate El Pedregal, and a more affordable bar called Palmira that also features Porcelana and other Criollos from Valrhona's farm in the Sur del Lago region, as well as single-origin couvertures from half-a-dozen countries.

Vintage Plantations Chocolates
The University of Chocolate
Ecuador
www.echocolates.com

Vintage Plantations is a line of couvertures manufactured in Ecuador with Ecuadorian beans and sold throughout the U.S.; a project created by French-born cacao entrepreneur Pierrick Chouard. He is also known for his University of Chocolate, a combination of lectures and guided tours through Ecuador's cacao producing regions.

Mail Order and Retail

Chocosphere
Portland, Oregon
www.chocosphere.com
(887) 99-CHOCO

A reliable online supplier of fine couvertures from all over the world, with attentive and helpful customer service.

Susana Trilling's Seasons of My Heart Cooking School
Oaxaca, Mexico
www.seasonsofmyheart.com
info@seasonsofmyheart.com
011 52 1 951 508 0469
Direct U.S. purchases:
SOMHimports@gmail.com

Cookbook author and cooking teacher Susana Trilling makes artisanal Oaxacan-style chocolate and authentic mole sauces at her ranch and cooking school in the wilds of Oaxaca. She will ship anywhere in the United States. She also organizes tours to Tabasco and Chiapas during the cacao harvest season.

The Chocolate Path
Montclair, New Jersey
www.chocolatepath.com
info@chocolatepath.com
(973) 655-0822

Susan Fine's shop in tony Montclair specializes in quality dark chocolate couvertures, saving northern New Jerseyans a trip to NY when a special chocolate is needed. Online sales also available.

Ultramarinos
Hoboken, New Jersey
www.ultramarinos.biz • sales@ultramrinos.biz
(201) 238-2797

Retail and mail-order source for Latin American and Spanish ingredients: *cazuelitas* for crema catalana and Spanish salamanders, mole sauces, chiles, Latin brown loaf sugars, cacao spice blends, single-origin chocolates, nibs, Venezuelan beans, and Corona plate mills for grinding cacao.

World Wide Chocolate
www.worldwidechocolate.com

An Internet-only source for fine chocolates based in New Hampshire.

Zingerman's Mail Order
Ann Arbor, Michigan
www.zingermans.com • zing@chamber.ann-arbor.mi.us
(888) 636-8162

The best little deli in the Midwest offers a complete selection of fine chocolates, cocoa powder, cacao nibs, premium estate-grown Mexican vanilla and vanilla extracts, and Askinosie's El Rústico bar.

Chocolate Classes

Ecole Chocolat
Vancouver, Canada
www.ecolechocolat.com
(604) 484-1872 (Canada) • (213) 291-8309 (U.S.)

Pam Williams' unusual online school offers three courses that take students from basic skills to advanced chocolate work, including making chocolate from scratch.

Elaine González
Northbrook, Illinois
chocartist@sbcglobal.net
(847) 498-3971

Elaine González, known for her sophisticated confections and her passion for all things chocolate is a chocolate consultant specializing in instructional services for the trade.

French Pastry School
Chicago, Illinois
www.frenchpastry.com
(312) 726-2419

At this one-of-a-kind school students learn about chocolate with Sebastien Canonne and Jacquey Pfeiffer, two pastry chefs recognized for their chocolate artistry. The school's professional pastry program devotes five weeks to chocolate training and there are also continuing education classes on chocolate.

Retail Confectioners International
Springfield, Missouri
www.retailconfectioners.org
kelly@retailconfectioners.org
(417) 883-2775

RCI holds a Chocolate Boot Camp every two years at the University of Wisconsin at Madison. The three-day, hands-on course is a basic but intensive overview of working with chocolate.

Richardson Researchers, Inc.
Davis, California
www.richres.com
(530) 754-9813

Terry Richardson, a respected teacher, and industry consultant, now teaches two courses a year at the University of California at Davis, combining technical background knowledge and hands-on practice as well as guest lectures by co-instructors Thalia Hohenthal of Guittard and Peter Dea of Mattson. His classes are good resources for serious pros who want to learn the nuts and bolts of chocolate processing and confectionery techniques.

Confectioners, Pastry Shops, and Bakeries

Chuao Chocolatier
Carlsbad, California
www.chuaochocolatier.com
info@chuaochocolatier.com
(888) 635-1444

Named after Chuao, Venezuela's premier cacao plantation, this dynamic San Diego chocolate company was founded in 2001 by Michael Antonorsi and his brother who hail from Venezuela. Known for adventurous flavor combinations, the company produces a wide array of confections made with Venezuelan chocolate and has expanded to two cafés in San Diego and a shop in Miami.

Donna & Company
Cranford, New Jersey
www.shopdonna.com
(908) 272-4380

Dina Pinder's delightful chocolate shop might be New Jersey's best-kept secret. Here you will find custom-made chocolates flavored with pure ingredients that speak of Italy like olive oil, balsamic vinegar, and salt.

Fran's Chocolates
Seattle, Washington
www.franschocolates.com
(800) 422-FRAN

Fran Bigelow, one of America's premier chocolatiers, delivers intense flavor in a large range of candies and truffles made from first-rate chocolate, especially El Rey's Venezuelan cacao. Three Seattle-area retail locations (University Village, Bellevue, and Downtown in the New Four Seasons Hotel) sell such Fran's specialties as figs coated in chocolate.

Jacques Torres Chocolate
www.mrchocolate.com • info@mrchocolate.com

Celebrity chocolatier Jacques Torres's company has become a nationally known brand name with several locations in New York and across the United States.

L. A. Burdick Chocolates
Walpole, New Hampshire
www.burdickchocolate.com
(800) 229-2419

Famed for his trademark chocolate mice (and also whimsical penguins), Larry Burdick is also known for his uncompromising allegiance to the finest, freshest ingredients and exploratory vigor in expanding the palette of flavorings used in fine chocolate. Recently, Larry has started importing Grenada beans for Swiss-made couvertures for some of his chocolates. For a taste of Larry's serious hot chocolate and Viennese pastries, visit Burdick's Cafés in Walpole, New Hampshire, and Cambridge, Massachusetts.

La Praline
Caracas, Venezuela
011 58 212 285 2475

At La Praline, Venezuela's most famous chocolate shop, Belgian-born Ludo and Lisette Gillis apply their Old World expertise to 100 percent Venezuelan chocolate.

Maison du Chocolat
Paris, France
www.lamaisonduchocolat.com
011 33 1 42 27 39 44

U.S. Location:
New York, New York
(800) 988-5632

Founder of an exclusive Paris shop with two in New York and other international branches, Robert Linxe is obsessed with the intrinsic flavor of the raw material as it comes from the world's cacao farms.

Oliver Kita Fine Confections

Rhinebeck, New York
www.oliverkita.com • okita@hvc.rr.com
(845) 876-2665

In the heart of the Hudson Valley, beautifully crafted confections elaborated with Valrhona chocolate and brimming with unexpected flavors.

Payard Patisserie & Bistro

New York, New York
www.payard.com
(212) 717-5252

A showcase for pastry chef François Payard's considerable talent, this pastry shop and bistro with an Old World feel is the home of delicious chocolate confections and desserts.

Recchiuti

San Francisco, California
www.recchiuti.com
(800) 500-3396

San Francisco-based Michael Recchiuti likes to make the pastry kitchen a garden by flavoring his elegant chocolate confections with freshly harvested flowers and herbs. His creative chocolates, sold at Recchiuti's Ferry Building Marketplace store, are made at an intimate production space that resembles an artisan European setup.

Rococo

London, England
www.rococochocolates.com
321kingsroad@rococochocolates.com
011 020 7352 5857

Taste a violet or a geranium-scented dark chocolate artisanal bar at Chantal Coady's charming Chelsea shop and her other branches, and you'll understand why this is a haven for London's chocolate lovers. Coady is one of the founders of London's Chocolate Academy, which awards annual prizes for excellence in chocolate making.

Romanicos

Miami, Florida
www.romanicoschocolate.com
(877) 848-4857

Hand-rolled truffles made with El Rey's Venezuelan chocolate in the heart of Latin Miami.

Chocolate-Making Equipment, Beans, Nibs, and Cacao Pulp

Cacao nibs

Most of the major chocolate makers like Guittard, Valrhona, and Scharffen Berger sell roasted cacao nibs through their websites and distributors. Whole Foods also carries raw organic nibs.

The Perfect Purée of Napa Valley, LLC.

Napa, California
www.perfectpuree.com • info@perfectpuree.com
(800) 556-3707

You can often find the frozen pulp of cacao and its Amazonian relative cupuaçu in Brazilian markets. Sweetened cacao pulp of excellent quality is also sold as Fruit of the Cocoa Fruit Purée by The Perfect Purée of Napa Valley. Delicious in cocktails and savory sauces.

Chocolate Alchemy

Yoncalla, Oregon
www.chocolatealchemy.com

John Nanci has a cult following among micro-batch chocolate makers. His online shop sells what you need to make homemade chocolate from scratch, from a mill to crack the roasted cacao beans into nibs to a wet grinder to grind and smooth out the cocoa liquor. Nanci also sells beans from several origins and gives detailed, illustrated instructions on how to work with chocolate starting at square one.

Chocolate Festivals

Fairchild's International Chocolate Festival

Coral Gables, Florida
www.fairchildgarden.org
(305) 667-1651

This yearly chocolate event on the grounds of the legendary Fairchild Tropical Garden in Coral Gables is attended by thousands. There are lectures and chocolates tastings, cacao plants for sale, and useful classes on grafting by horticulturists Noris Ledesma and Richard Campbell.

Select Bibliography

Note: I have deliberately chosen sources concerning chocolate history and cacao agriculture and science.

Acosta, Joseph de. *Historia natural y moral de las Indias.* México DF: Fondo de Cultura Económica, 1985. [First published in 1590.]

Alemán, Carmen Elena. *Corpus Christi y San Juan Bautista: Dos manifestaciones rituales en la comunidad de Chuao.* Caracas: Fundación Bigott, 1997.

Amado, Jorge. *Gabriela, Clove, and Cinnamon.* Translated by James L. Taylor and William Grossman. New York: Avon, 1962.

Are, L. A. *Cacao in West Africa.* Ibadan, Nigeria: Oxford University Press, 1974.

Balzer, Jan, et al. "Sustained Benefits in Vascular Function Through Flavanol-Containing Cocoa in Medicated Diabetic Patients: A Double-Masked, Randomized, Controlled Trail." *Journal of the American College of Cardiology* (2009) 51: 2141–2149.

Bartley, B.G.D. *The Genetic Diversity of Cacao and its Utilization.* Oxfordshire: CABI Publishing, 2005.

Bell, Ellen E., Marcello A. Canutto, and Robert J. Sharer, eds. *Understanding Early Classic Copan.* Philadelphia: University of Pennsylvania Museum of Archaeology and Anthropology, 2004.

Berdan, Frances F., and Patricia Rieff Anawalt. *The Essential Codex Mendoza.* Berkeley: University of California Press, 1997.

Bergmann, John F. "The Distribution of Cacao Cultivation in Pre-Columbian Mesoamerica." *Annals of the Association of American Geographers.* Vol. 59 (1), March 1969: 85–96.

Blegny, Nicolas de. *Le bon usage du thé, du caffé et du chocolat.* Paris: Estienne Michallet, 1687.

Borrone, James W., David N. Kuhn, and Raymond J. Schnell. "Isolation, Characterization, and Development of WRKY Genes as Useful Genetic Markers in Theobroma cacao." *Theoretical and Applied Genetics* (2004) 109: 495–507.

Brenner, Joel Glenn. *The Emperors of Chocolate: Inside the Secret World of Hershey and Mars.* New York: Random House, 1999.

Brown, Stephen J. et al. "Mapping QTLs for Resistance to Frosty Pod and Black Pod Diseases and Horticultural Traits" *Theobroma cacao L. Crop Science* (2007) 47: 1851–1858.

———. "A Composite Linkage Map from Three Crosses Between Commercial Clones of Cacao, *Theobroma cacao L.*" *Tropical Plant Biology* (2008) 1: 120–130.

Cadbury, Richard. *Cocoa: All about It.* By "Historicus" (pseud.). London: S. Low, Marston and Co., 1896.

Cárdenas, Juan de. *Problemas y secretos maravillosos de las Indias.* Madrid: Alianza Editorial, 1988. [First published in 1581.]

Chinchilla Mazariego, Oswaldo, ed. *Kakaw. El chocolate en la cultura de Guatemala.* Guatemala: Museo del Popul Vuh, 2005.

Ciferri, R. *Varietá, forme, e razze di cacao coltivate in San Domingo.* Roma: Reale Accademia d'Italia, 1933.

Christenson, Allen J. *Popol Vuh: The Sacred Book of the Maya.* Translated from the original Maya text. Oklahoma: University of Oklahoma Press, 2007.

Clarence-Smith, William Gervase. *Cocoa and Chocolate, 1765–1914.* London: Routledge. 2000.

Clapperton, J., et al. "The Contribution of Genotype to Cocoa *(Theobroma cacao)* Flavor." *Tropical Agriculture* 71 (October 1994): 303–8.

———. "Effects of Planting Materials on Flavor." *Cocoa Growers Bulletin 48* (December 1994): 47–63.

Cheesman, E. E. "Notes on the Nomenclature, Classification, and Possible Relationships of Cacao Populations." *Tropical Agriculture* (1944) 21 (8): 265–85.

Chevaux, Kati A., et al. "Proximate, Mineral, and Procyanidin Content of Certain Foods and Beverages Consumed by the Kuna Amerinds of Panama." *Journal of Food Consumption and Analysis* (2001) 14: 553–563.

Coe, Michael D. *Breaking the Maya Code.* New York: Thames and Hudson, 1992.

Coe, Sophie D., and Michael D. Coe. *The True History of Chocolate* (revised edition). New York: Thames and Hudson Ltd., 2007.

Coe, Sophie. *America's First Cuisines.* Austin: University of Texas Press, 1994.

Colmenero de Ledesma, Antonio. *Curioso tratado de la naturaleza y calidad del chocolate.* Madrid, 1631.

Cook, Russell L. *Chocolate Production and Use.* New York: Harcourt Brace Jovanovich, 1982.

Corti, MD, Roberto, et al. "Cocoa and Cardiovascular Health." *Circulation* (2009) 119: 1433–1441.

Crespo, Luis Alberto. "Aquel Sabor a Chuao." In *Venezuela Tierra Mágica.* Caracas, Venezuela: Corpoven S.A., 1992.

238

Crespo, Silvio. *Cacao Beans Today*. Lititz, PA: by author, 1986.

Crown, Patricia L. and W. Jeffrey Hurst. "Evidence of cacao use in the Prehispanic American Southwest." *Proceedings National Academy of Science* (2009) 106 (7): 2110–2113 Cuatrecasas, José. *Cacao and Its Allies: A Taxonomic Revision of the Genus Theobroma*. Washington, DC: Smithsonian Institution, 1964. [*Contributions from the United States National Herbarium*] v. 35, pt. 6.

Davis-Salazar, Karla L. and Ellen E. Bell. *Una Comparación de los Depósitos Funerarios de Dos Mujeres Elites en la Acrópolis de Copan, Honduras* In *XIII Simposio de Investigaciones Arqueológicas en Guatemala*, edited by J. P. Laporte et al. Ciudad de Guatemala: Ministerio de Cultura y Deportes, Instituto de Antropología e Historia, y Asociación Tikal, 2000, 1113–1128.

De León Pinelo, Antonio. *Question moral si el chocolate quebranta el ayuno eclesiastico*. México, DF: Centro de Estudios de Historia de México, 1994. [First published in Madrid, 1636.]

Díaz del Castillo, Bernal. *Historia verdadera de la conquista de la Nueva España. Texto Comparado: Edición de Alonso Remón, 1632, paleografía de Genaro García 1904.* 3 vols. [Facsimile autographed edition.] Mexico DF: Miguel Angel Porrúa, 1992–2001.

Diego de Landa, Friar. *Yucatan Before and After the Conquest*. Translated with notes by William Gates. New York: Dover Publications, 1978.

Enríquez, G. A. "Characteristics of Cacao 'Nacional' of Ecuador." In *International Workshop on Conservation, Characterization, and Utilization of Cocoa Genetic Resources in the 21st Century*. Trinidad: Cocoa Research Unit, 1992, 269–78.

Estrada Monroy, Agustín. *El mundo K'ekchi de la Alta Vera-Paz*. Guatemala: Editorial del Ejercito, 1979.

Fernández Pérez, Joaquín, and Ignacio González Tascón. *La agricultura viajera: Cultivos y manufacturas de plantas industriales y alimentarias en España y en la América Virreinal*. Real Jardín Botánico (CSIC), n.d.

Freud, Ellen Hanak, Philippe Petithuguenin, and Jacques Richard. *Les champs du cacao. Un défi de compétitivité Afrique-Asie*. Montpellier: CIRAD, 2000.

Fuentes, Cecilia, and Daría Hernández. *Cultivos Tradicionales de Venezuela*. Caracas: Fundación Bigott, 1992.

García Fuentes, Lutgardo. *El comercio español con América (1670–1700)*. Sevilla: Excma. Diputación Provincial de Sevilla, 1980.

García Ponce, Antonio. "Los esplendores y las amarguras del cacao venezolano." *Revista M*, 7 (1992): 30–39.

Gómez-Pompa, Arturo, et al. "The Sacred Cacao Groves of the Maya." *Latin American Antiquity* 1, 3 (1990): 247–57.

Grant, Lynn A. *The Maya Vase Conservation Project* (with contributions by Elin C. Danien). Philadelphia: University of Pennsylvania Museum of Archaeology and Anthropology, 2006.

Grivetti, Louis Evan and Howard-Yana Shapiro, eds. *Chocolate: History, Culture, and Heritage*. Hoboken, NJ: John Wiley & Sons, Inc., 2009.

Gumilla, Joseph. *El Orinoco Ilustrado*. 2 vols. Facsimile edition. Valencia: Generalitat Valenciana, 1988. [First published in 1741.]

Hall, Carolyn, et al., eds. *Historical Atlas of Central America*. Oklahoma: University of Oklahoma Press, 2003.

Heiss, MD, Christian, et al., "Acute Consumption of Flavanol-Rich Cocoa and the Reversal of Endothelial Dysfunction in Smokers." *Journal of the American College of Cardiology* (2005) 46: 1276–1283.

Heyden, Doris, trans. *The History of the Indies of New Spain by Fray Diego Durán*. Oklahoma: The University of Oklahoma Press, 1994.

Hollenberg, Norman K., et al. "Aging, Acculturation, Salt Intake, and Hypertension in the Kuna of Panama." *Hypertension* (1997) 29: 171–176.

Hollenberg, N.K. and N.D. Fisher. "Is it the Dark in Dark Chocolate?" *Circulation* (2007) 116: 2376–2382.

Hughes, William. *The American Physitian; or treatise of the roots, plants, herbs, growing in the English plantations in America. Describing the place, time, kindes, temperature, vertues and uses of them, either for diet, physick, &c. Whereunto is added a discourse of the cacao-nut tree, and the use of its fruit; with all the ways of making of chocolate*. London: Printed by J.C. for William Crook, 1672.

Humboldt, Alexander von. *Ensayo político sobre el reino de la Nueva España*. México DF: Editorial Porrúa, 1991. [First published as *Essai politique sur le royaume de la Nouvelle-Espagne* (Paris: F. Schoell, 1807–11, 2 vols.).]

———. *Viaje a las Regiones Equinocciales del Nuevo Continente*. 5 vols. Caracas: Monte Avila Editores, 1991. [First published as *Voyage aux régions équinoxiales du nouveau continent* (Paris: F. Schoell, 1814).]

International Workshop on Cocoa Breeding Strategies. 18–19 October 1994, Kuala Lampur, Malaysia.

Kean, B.H. "The Blood Pressure of the Cuna Indians." *American Journal of Tropical Medicine* (1944) 1–24 (6): 341–343.

Knapp, Arthur William. *Cacao Fermentation: A Critical Survey of its Scientific Aspects*. London: J. Bale, 1937.

Laurent,Valerie. "Etude sur la diversité génetique du cacaoyer *(Theobroma cacao)*," PhD diss. University Paris-Sud. Centre D'Orsay, 1993.

Libro de Chilam Balam de Chumayel. Trans. from the Maya by Antonio Mediz Bolio. México DF: Secretaría de Educación Pública, 1985.

López de Gómara, Francisco. *Historia general de las Indias.* 2 vols. Barcelona: Editoral Iberia, 1966. [First published in 1552.]

López, Rosado. *El abasto de productos alimeticios en la ciudad de México.* México DF: Fondo de Cultura Económica S.A., 1988.

Martínez Llopis, Manuel. *Historia de la gastronomía Española.* Madrid: Editorial Nacional, 1981.

Matthew, Restall et al, eds. *Mesoamerican Voices: Native Language Writings from Colonial Mexico, Oaxaca, Yucatan, and Guatemala.* Cambridge: Cambridge University Press, 2005.

Martínez, Máximino. *Catálogo de nombres vulgares y científicos de plantas mexicanas.* México DF: Fondo de Cultura Económica, 1979.

McCullough, Marjorie L., et al. "Hypertension, the Kuna, and the Epidemiology of Flavanols." *Journal of Cardiovascular Pharmacology* (2006) 47 (Supplement 2): 103–109.

McNeil, Cameron L., ed. *Chocolate in Mesoamerica.* Gainesville: University of Florida, 2006.

McNeil, Cameron L. *Maya Interactions with the Natural World: Landscape Transformation and Ritual Plant Use at Copan, Honduras."* Ph.D. diss., The Graduate Center, City University of New York, 2006.

Miller, Kenneth B., William Jeffrey Hurst, et al. "Impact of Alkalization on the Antioxidant and Flavanol Content of Commercial Cocoa Powders." *Journal of Agricultural and Food Chemistry* (2008) 56: 8527–8533.

Minifie, Bernard W. *Chocolate, Cocoa, and Confectionery.* Maryland: Aspen Publishers, Inc., 1999.

Motamayor, Juan Carlos, et al. "The Genetic Diversity of Criollo Cacao and its Consequence in Quality Breeding. In *Memorias del primer congreso Venezolano del cacao y su industria* (Nov. 17–21, 1997). Maracay, Venezuela.

———. "Cacao Domestication I: the Origin of the Cacao Cultivated by the Maya." *Heredity* (2002) 89: 380–386.

———. "Cacao Domestication II: Progenitor Germplasm of the Trinitario Cacao Cultivar." *Heredity* (2003) 91: 332–30.

———. "Geographic and Genetic Population Differentiation of the Amazonian Chocolate Tree *(Theobroma cacao L)" PLoS ONE* (October 2008) 3 (10): 1–8.

Mooleedhhar, V., and W. Maharaj. "Mayan Cacao for the ICG, T." *Cacao Research Unit Newsletter* 2 (June 1995): 4–5.

Morison, Samuel Eliot, trans. *Journals and Other Documents on the Life and Voyages of Christopher Columbus.* New York: Heritage Press, 1963.

Mossu, Guy. *Cocoa.* Translated by Shirley Barrett. London: Macmillan, 1992.

Mota, Ignacio H., de la. *El libro del chocolate.* Madrid: Ediciones Pirámide, 1992.

Nestlé, Inc. *Cacao: Historia, economía y cultura.* México DF: Comunicación y Ediciones Tlacuilo, 1992.

Norton, Marcy. *Sacred Gifts, Profane Pleasures: A History of Tobacco and Chocolate in the Atlantic World.* Ithaca: Cornell University Press, 2008.

———. "Tasting Empire: Chocolate and the European Internalization of Mesoamerican Aesthetics." *The American Historical Review* 111 (June 2006): 660–691.

Núñez González, Niurka and Estrella González Noriega. *El cacao y el chocolate en Cuba.* La Habana: Centro de Antropología, 2005.

Olivas Weston, Rosario. *La cocina en el virreinato del Perú.* Lima: Escuela Profesional de Turismo y Hotelería Universidad de San Martín de Porres, 1996.

———. *La cocina cotidiana y festiva de los limeños en el siglo XIX.* Lima: Escuela Profesional de Turismo y Hotelería Universidad de San Martín de Porres, 1999.

Popenoe, Wilson. "Batido and other Guatemalan Beverages Prepared with Cacao." *American Anthropologist* (1919) 21 (1): 403–409.

Posnette, A. F. *Fifty Years of Cocoa Research in Trinidad and Tobago.* St. Augustine, Trinidad: Cocoa Research Unit, University of the West Indies, 1986.

Pound, F. J. "Cacao and Witches' Broom Disease *(Marasmius perniciosa)* of South America." Reprint in *Archives of Cocoa Research Institute* (1981) I: 20–72.

Quelus, D. de. *Histoire naturelle du cacao, et du sucre: divisée en deux traités, qui contiennent plusiers faits nouveaux, & beaucoup d'observations également curieuses & utiles.* Paris: L. d'Houry, 1719.

Reents-Budet, Dorie. *Painting the Maya Universe. Royal Ceramics of the Classic Period.* Durham: Duke University Press, 1994.

Reyes, Humberto et al. *Catálogo de cultivares del cacao Criollo venezolano.* Venezuela: Fonaiap, n.d.

Román de Zurek, Teresita. *Cartagena de Indias en la olla.* Bogotá: Ediciones Lerner, 1963.

Ruf, François. *Booms et crises du cacao. Les vertiges de l'or brun.* Ministére de la Coopération, CIRAD-SAR et Karthala, 1995.

Ruz, Mario Humberto. *Un rostro encubierto: Los indios del Tabasco colonial.* México DF: Instituto Nacional Indigenista, 1994.

Sahagún, Fray Bernardino de. *Historia general de las cosas de Nueva España.* México DF: Editorial Porrúa, 1992.

Schnell, R.J., D.N. Kuhn. J.S. Brown, C. T. Olano, et al. "Development of a Marker Assisted Selection Program for Cacao." *Phytopathology* (2007) 97: 1644–1699.

Simón Palmer, María del Carmen. *La cocina de palacio.* Madrid: Editorial Castalia, 1997.

Schroeter, Hagen, et al. " (-) –Epicathechin Mediates Beneficial Effects of Flavanol-Rich Cocoa on Vascular Function in Humans." *Procedings of the National Academy of Sciences* (January 2006) 103 (4): 1024–1029.

Smith, Nigel J. H., et al. *Tropical Forests and Their Crops.* New York: Cornell University Press, 1992.

Sotelo, Angela and Reyna G. Alvarez. "Chemical Compositon of Wild Theobroma Species and their Comparison to the Cacao Bean." *Journal of Agricultural Food Chemistry* (1991) 33: 1940–1943.

Sounigo, O., et al. "Assessing the Genetic Diversity in the International Cocoa Genebank, Trinidad (ICG, T) using Isozyme Electrophoresis and RAPD." *Genetic Resources and Crop Evolution* (2005) 52: 111–1120.

Szogyi, Alex, ed. *Chocolate: Food of the Gods.* Westport, CT: Greenwood Press, 1997.

Tienush, Rassaf and Matte Kelm. "Cocoa Flavanols and the Nitric Oxide-Pathway: Targeting Endothelial Dysfunction by Dietary Intervention." *Drug Discovery Today: Disease Mechanisms* (2008) 5 (3–4): e273–e278.

Touzard, Jean-Marc. *L'economie coloniale du cacao en Amérique centrale.* Montpellier: CIRAD, 1993

Toxopeus, H., and G. Geisberger. "History of Cocoa and Cocoa Research in Indonesia." In *Archives of Cocoa Research* (1983).

Viso, Carlos. "En la almendra de cacao cabe el mundo." *Revista Bigott* 44 (1997–1998): 109–15.

Young, Allen M. *The Chocolate Tree: A Natural History of Cacao.* Revised and expanded edition. Gainesville: The University Press of Florida, 2007.

Cacao Journals and Newsletters

Agrotropica. Itabuna, Bahia: Centro de Pesquisas de Cacao (CEPEC).

Annual Report on Cacao Research. St. Augustine, Trinidad: Cocoa Research Unit.

Archives of Cocoa Research. Washington, DC: American Cocoa Research Institute.

Cocoa Research Unit Newsletter. St. Augustine, Trinidad: Cocoa Research Unit.

INGENIC (International Group for Genetic Improvement of Cocoa) Newsletter.

Tropical Agriculture. St. Augustine, Trinidad: The University of the West Indies Press.

Cacao Research Institutes

CATIE Centro Agronómico Tropical de Investigaciones y Enseñanza (Turrialba, Costa Rica)

CEPLAC Comissão Executiva de Planejamento da Lavoura Cacaueira (Ilheus, Brazil)

CIRAD Centre de Coopération Internationale en Récherche Agronomique pour le Développement (Montpellier, France)

CRIG Cocoa Research Institute of Ghana

CRU Cocoa Research Unit (St. Augustine, Trinidad)

ICG, T International Cocoa Genebank of Trinidad

ICCO International Cocoa Organization

WCF World Cocoa Foundation

This influential organization, created in 2000, is funded by more than seventy chocolate companies and trade associations from all over the world. One of its primary goals is to support sustainable cacao economies in Latin America, Africa, and Southeast Asia by providing production technologies and marketing tools to small-scale farmers in very remote areas of the tropics. Another important mission is to fund applied research for breeding disease-resistant cacao strains to improve productivity.

Cacao Websites

To take the pulse of today's current obsession with chocolate, visit the following websites, all known for passionate opinions:

The Chocolate Life: www.thechocolatelife.com

The Chocolate C-Spot: www.c-spot.com

Seventy Percent: www.seventypercent.com

Index